Sri Lanka and the Responsibility to Protect

This book provides a study of the war by Liberation Tigers of Tamil Eelam (LTTE) to create a separate state in Sri Lanka. It examines the ways in which this war should, in principle, have invoked 'responsibility to protect' principles, as well as the political, legal and practical problems involved and, ultimately, why the international community failed to act.

Over the years there have been several events, including those in Rwanda, Sierra Leone, Timor-Leste, Darfur and Kosovo, that have led the international community to accept a responsibility to protect. However, despite its overwhelming preliminary endorsement, the principles of this concept are still not universally sanctioned and there are some strong international opponents, including some countries that were initial signatories of the convention.

By considering the example of Sri Lanka, the text focuses on what conditions could satisfy or demand the application of responsibility to protect. It further presents a case as to why this conflict was, and may still be, the normative responsibility of the international community.

Sri Lanka and the Responsibility to Protect will be of great interest to students of South-East Asian politics, human rights, international law, ethnic conflict, security studies and IR in general.

Damien Kingsbury is Professor at the School of International and Political Studies, Deakin University, Melbourne. He is the author and editor of a number of books and numerous journal articles on political and security matters.

Asian Security Studies

Series Editors: Sumit Ganguly, Indiana University, Bloomington and Andrew Scobell, US Army War College

Few regions of the world are fraught with as many security questions as Asia. Within this region it is possible to study great power rivalries, irredentist conflicts, nuclear and ballistic missile proliferation, secessionist movements, ethnoreligious conflicts and inter-state wars. This book series publishes the best possible scholarship on the security issues affecting the region, and includes detailed empirical studies, theoretically oriented case studies and policy-relevant analyses as well as more general works.

China and International Institutions
Alternate paths to global power
Marc Lanteigne

China's Rising Sea Power
The PLA Navy's Submarine Challenge
Peter Howarth

If China Attacks Taiwan
Military strategy, politics and economics
Edited by Steve Tsang

Chinese Civil–Military Relations
The transformation of the People's Liberation Army
Edited by Nan Li

The Chinese Army Today
Tradition and transformation for the 21st century
Dennis J. Blasko

Taiwan's Security
History and prospects
Bernard D. Cole

Religion and Conflict in South and Southeast Asia
Disrupting violence
Edited by Linell E. Cady and Sheldon W. Simon

Political Islam and Violence in Indonesia
Zachary Abuza

US–Indian Strategic Cooperation into the 21st Century
More than words
Edited by Sumit Ganguly, Brian Shoup and Andrew Scobell

India, Pakistan and the Secret Jihad
The covert war in Kashmir, 1947–2004
Praveen Swami

China's Strategic Culture and Foreign Policy Decision-Making
Confucianism, leadership and war
Huiyun Feng

Chinese Military Strategy in the Third Indochina War
The last Maoist war
Edward C. O'Dowd

Asia Pacific Security
US, Australia and Japan and the new security triangle
Edited by William T. Tow, Mark J. Thomson, Yoshinobu Yamamoto and Satu P. Limaye

China, the United States, and Southeast Asia
Contending perspectives on politics, security, and economics
Edited by Evelyn Goh and Sheldon W. Simon

Conflict and Cooperation in Multi-Ethnic States
Institutional incentives, myths, and counter-balancing
Brian Shoup

China's War on Terrorism
Counter-insurgency, politics and internal security
Martin I. Wayne

US Taiwan Policy
Constructing the triangle
Øystein Tunsjø

Conflict Management, Security and Intervention in East Asia
Third-party mediation in regional conflict
Edited by Jacob Bercovitch, Kwei-Bo Huang and Chung-Chian Teng

South Asia's Cold War
Nuclear weapons and conflict in comparative perspective
Rajesh M. Basrur

The Rise of China and International Security
America and Asia respond
Edited by Kevin J. Cooney and Yoichiro Sato

Nuclear Proliferation in South Asia
Crisis behaviour and the bomb
Edited by Sumit Ganguly and S. Paul Kapur

Nuclear Weapons and Conflict Transformation
The case of India–Pakistan
Saira Khan

Managing the China Challenge
Global perspectives
Edited by Quansheng Zhao and Guoli Liu

India and Counterinsurgency
Lessons learned
Edited by Sumit Ganguly and David P. Fidler

Cooperative Security in the Asia-Pacific
The ASEAN Regional Forum
Edited by Jürgen Haacke and Noel M. Morada

US–China–EU Relations
Managing the new world order
Edited by Robert S. Ross, Øystein Tunsjø and Zhang Tuosheng

China, Europe and International Security
Interests, roles and prospects
Edited by Frans-Paul van der Putten and Chu Shulong

Crime–Terror Nexus in South Asia
States, security and non-state actors
Ryan Clarke

US–Japan–North Korean Security Relations
Irrepressible interests
Anthony DiFilippo

Pakistan's War on Terrorism
Strategies for combating jihadist armed groups since 9/11
Samir Puri

Indian Foreign and Security Policy in South Asia
Regional power strategies
Sandra Destradi

Sri Lanka and the Responsibility to Protect
Politics, ethnicity and genocide
Damien Kingsbury

The Chinese Army Today
Tradition and transformation for the 21st century
Second edition
Dennis Blasko

Sri Lanka and the Responsibility to Protect

Politics, ethnicity and genocide

Damien Kingsbury

Routledge
Taylor & Francis Group
LONDON AND NEW YORK

First published 2012
by Routledge
2 Park Square, Milton Park, Abingdon, Oxon, OX14 4RN

Simultaneously published in the USA and Canada
by Routledge
711 Third Avenue, New York, NY 10017

Routledge is an imprint of the Taylor & Francis Group, an informa business

British Library Cataloguing in Publication Data
A catalogue record for this book is available from the British Library

Library of Congress Cataloging-in-Publication Data
Kingsbury, Damien.
Sri Lanka and the responsibility to protect: politics, ethnicity and genocide/ Damien Kingsbury.
p. cm.
Includes bibliographical references and index.
1. Sri Lanka—History—Civil War, 1983–2009. 2. Humanitarian intervention—Sri Lanka. 3. Humanitarian intervention—Philosophy. I. Title.
KZ6795.S65K56 2011
954.9303'2–dc23
2011024492

ISBN13: 978–0–415–58884–3 (hbk)
ISBN13: 978–0–203–80434–6 (ebk)

Typeset in Times New Roman by Prepress Projects Ltd, Perth, UK

MIX
Paper from responsible sources
FSC www.fsc.org FSC® C004839

Printed and bound in Great Britain by
CPI Antony Rowe, Chippenham, Wiltshire

Contents

Acknowledgements

I would like to extend my gratitude for the assistance I have received in the writing of this book from a number of friends and colleagues. In particular, I would like to thank David Feith, Jay Maheswaran and Murugesu Paramanathan for the information, advice, support and assistance they have each offered me, as well as extending my thanks to the Tamil community of Australia for their warmth and generosity. As an extension of this, I would also like to thank those Tamils of Jaffna and the Vanni who showed me such hospitality during my visit in 2006. They demonstrated what might be possible should the people of Tamil Eelam again achieve the opportunity to be responsible for their own affairs.

Finally, and in particular, I would like to thank my friend, colleague, comrade and wife, Rae, for her love, support and encouragement in the writing of this book and a great deal else. Rae and I came together over issues of injustice, and this remains at the core of our shared values, commitment and work.

I would also like to acknowledge the support provided by Deakin University in allowing me time to research and write this book, and other related work. Finally, I acknowledge the financial support of the Australia Research Council for the awarding of grants that, although not on this subject in particular, have greatly assisted with my broader understanding of the role and responsibility of the international community in conflict and post-conflict environments.

Introduction

This book is about the idea of a responsibility to protect (R2P) in relation to the Tamil separatist war in Sri Lanka and how and why the international community failed to fulfil its obligations under the terms of the R2P paradigm. This failure to invoke and act upon R2P allowed a brutish war to continue for more than three decades and at the end led to the massacre of some 40,000 people. Some in the international community expressed concern over these events but, in the end, were powerless to stop them. If the idea of R2P might have seemed compelling, implementing it proved much more difficult. That it was not able to be invoked and that 40,000 people died would, by any reasonable assessment, have to be understood as a practical failure of the R2P principle.

Any book on R2P, and especially in relation to the separatist war in Sri Lanka, will necessarily engage with a range of difficult, complex and often controversial issues. Despite attempting to keep this book as accessible as possible, it too cannot help but sometimes test the engagement of the reader not already familiar with some of the ideas that it is required to address. Similarly, although coming from a distinctly humanitarian perspective, in this case focusing on the failure of R2P in Sri Lanka, it will by definition arouse the opposition and indeed ire of both people who disagree with the general principles of both international responsibility and the duty of care that is embedded in protection, and those who will object specifically to cases in which they have a vested interest or which stand as examples of how such vested interests could be compromised. Finally, the subject matter of R2P addresses issues that highlight the very worst aspects of human behaviour and the misery and profound suffering that it leaves in its wake. This does not make for easy or happy reading and for any of these reasons one would be unlikely to read this or similar material without good reasons.

However, one would like to think that, despite the difficulty associated with such a text, the reason a reader would want to engage with this field is because it matters. It matters a lot. Anyone who thinks from time to time about any of the constituent elements of this subject will find not only much challenging, but also much to engage with. This may be as a point of argument, perhaps as reaffirmation and perhaps, one might dare to hope, as an opportunity to reflect and by doing so to develop. Regardless of the point of interest that a reader might bring to this book, it is difficult to argue against its underlying principle: that certain forms of behaviour, such as crimes against humanity, war crimes and genocide, have never been socially acceptable – anywhere in the world – other than to those employing them. Similarly, for very good, compelling and widely agreed reasons there are now sanctions able to be imposed against people responsible for them. To employ a quote that neatly summarises this equation: ‘a deliberate and systematic attempt to terrorise, expel or murder an entire people must be met decisively with all necessary means, and with the political will to carry the policy through to its logical conclusion’ (Lederer 1999).

The idea of R2P is relatively new in formal terms, bringing a sense of an international duty of care to the conduct of world affairs. In another, less formal sense, however, the idea of having an R2P or a duty of care towards others is perhaps as old as humanity, evoking as it does the very basic notion of humanity being shared and, consequently, of empathy and kindness. It also evokes a common opposition to abuses of these normative and sometimes self-sustaining qualities. Most cultures and each of the world’s major religions exhort the protection of the weak and vulnerable; do we not feel a sense of compulsion to intervene when a vulnerable person suffers undue attack? Most laws – the rules by which we agree to live – are similarly codified to ensure that all to whom the law applies are equally accountable to it but all are equally protected by it. These are the rules that govern, or are supposed to govern, the actions of states.

Yet although composed of them, states are not people, and their concerns for the welfare of others, although often common and usually normative, are not absolute. In this, a particular society might agree to a set of laws by which it regulates social conduct, thus ensuring the protection of all within the law by the agreement of all within the law. But the extent to which such laws exist within the community of states and, more importantly, the extent to which they are enforceable is less clear and much more open to debate. To illustrate this point, the ‘realist’ interpretation of international relations theory posits, among other things, that the internal affairs of states are of no necessary interest or concern to other states; that international relations is conducted between states as free entities in an unregulated environment abstracted from their internal systems and conditions (e.g. see Waltz 1979). That is, in such a system, what happens in one country is relevant to the citizens of another country only if they are directly affected.

In particular, states have historically resisted or actively opposed intervention in their internal affairs by external parties both as a principle of sovereignty and as a practical means by which they have safeguarded their territory and the interests that territory represents. That is, although societies of peoples have construed laws to govern their common behaviour, states have not also construed laws to regulate their behaviour, or at least not in ways that are always or consistently recognisable or enforceable. This may then start to help explain why the principle of R2P was not invoked in the case of Sri Lanka, which subsequently allowed a massacre of innocents to occur. That there was no intervention to prevent the deaths of around 40,000 people was fairly clearly a failure of R2P as a binding international obligation.

As with a small community of people, when a larger or more powerful individual behaves in an anti-social manner, the rest of the community is sometimes limited as to its potential response. This is especially so if the behaviour in question is conducted within the home of the individual concerned and relates, perhaps, only to their immediate family. There may be social concern or even opprobrium over the behaviour of the individual concerned, but there may also be reluctance to intervene in a 'domestic' matter. Further, by intervening, a precedent can be set that may be used against others of the community whose behaviour from time to time runs contrary to accepted behavioural norms. A sense of commitment to assist the citizens of other states, then, may be strong or even compelling, but for a range of reasons states may choose not to act on the compulsions of their own citizens, or to go slowly and reluctantly even when a compelling case is accepted. This is particularly so when states (or their leaders) sometimes claim that such notions of international responsibility are recent, impractical and untested. Yet the ideas and actions that precede R2P have a considerable history, both as ideas and as actions.

Although arguments in its favour can be found earlier, R2P finds its philosophical home in the legal 'classicist' tradition developed principally in the United States from the late nineteenth century (see Hovenkamp 1985) and which reached its high point in the doctrine of Wilsonian self-determination, which is parallel, if formally unrelated, to R2P. Such classicism, which sees the origins of law as transcendent, also finds parallels with assertions of natural justice, which more directly fits into notions of R2P. The key element of the classicist argument is that law changes over time, following social, political and economic changes. What is acceptable to one generation may become unacceptable to another (such as slavery) and vice versa (such as gay rights). Indeed, the notion that there is and can be international law, beyond the confines of the narrowly conceived sovereign state, graphically illustrates this point about the dynamism of legal values.

But at what point does one cease to turn a blind eye to actions that would not be acceptable otherwise? At what point is self-interest overcome by social responsibility? And, perhaps most importantly, at what point does refusal or failure to act become complicity?

Individuals – and states – do have a responsibility to behave in a manner that accords to a more comprehensive and arguably universal norm. International behaviour is properly the concern of the international community, which is the subject of international law and the potential adjudication of international bodies such as the UN Security Council. But even internally – at home – states have a responsibility towards their own citizens. Francis Deng *et al.* (1996) articulated the state's responsibility towards its own citizens as a duty of care, based on the state as the cumulative political manifestation of its citizens. This followed earlier articulations of concern over the 'predatory' behaviour of some states or the elites that lead them towards their citizens (e.g. see Evans 1995). This then came to be one of the foundation principles behind R2P, that 'Each individual State has the responsibility to protect its populations from genocide, war crimes, ethnic cleansing, and crimes against humanity' (UNGA 2005: 138).

Hence, although there is a strong moral argument for intervention and there is also considerable basis in international law and there is some precedent, enacting R2P principles is rarely straightforward and very often confounded by a range of competing and mutually exclusive considerations. It is not always possible, or even desirable, to extrapolate from the personal to the universal, but the sense of social order, concern for the welfare of others and a desire to protect at least obviously innocent victims that exemplifies the better aspects of human social behaviour does find a parallel in international behaviour. If such social behaviour can be said to reflect the better qualities of the human condition within a social context, one might posit that it has taken so long for the community of states to arrive at a broad consensus around the idea of R2P because it has been only in relatively recent times that there has been sufficient global cohesion or a sufficient sense of global community, such that it exists, for the idea to have some practical meaning. R2P can be said to be one more element of what has long been recognised as the phenomenon of globalisation.

Despite the prevalence of realpolitik in international affairs and the general reluctance of states to become involved in each other's affairs, there has also long been a moral counter-argument for intervention in the affairs of other states, which has in some cases been borne out in practice. These interventions cannot be equated with R2P as such, but they do indicate the various streams of thinking and some of the actions that have underpinned the development of the concept. For example, the United Kingdom's intervention in Burma took place in three stages in the nineteenth century (1824–86), with the third and final phase of its invasion predicated upon the supposed outrage of the Burmese royalty engaging in its traditional practice of murdering royal relatives upon the ascension to the throne of the new king. So, too, France invaded what was then Indochina in 1858 following the pretext of protecting Christian priests, while the United States declared war on Spain, securing its remaining colonial possessions and asserting strategic primacy in the Americas, on the pretext of supporting Cuban independence. Indeed, many of the nineteenth century's colonial adventures were predicated upon some nominal excuse about protection of ethnic or religious minorities or the freedom of unfettered internal or international trade. More recent illustrations of the types of interventions that contributed to thinking about the legitimacy (or otherwise) of R2P being used in ambiguous circumstances include, for example, the US-led invasion of Kuwait or the later, post-'weapons of mass destruction' rationale for the invasion of Iraq – that Saddam was an evil dictator who murdered his own people. Although true, it is a rationalisation not similarly used elsewhere. This, then, has caused many citizens of liberal states to regard the potential for R2P as being but a subterfuge for invading another state in order to seek unrelated material advantage and, as such, a more contemporary form of traditional colonialism (e.g. see Fenton 2005).

Importantly, however, is that, although there may be legitimate concerns with the application of R2P in practice, especially as a subterfuge for other agendas, the underlying principle of protecting the world's most vulnerable peoples remains a compelling moral and legal obligation. This applies especially given that such peoples are subject to depredations by the governments that are nominally in office to protect and advance the interests of their states' citizens. All too often, governments in some countries exist primarily to advance their own narrow personal or sectional interests by preying on those people they are supposed to serve.

This then raises the spectre of the 'just war' paradigm and the complex and competing issues it in turn raises. The notion of 'just war' derives from mediaeval Christian theology (although parallels can also be found in other moral philosophies, not least in Islam) and was used as a rationale for numerous colonial adventures. It posits that, in certain circumstances, it can be acceptable and indeed obligatory to go to war against another state or country in defence of the unprotected. The Catechism of the Catholic Church, section 2309, states:

> The gravity of such a decision makes it subject to rigorous conditions of moral lcgitimacy. At onc and thc samc timc:
>
> - the damage inflicted by the aggressor on the nation or community of nations must be lasting, grave, and certain;
> - all other means of putting an end to it must have been shown to be impractical or ineffective;
> - there must be serious prospects of success;
> - the use of arms must not produce evils and disorders graver than the evil to be eliminated. The power of modern means of destruction weighs very heavily in evaluating this condition.
>
> These are the traditional elements enumerated in what is called the 'just war' doctrine.
>
> The evaluation of these conditions for moral legitimacy belongs to the prudential judgment of those who have responsibility for the common good. (CCC 1997)

Although secular theorists may also argue in favour of a 'just war', they do so not on the basis of religious precepts but on the basis of universal moral values. Other secular conditionalities concerning 'just war' include protection of life from imminent threat, that injustice is suffered disproportionately, that only constituted public authorities, for example states or a coalition of states, may wage such a war, that the war must be proportionate to the harm it seeks to redress and that it should be engaged only with enemy combatants and in a manner that is consistent with the rules of war.

In both the religious and the secular sense, the conditions informing the notion of 'just war' are similar to, or much the same as that of, R2P, requiring the establishment of a particular set of conditions and, to a lesser extent, its management and conduct. The principle difference is that the 'just war' paradigm may be used in, and was largely developed for the purpose of, self-defence, whereas the notion of R2P is based on the protection of others rather than oneself.

Although 'just war' in defence of others is a divisive concept, there are clearly legitimate examples of R2P being employed. In 1999, the international community pressured the Indonesian government[1] to accept the entry of an international peacemaking/peacekeeping force in Timor-Leste to end violence against a people who had voted for independence under an agreement between the Indonesian government and the UN. The decision to intervene and that the Indonesian government acceded to the UN-sanctioned force, if under a high degree of economic compulsion, militates in favour of this being a conventional R2P situation.[2] Despite later claims by some Indonesian 'nationalists', there was no manipulation of the vote to lead inevitably to such intervention, nor was there any demonstrable ulterior motive for it. Indeed, the lead country in that intervention, Australia, had actually stated that it wished to see a continuation of its long-held policy of supporting Timor-Leste's integration into Indonesia (see Fernandes 2004). After being compelled to act by Australian public opinion, the Australian government then withdrew its forces from Timor-Leste as soon as possible and, according to some critics at the time and with the benefit of hindsight, precipitously in 2003.[3]

The behaviour of Indonesian state agents in 1999, including its army, their proxy militias and its police, illustrated the ways in which states sometimes turn against the people they are ostensibly employed to protect or defend. Yet even if it was possible to accept the Indonesian government's otherwise facile claim that the violence of Timor-Leste in 1999 was perpetrated by 'rogue elements', this continued to illustrate the weakness of the central government's capacity to protect its own citizens (or its claimed citizens) from serious harm. Under precisely the types of terms that were later incorporated into the R2P paradigm, this state incapacity (or culpability) then legitimised international intervention.

Such circumstances then reflect on the situations in which states fail to fulfil those criteria by which they are conventionally measured and understood. Conventional criteria for statehood includes maintaining a monopoly on the legitimate use of violence, maintaining territorial integrity (which in turn finds some contradiction with and is one of the stumbling blocks for R2P) and the equitable provision of services by which a state is conventionally identified, including raising taxes or other forms of standardised income, rule of law and social services such as education, health and communication. That is, when a state fails in its duty of care as a state, that duty of care devolves to another, more competent authority. In ensuring that this authority does not then exploit said state weakness, its greatest guarantee of impartiality is agreement by other states in concert.

There have been numerous other cases cited where R2P has applied, where it has been argued that it should be applied or where, after the fact, it appears that the international community has been remiss is not applying it. NATO's 1999 intervention in Kosovo stands, alongside Timor-Leste, as an example of the application of R2P; the situation in the Sudanese region of Darfur illustrates a case in which it has been argued that R2P should apply; and the Rwandan genocide stands as a strong example of a case in which, after the fact, it is widely agreed that R2P should have applied. In the case of Rwanda, over three months in 1994, ethnic Hutu militias and army members murdered perhaps 800,000[4] mostly ethnic Tutsi men, women and children and would probably have continued their rampage had they not been stopped by the predominantly ethnic Tutsi Rwandan Patriotic Front operating out of neighbouring Uganda. The UN-mandated commander in Rwanda, Lieutenant General Romeo Dallaire, pleaded before and during the massacre for greater support and a more open mandate from the UN Security Council (UNSC), which at that time included Rwanda as a non-permanent member and France, which has been argued to have supported the then Hutu-dominated government. The USNC was, however, slow to respond and eventually offered too little too late. US president Bill Clinton acknowledged that the international community had failed to act in Rwanda when it had a responsibility to do so (PBS 1998). It was, he said at the time, a case of 'never again'.

Despite being around in other forms for a much longer period, R2P as it is now understood has come a long way in a relatively short time. From inauspicious beginnings, the principle of R2P was endorsed by the General Assembly in 2005 and unanimously reaffirmed by the Security Council in 2006 (Resolution 1674). There have been numerous events that have highlighted the need for or led to the acceptance of R2P, including the following wars or other forms of conflict:

- India–Pakistan–Bangladesh war in 1971;
- Angolan civil war in 1971;
- Cambodia in 1978;
- Kurdish genocide in Iraq in 1987;
- Liberia in 1990, 2003;
- Gulf War in 1990;
- Northern Iraq (Kurdish area) in 1991;
- Yugoslav wars from 1991;
- Somalia in 1993;
- Rwandan genocide in 1994;
- Sierra Leone's civil war in 1998;
- Kosovo in 1999;
- Timore-Leste in 1999;
- Haiti in 2004;
- Cote D'Ivoire in 2002, 2005;
- Darfur from 2003.

In each of these cases the event was significant in terms of crimes against humanity or war crimes, and where there was an intervention it was of a military nature. This does not, then, go to the full range of R2P-type responses, but it does highlight that the need for intervention had been established before the formal adoption of R2P. In cases in which the intervention was carried out by organisations of states, it was or was intended to be under the UN Charter Chapter VIII, Article 53 with reference to Security Council-approved enforcement under regional arrangements. In each of these cases, there has been a trend towards more liberal interpretations of the Charter for the purpose of allowing such military intervention (see Farer 2003: 71–3). Moreover, Walzer argued that India's invasion of Pakistan in 1971 averted a mass slaughter and was therefore no less defensible than an approved UN intervention (Walzer 2000: 71). Yet as Walzer notes, both governments and coalitions of governments have a mixture of motives in acting solely or together. Vietnam's invasion of Cambodia in 1978 has often been cited as a humanitarian intervention and, in that it toppled the Khmer Rouge regime that had perpetrated one of the most grave slaughters of the twentieth century, this was an accurate characterisation. However, the overriding motivation for this intervention was the increasing Khmer Rouge incursions into sovereign Vietnamese territory, the persecution of ethnic Vietnamese in Cambodia and strategic rivalry between the Soviet Union and China as played out by their respective proxies, Vietnam and Cambodia.

The main difference between R2P and humanitarian intervention is that the latter can be applied to situations beyond mass atrocities, and it can be implemented unilaterally. Intervention under R2P is applied strictly multilaterally through a consensus within and under the auspices of the UN Security Council in cases of actual or imminent mass atrocities. The extent (or lack) of international intervention in each of the above cases differs, but each raised the question of the responsibility of the international community and the role of international law.

R2P has a number of precedents and, apart from economic and diplomatic interventions, illustrations of R2P in practice arguably include:

- Kuwait 1990 (UN-authorised US-led coalition);
- Sierra Leone 1991–2000 (Nigeria–UN);
- Somalia from 1993 (UN and UN-authorised US-led coalition and again UN);
- Timor-Leste 1999 (UNSC-authorised Australian-led coalition);
- Kosovo 1999–2008 (NATO and then the UN);
- Darfur 2004 (UN-authorised African Union).

Despite the obvious necessity of each of these interventions, not only is R2P not universally endorsed but also it has strong international opponents, including many countries noted to be signatories to the R2P convention who have subsequently said they oppose it. Critical among those opponents to R2P, not least because it could be subject to its provisions, is Sri Lanka.

There are many wars and other forms of conflict, both internal and external, that deserve the attention of R2P. High among them for longevity, brutality and structural intransigence is the separatist 'Eeelam' war in Sri Lanka, beginning in 1976[5] and concluding in a massacre on a remote stretch of beach in 2009. In the intervening period, there have been widespread and often indiscriminate attacks against civilians, the profound entrenchment of ethnic enmities and the state-sponsored displacement (see Aluwihare 2000) of hundreds of thousands, perhaps millions, of ethnic Tamils. This displacement and the structural discrimination against and exclusion from the state of ethnic Tamils has been referred to as 'demogracide', meaning to exclude a people geographically, economically, socially and politically.

This book aims to provide a study of the war by Liberation Tigers of Tamil Eelam to create a separate state in Sri Lanka and the ways in which and extent to which this war might have invoked R2P principles and the ways in which the continuing humanitarian and political crisis in Sri Lanka may still do so. By considering the example of Sri Lanka, this book will focus on what conditions could satisfy, or in principle demand, the application of R2P. It will further offer an insight into the nature and consequences of the Sri Lanka war, presenting a case as to why this conflict was and may still be the normative responsibility of the international community. The question, then, is at what point can a state, or the government of a state, be said to be engaging in activities that undermine its claim to legitimacy, and at what point can the international community be reasonably expected to take action to remedy such a situation. The question then arises as to types of action that might be taken to implement R2P principles. This book addresses the issues and challenges facing the implementation of the R2P principles, and employs as its main case study the circumstances that have confronted Sri Lanka. It will address the political, legal and practical challenges that such possible implementation could confront.

The main themes of the book include:

- a restatement of the principles of R2P, including identification of the types of military, economic and diplomatic action that might be taken by third parties in cases in which a large number of people are under serious threat;
- a brief history of post-colonial war in Sri Lanka;
- the ethnically specific nature of the war with the LTTE;
- an outline and analysis of the manner in which the war and subsequent policies have been waged;
- the extent to which the war and policies constitute the deliberate and systematic destruction, in whole or in part, of Sri Lanka's Tamils as an ethnic, racial, religious and, as perhaps most Sri Lankan Tamils claim, national group;
- the relationship between the actions of the government of Sri Lanka and its potential or actual contravention of international law;
- government of Sri Lanka opposition to R2P in theory and in practice;
- geo-strategic factors against implementing R2P;
- geo-strategic factors in favour of R2P;
- the extent to which Sri Lanka could become a site of R2P intervention, the reasons for such intervention and the lessons that come from such an analysis.

There is little doubt that the war in Sri Lanka and in particular how it was conducted in its final six months and especially the last few weeks represented a fairly clear-cut case for the implementation of R2P. Following the war, more than 200,000 Tamils were held in internment camps in which they did not have access to adequate food, clean water or health care. Most were eventually released, even if to an uncertain future, in many cases not being able to return to the homes or the land they once owned. In some cases they were destroyed but in many cases they had become the site of or were in close proximity to army camps in what remained an occupied area, and to where poor Sinhalese were increasingly brought in to permanently displace them. The 'disappearances' of thousands of individuals from internment camps, presumably murdered by soldiers or police without recourse to trial or any other form of justice, continued as a profound reminder of the nature of the state that had evolved to assume authority of its sometimes reluctant peoples.

In the period after the war, Tamils continued to flee Sri Lanka, in substantial fear of their lives. Despite the clear grounds they were able to present for seeking refugee status, receiving countries such as Australia and Canada treated them not with compassion but as, in effect, criminals or at least potential criminals. The government of Sri Lanka meanwhile continued its shrill calls for Tamil asylum seekers to be returned to Sri Lanka, employing the logic that if they fled they necessarily had something to be afraid of and they would be afraid only if they were members or sympathisers of the LTTE. Apart from the obvious fact that many were just ethnic Tamils wishing to escape persecution, many LTTE sympathisers simply sought equity under the state. And even though many LTTE soldiers had been forced to join the organisation, the assumption was that they were all 'terrorists'. Being returned to Sri Lanka, then, meant at least a brutal interrogation and a period of detention without trial, and at worse joining the legion of 'disappeared'. The grounds for international concern were overwhelming in practice yet remained underwhelming in terms of response. The grounds for implementing R2P in Sri Lanka were clear, but the lack of such intervention illustrated much of the weakness of the idea as currently constructed. Also clearly illustrated were the debilitating qualities of international division and sectional self-interest that precluded effective action and, in a time when much of the world and many of its leaders believe we have moved beyond barbarism, allowed it to continue. We would like to think 'never again', as President Clinton so passionately promised, but all too often we find excuses to avoid a common responsibility, and we do little or nothing to protect.

R2P as a norm

R2P developed as a norm in light of the lead-up to the 2005 World Summit agreement, the UN Secretary-General's High Level Panel, and the subsequent agreement. It was applied in practice, even if outside (primarily before) the formal parameters of the UN's 2005 agreement. In particular, there were both correspondence and distinctions between R2P and the interventions in Kuwait in 1990 by a US-led coalition, Sierra Leone in 1991–2000 by Nigeria and the UN, Somalia in 1993 by the United States (and subsequently Ethiopia), Timor-Leste in 1999 by the Australian-led, UN-endorsed Interfet, Kosovo in 1999 by the UN, and Darfur in 2003 by the UN.

In attempting to explore the conditions for the implementation of R2P and its application to Sri Lanka, the 'norm life cycle' model, as developed by Martha Finnemore and Kathyrn Sikkink, is useful in understanding how a new norm (shared expectations of appropriate behaviour for a given identity) has been accepted at the declaratory level in a global institution, and then diffused into institutions and practice (Finnemore and Sikkink 1998). The 'norm diffusion' process helps identify both the drivers and the obstacles to implementation that may assist or preclude R2P from achieving a 'taken-for-granted' quality which would embed the principle into localised state behaviour. Importantly, this diffusion and acceptance is based, according to Acharya (2004, see also Acharya 2009), on congruence building based upon pre-existing norms. In this model, 'universal' norms are reconstructed and 'localised' and thus acculturated.

If there is a small element of Acharya's thesis that is questionable, it is not this diffusion through a dynamic congruence with local norms, but his initial proposition that constructivist scholarship posits moral transformation as a case of 'good' global norms prevailing over 'bad' local norms. This false dichotomy does not in fact accurately reflect 'constructivist' (or behavioural) understandings of norm diffusion, which actually tend to support Acharya's central position (e.g. see Kravtsov 2006). What appears to have happened is that Acharya has put up a 'straw man' argument in order to knock it down again with his own proposition, if within the politically specific context of his own institution. That is, on one hand Acharya attempts to explain how universal norms find acceptance in specific environments while on the other he criticises the putative suggestion that the universal is necessarily more positive and the local necessarily more negative. This intellectual juggling act is a prerequisite for public scholarship under Singapore's highly interventionist political order. In short, Acharya identified the relatively obvious, that, for example, global conventions on the equitable and consistent rule of law find correspondence with locally applied *syariah* (Islamic law) or just and accountable government. The problems of congruence are usually not on the part of 'local' people, but the elites that benefit from constructing 'norms' on their behalf. On this, Acharya is silent, as is to be expected within the closed Singaporean political context.

Beyond that, the norm diffusion process follows a 'norm life cycle' model that Finnemore and Sikkink identify as occurring in three stages. The first stage is when the incipient norm is introduced by 'norm entrepreneurs' who seek to persuade a critical mass of states to adopt the new norm. Regarding R2P, Gareth Evans might be such a 'norm interpreter'. If they are successful in doing so a 'tipping point' is reached, leading to the second stage of the new norm. At this stage, also referred to as 'norm cascade', the norm is to be prioritised with the understanding that there will be alterations to state behaviour as a result of unanimously adopting this new norm. At this stage it is also common for there to be some 'back and forth' contestation as states determine the significance of the new norm in terms of how it alters existing behaviour and competing norms. In the final stage, the norm is then internalised by states at the domestic level.

However, Acharya argues that it is at this stage that norm diffusion becomes crucial, as for global norms to be internalised and thereby implemented the norm does not need to just be accepted at the domestic level – it also needs to be 'localised'. According to Acharya (2004: 251), norm localization is the 'process in which external ideas are simultaneously adapted to meet local practices'. This localisation is important because it is only when domestic states have adopted the norm to an extent that it becomes an accepted 'local' practice that we see their contribution to strengthening the norm at the regional and international level.

> A new norm is created only when the initial behaviour is repeated consistently by a preponderance of states over a considerable period of time and only when there is a shift in the legal consciousness of all or most states as to the juridical status of the behaviour.
>
> (Buchanan 2003:135)

Having outlined the origins and purpose of R2P, the question is then what application might this have to the case of Sri Lanka. In an era in which political solutions to internal conflicts have become increasingly successful, Evans (2008: 235) has identified Sri Lanka as being one of the conflicts in which R2P has '*prima facie* application' (Evans 2008: 6, 76). This is, he notes, because of its 'ethnic dimension and the kinds of atrocities that have occurred in the past' (Evans 2008: 73) and which has failed in terms of finding a political or diplomatic resolution because the parties were 'too dug in and too far apart' (Evans 2008: 109). Or, as noted by Traub (2009):

> The fighting threatens to produce exactly the kind of cataclysm that states vowed to prevent when they adopted 'the responsibility to protect' at the 2005 U.N. World Summit. This doctrine stipulates that states have a responsibility to protect peoples within their borders from genocide, war crimes, crimes against humanity and ethnic cleansing. When states are found to be 'manifestly failing' to protect citizens from such mass violence, that responsibility shifts to the international community, acting through the United Nations. At the core of this norm is the obligation to act preventively rather than waiting until atrocities have occurred, as has happened too often.

The UN Secretary-General, Ban Ki-moon, identified the challenge of implementing R2P as one of the cornerstones of his tenure as Secretary-General. Yet at the first hurdle, Sri Lanka in 2009, the UN was unable or unwilling to act. The principle of R2P, then, was such that it was logically consistent with other global norms and values and was sufficiently supported to be passed into the global body of requirements around rights and obligations. But it was too problematic in practice for a world in which the interests of individual states and alliances between such states were able to thwart consensus.

1 The meaning, theory and application of R2P

This first substantive chapter will provide a brief overview of the key principles of and background to R2P. It will do so in two main parts. The first part will address the origins of the idea of R2P and the specific instances that gave rise to its perceived necessity. The second part will identify the shift, in particular in the post-Cold War environment, that has allowed and indeed encouraged the development of R2P as a coherent set of principles located in normative global behaviour and international law. It will also discuss issues of R2P within a human rights framework and the issue of legitimate and illegitimate violence, employed by both state and non-state actors.

Ideas such as R2P do not, of course, spring fully formed into life but are the product of circumstances, time and necessity. Like all such emerging ideas, R2P has enjoyed proponents and interlocutors as well as detractors and opponents. However, from its earliest forms of enunciation and application, R2P and its precedents have developed and grown as an intellectually coherent idea, increasingly taking hold of the imagination of leading thinkers and heads of state and, in the negative, establishing itself as something to be feared on the part of political actors whose methods have continued to exhibit characteristics consistent with 'might over right', or simple brute force over reason, equity and humanity.

The origins of R2P date to concerns over the atrocities of World War II, notably the genocide perpetrated principally against European Jews, Gypsies and others, but also over mass slaughter in China and elsewhere. Before this time, in that such concerns existed, they foundered on the realpolitik of Westphalian state sovereignty, not withstanding the brief and unsuccessful period of the League of Nations. However, with the advent of the United Nations came the requirement to formalise a range of international normative criteria, including various human rights instruments and the theoretical formalisation of international solidarity in cases of arbitrary attacks against sovereign states. The ideological divisions of states during the Cold War, however, put paid to much of the potential for the UN to act in either a pre-emptive or corrective manner. States that might have otherwise been more benign all too often supported strategic allies who shared little or none of their humanitarian concern and who at a later time might have been vulnerable to the application of R2P.

Of the various concerns that have been raised in relation to R2P, in Sri Lanka and elsewhere, Weiss (2004) cited shortcomings that were less critical of its intent and more critical of its *lack* of application. Arguing that R2P was beginning to decline as a global moral imperative, Weiss identified four basic shortcomings of R2P. The first was that R2P is actually quite constrained in its possible use, failing to live up to the ideals held for it and not being nearly as forward looking as its proponents had suggested. The second was that, globally, and in contrast to what the critics said, there was too little humanitarian intervention rather than too much. Weiss also noted that any wider concern over intervention as a consequence of R2P was misdirected, with that concern being more properly aimed at pre-emptive or preventative armed intervention. In his final critique of R2P, Weiss argued that reform of the UN Security Council, which formally has carriage of legitimising R2P, was illusory and that the real challenge was to identify where US multilateralism could and should be applied (Weiss 2004), given the UN Security Council's failures.

Weiss's concerns were echoed by the UN High Commissioner for Refugees (UNHCR) and the International Committee of the Red Cross (ICRC). A UNHCR-led 'protection cluster' was formed as part of the humanitarian reforms and the issue of 'protection' is included in most of its humanitarian appeals. However, the cluster noted that the term 'protection' means different things to different agencies. UNHCR and ICRC protection mandates are defined by international law whereas other humanitarian agencies tend to focus on protecting people from harm, abuse and exploitation, or take a wider approach of protecting all civilian rights, including shelter, water or education, or embrace both. 'But protection as a response by the humanitarian community is still relatively new, not very well defined, and some experts warn of the danger of over-promising what cannot be delivered' (IRIN 2010a). In discussing humanitarian responses to circumstances requiring protection, Weiss opened up a twofold discussion. The first part of his discussion identified the broad range of activities that could and should be considered part of protection – including intervention – and why they should be acted upon. The second part of his discussion noted that focusing solely on protection directed attention away from the responsibilities and actions, inaction or malignant action of responsible governments.

By way of illustration, the British head of the global medical charity, Médecins Sans Frontières, Marc DuBois, commented widely on what he saw as the dangers of humanitarian agencies over-promising how much protection they could deliver, which, he said, could mask the responsibility of the perpetrators of violence and abuse in crisis situations. DuBois characterised this tendency as the 'fig leaves and other delusions of protection' (DuBois 2008). When asked to define his organisation's protection role and where its protection limits lie, DuBois said:

> We struggle even with the word, 'protection' – different people in MSF have different approaches to it and there is no consensus. Responding to humanitarian crises requires more than the sterile distribution of goods and services; if a population is being abused, it requires more than assistance, and humanitarians should pat themselves on the back for breaking through the 'aid alone' barrier'.
>
> MSF's protection limits are not hard and fast. We can try to stop people

at checkpoints from harassing patients crossing in search of healthcare; we can design our own programmes to minimize violence, [like] delivering tents to Haitians in a way that will not end up in a riot, but we cannot go out and stop physical violence and abuse – that is a clear limit.

(IRIN 2010a)

On defining 'protection', UNICEF's Bo Viktor Nylund said:

> The way we define protection varies a lot. UNICEF's [2008] child protection strategy states [that it] is 'preventing and responding to violence, exploitation and abuse to ensure children's rights to survival, development and well-being,' but UNICEF also signs up to a broader, rights-based inter-agency definition of protection through the protection cluster. Whenever you engage with governments or non-state actors on protection of civilians against harm or abuse, you always have to have in mind their accountability. You are there to assist them, to see how they will protect people from abuse. You can't . . . be the agency taking on those responsibilities. In Haiti, when there was no police force up-and-running, and displaced people were experiencing abuse, we could not just stand by and do nothing, but we tried to build the capacity of remaining police forces to address it. We helped them establish police brigades. It was then the police who started monitoring airports to make sure children had appropriate documentation so they weren't trafficked out of the country. In Sri Lanka we advocated for the release of children in the government armed forces, but we wouldn't start sending supplies to strengthen police forces, or hand out money that could be used to fuel conflict. It's a thin line we tread. It can be more difficult to get . . . non-state actors to address violations . . . for instance, the LTTE [Tamil Tigers rebel group] in Sri Lanka was an organized rebel group, [so] the government of Sri Lanka would not accept if outsiders try to build up the LTTE's capacity to protect.
>
> (IRIN 2010a)

World Vision, on the other hand, was:

> committed to doing everything possible to ensure that our activities do not put children at risk. We define this as being a 'child-safe organization' . . . [which] includes efforts at prevention, responding and protecting related to abuse, neglect, exploitation and other forms of violence against children.
>
> (IRIN 2010a)

But according to World Vision's Bill Forbes:

> We do not promise that children in our target communities will be safe. We do not take on the responsibility for security, other than ensuring all efforts to not put people at risk of harm through participation in activities. However, since we work in volatile environments, even this must be spelled out in each crisis.
>
> (IRIN 2010a)

The UNHCR's Ruvendrini Menikdiwela defined 'protection' in terms of

> content and the people we cover, which includes refugees, stateless people, returnees, and internally displaced persons [IDPs]. We don't have a generic protection definition. For refugee protection we follow the gamut of rights in the 1951 Refugee Convention, and 1954 and 1961 Conventions. With IDPs there is no internationally binding legal treaty, but our work is mainly based on the 1988 guiding principles. The protection cluster's 40 or so members have adopted a definition, which states [that] protection activities will respect the rights of the individual in accordance with the letter and spirit of all relevant bodies of law, including international humanitarian law, human rights law or refugee law.
>
> (IRIN 2010a)

MSF's DuBois said that although there was criticism of the term 'protection' it remained useful.

> The term works internally for us, and we do break protection into projects. We know what we mean by humanitarian protection, it is just not what the public understands by it. They think it is mainly provision of physical safety: when the armed forces stop bad people doing bad things to good people.
>
> (IRIN 2010a)

In the magazine *Humanitarian Exchange*, DuBois (2008) posited the following rhetorical question:

> If you were walking in the street and saw a group of people beating a child on the ground, which of the following activities would you consider protection?
>
> 1 Run across the street and stop the attacker.
> 2 Keep walking. Lobby for better street lighting.
> 3 Run home and write down everything you witnessed as a report for publication.
> 4 Visit the family of the victim to offer replacements for torn clothing.

DuBois said that 'humanitarians' considered all of the responses as examples of humanitarian protection, whereas the public overwhelmingly thought that only the first response was correct. To extrapolate from this, although all responses are legitimate, 'running across the street and stopping the attacker' – intervention – was widely seen as legitimate. This then raised the vexing question of when does knowledge but inaction become complicity?

UNICEF's Nylund said that:

> The risk [of scrapping humanitarian protection] would be that the 20 years we have spent trying to get coherence on what . . . [it] means would be lost. We each feel a bit differently about what protection means, but hopefully we

complement each other in the field. If we all did the same thing, our services would not be wide enough.

(IRIN 2010a)

The UNHCR's Menikdiwela said that:

> Whatever category of assistance you use relates to fundamental human rights, which is protection. You can't scrap it. Each agency interprets the parameters through their own lens: UNICEF through child protection, OHCHR through human rights protection, UNHCR as refugee protection. The beauty lies in the diversity. We are clearly a long way from being perfect entities, but there are merits to diversity. The challenge is to ensure all protection responses encompass different aspects . . . [and] displaced people, women at the risk of sexual violence, and unaccompanied children are all covered in a crisis.
>
> (IRIN 2010a)

One of DuBois' criticisms was that humanitarian agencies defined protection too much in terms of what they could or could not deliver. As a result, responsibility was shifted away from perpetrators. World Vision's Forbes agreed that non-governmental organisations (NGOs) can take on too much responsibility for a situation as it exists, 'as though their lack of effectiveness causes the situation, which is delusional and misplaced' (IRIN 2010a).

> However, I also think that the dichotomy between what NGOs can deliver and the situation in the community is a false one, since the focus of much protection work is to strengthen the protective environment in communities, or to advocate against root causes of violence. NGOs doing good protection work are actually strengthening the capacity of communities and stakeholders to address protection issues, including responding to and stopping perpetrators.
>
> (IRIN 2010a)

However, the UNCHR's Menikdiwela disagreed with DuBois:

> If you look at what humanitarians are doing in Democratic Republic of Congo, eastern Chad, Darfur, South Sudan, these are all complex political situations, but no humanitarians are saying, 'this is what we can do to solve the crisis'. They are just doing what they can to their best ability. Bringing perpetrators to justice is beyond the gambit of any humanitarian agency. If we do that, we compromise the humanitarian mandate. We still need to maintain humanitarian space from the political wings of the UN – that is a concern for all humanitarian agencies – but getting more involved in protection is not a bad thing.
>
> (IRIN 2010a)

In this, Menikdiwela implicitly acknowledged that, although humanitarian agencies could not bring perpetrators to justice, there was a role for doing so, which devolved to the UN's 'political wings'. That is, there was a responsibility of the UN's political – and legal – agencies to actively intervene in the perpetration of humanitarian abuses, which amounted to a practical need for R2P. Considering the proposition that donors are funding a growing protection bureaucracy rather than engaging in other types of protection and, in effect, are excusing abusive state actors, DuBois said that he believed that states with duties to act are constrained by real-world politics, but that funding protection can shield abusive states in the same way that humanitarian aid has been given to address a political crisis, as opposed to addressing it as a political problem. 'Funding protection is no bad thing – advocates and human rights organisations who can speak up on abuses are needed – but it is only part of a bigger puzzle' (IRIN 2010a). According to Forbes, both security-related funding and bureaucracy-related protection are underfunded, while Nylund said that in Sudan UNICEF supported police to establish child and family protection units, which had also been invested in by the police themselves (IRIN 2010a). Menikdiwela said that, from the perspective of the UNHCR, there were no gaps in funding that were not being addressed:

> Ten years ago governments wouldn't be talking about 'responsibility to protect'. In some cases where states are not living up to their duties . . . the gap is more about translating concepts at a [UN] policy level in Geneva and New York into the field of operations; transitioning from concepts to reality on the ground.
>
> (IRIN 2010a)

The tactics of certain governments being explicitly identified as needing to be addressed logically lead to the need for R2P. The question is, though, perhaps less one of 'pre-empting' such tactics and more one of intervening to ensure that the framework for such tactics does not exist.

The birth of R2P

The formal idea of R2P can be said to have had its birth with the appointment by the Canadian government in September 2000 of an International Commission on Intervention and State Sovereignty (ICISS). The ICISS was intended to assist the then UN Secretary-General, Kofi Annan, and other key international actors to find common ground on the question of the R2P. A little more than a year later, in December 2001, the ICISS produced a 90-page document (and appendices) outlining the key principles of R2P.

Insofar as R2P has been said to undermine the 'rules' pertaining to state sovereignty, it can equally be said to be an attempt to institute a new set of rules around the circumstances that might allow intervention in otherwise state sovereign matters, and under which authority (Lang 2010: 72–3).

The four key principles of these 'new rules' included that state sovereignty implies responsibility for the protection of its people and, where a state is unable or unwilling to protect its people from internal war, insurgency, repression or state failure, the principle of non-intervention in the affairs of sovereign states yields to an international responsibility to protect. The foundations of R2P are found in obligations inherent in conceptions of sovereignty, the responsibility of the UN Security Council under Article 24 of the UN Charter for the maintenance of international peace and security, legal obligations under human rights covenants and treaties, international humanitarian law and state law, and the increasing practice of states, regional organisations and the Security Council.

The ICISS document outlined as elements of R2P the responsibility to prevent (both direct and root causes of) conflict and other endangering crises; the responsibility to react to situations of compelling human need, including sanctions, international prosecution and in extreme cases military intervention; and the responsibility to rebuild, particularly after military intervention, including recovery, reconstructions and reconciliation. In all of this, the responsibility to prevent was the single most important consideration and should be exhausted before intervention is considered, which in the first instance should always be the least intrusive and coercive measures (see Evans 2008: 40–1). It is important to note that R2P does not equate with military intervention as such and that military intervention is only one possible response of last resort in situations of humanitarian crisis. Among the range of other possible interventions are early warning mechanisms, mediation, diplomatic and various forms of economic pressure, assistance or removal of assistance to principle parties and, finally, as a measure of last resort, direct intervention. Although not specifically undertaken under the rubric of R2P, the international community did intervene in the case of Sri Lanka, offering mediation and diplomatic and some economic pressure. However, to be expanded upon later, these measures met with only short-term or very qualified success. There was one military intervention in Sri Lanka, by India in 1987, and, although this had a humanitarian aspect to at least parts of it, this was well before the explication of the R2P principle. Moreover, this intervention ended up in failure, both in terms of engaging in fighting with the Liberation Tigers of Tamil Eelam and in terms of not halting the war in Sri Lanka. There is a strong argument to support the claim that, following the failure of other forms of persuasion, armed intervention in Sri Lanka was necessary to prevent the deaths of the 40,000. It was, however, never a likely proposition, for reasons to be outlined later.

The ICISS report of 2001 is broadly understood to be the formal progenitor of R2P (ICISS 2001). Sections 4.18–4.21 of the report show an eagerness to approach the issue of the scale of atrocity that necessitates humanitarian intervention:

> In both the broad conditions we identified – loss of life and ethnic cleansing – we have described the action in question as needing to be ‘large scale’ in order to justify military intervention. We make no attempt to quantify ‘large scale’: opinions may differ in some marginal cases (for example, where a number of small scale incidents may build cumulatively into large scale atrocity), but most will not in practice generate major disagreement. What we do make clear, however, is that military action can be legitimate as an anticipatory measure in response to clear evidence of likely large scale killing. Without this possibility of anticipatory action, the international community

would be placed in the morally untenable position of being required to wait until genocide begins, before being able to take action to stop it.

Formal adoption

R2P was formally adopted by the UN General Assembly at the 2005 World Summit. As Evans (2008: 31) notes, from conception to adoption (if not implementation), this was a remarkably short period of time. R2P finds its origins in (but is distinct from) the notion of 'humanitarian intervention', which was first enunciated in the early nineteenth century when the United Kingdom, France and Russia intervened in the Greek war of independence from Turkey following numerous significant massacres by both sides, although massacres of Greeks by Turks led many to believe that they intended to perpetrate genocide (Fisher 1984: 881). Notably and especially from the UK and French perspective, there was no intention of establishing territorial gains as a result of the intervention (Bass 2008: 19, 39, 58). Mill (1984: 109) also enunciated this principle in his discussion of grounds for intervention, in which he argued that it was morally defensible to go to war for reasons other than defence from attack or threat of attack, in particular against acts of barbarism.

In the wake of humanitarian crises, examples of which have been identified, humanitarian intervention, or a 'right to intervene', was more recently popularised by Bernard Kouchner.[1] This followed Mario Bettati's development of the idea of a 'duty to interfere' (e.g. see Bettati 1987, 2004; Bettati and Kouchner 1987). In the post-Cold War environment in which larger powers were less forgiving of grave human rights abuses on ideological grounds and in which there was a tendency towards coherence around a democratic norm, humanitarian intervention was an idea whose time had come (Evans 2008: 32).

The acceptance of this idea was nowhere more clear than in NATOs air strikes against Yugoslavia in the latter stages of the break-up of the federated Yugoslavian state. Following a series of massacres, the failure of the UN to secure Yugoslav compliance with a ceasefire agreement and ultimately ethnic cleansing of Kosovars by Serbians, between March and June 1999, NATO undertook some 38,000 air missions against Yugoslavia. The intention of the airstrikes was to have the Serbian army withdraw from Kosovo, peacekeepers sent in and Kosovar refugees returned to their homes. On 3 June, the Yugoslav president Slobodan Milosevich capitulated and nine days later, following the withdrawal of Yugoslav forces, peacekeepers began entering Kosovo. Defending the airstrikes, UK prime minister Tony Blair said that it was necessary to 'identify the circumstances in which we should get actively involved in other people's conflicts', setting out five aims for such intervention (Brown 1999). Not only did NATO's intervention in Kosovo set a precedent for humanitarian intervention as a form of R2P, but also insofar as the rules of intervention were being rewritten, or at least reformulated, this intervention followed a reinterpretation of the rules that concern the authority of the UN Security Council. That is, it was a reinterpretation of a reinterpretation of the rules, which stretched international law but for which there was no alternative authority able to impose a further sanction. As Lang (2010: 75) noted:

> The Kosovo intervention took place at a moment when global constitutional change was accelerating. The weakening of a fundamental rule in the international order, non-intervention, was being accompanied by a rise in emphasis on the moral dimension of human rights and humanitarianism.

The five aims of intervention set out by Blair included being certain of the circumstances in question; having exhausted all diplomatic options; undertaking sensible and prudent military operations; being prepared for long-term commitment; and national interests. Blair identified NATO's intervention in this war of 'values' as a manifestation of globalisation. It was, Blair said, 'a more subtle blend of mutual self-interest and moral purpose in defending the values we cherish' (Blair 1999). The question was and remains, however, whether the Kosovo case was *sui generis* or whether it set a precedent for other, non-UN Security Council-sanctioned interventions, as suggested by Weiss. However, although 'humanitarian intervention' and in particular coercive military action may be a component of R2P, it does not constitute R2P as such and may instead be seen as just the most extreme end of the R2P scale of concerns and potential actions. The circumstances in which coercive military action would be initiated were restricted to those that were 'a desperately serious, extraordinary, and exceptional matter' (Evans 2008: 59). Even so, proponents of R2P were careful not to conflate it with humanitarian intervention as such, despite the potential for overlap between the two at the point of armed force.

Following from these events, the 2005 World Summit statement on R2P was endorsed the following year by the UN Security Council (UNSC 2006a), followed by a specific endorsement in relation to the crisis in Darfur the following August (UNSC 2006b) and the Secretary-General's invocation in 2008 (Ban 2008). If there is legitimacy to the idea of R2P, which, on the face of it, would seem to be the case, then the question arises as to whether it is not better to prevent situations requiring the application of R2P from arising, rather than addressing them once they have arisen. 'Realising the Responsibility to Prevent' (Bellamy 2009: 106–31) took the R2P idea to a new level, employing early warning systems, diplomacy and an end to impunity. In this, the move away from a capacity to intervene in the affairs of another state in ways that impose on sovereignty to a 'responsibility' to protect that privileges humanity over sovereignty reflected a major change in how international intervention is understood. Moreover, instead of arguing that states might have the right to intervene in cases of humanitarian emergency, R2P asserts that states have an obligation or responsibility to intervene in such cases. This emphasis away from choice to responsibility changes the focus and rationale for international intervention.

The conditions that lead to circumstances that require R2P should, in an ideal world, not exist. Yet the world is complex, with myriad conflicts and competitions, any one of which can, at almost any time, spill over into something more critical and 'R2Pworthy'. It is not feasible to constantly monitor each and every situation all the time. However, some places are or have been more prone to violence than others, and programmes such as the United Nations Development Program's (UNDP) Threat and Risk Mapping Analysis in the Sudan and Columbia

University's Early Warning/Early Response Project in Timor-Leste, among others, have been useful steps in preventative monitoring. Similarly, the wider range of rights as envisaged by the UN, if implemented, would go a long way towards redressing the circumstances in which grievance and conflict occurs.

As with the societies of states, their members will have rules of legal and normative conduct but by and large will not be constantly monitored as to the possibility of their breach. Apart from the impracticability of such monitoring, many individuals – and many states – would regard such monitoring as interference in their internal affairs. Having said that, informal or non-governmental monitoring does take place, with organisations such as Amnesty International, Human Rights Watch, the International Crisis Group and others maintaining a close watch on most states and their performance with regard to issues of human rights and their transgression or abuse.

Despite these monitoring mechanisms, conflict still occurs, often in places where such monitors have been excluded or when circumstances have made it impractical or dangerous to remain. As a result, sanctions applying to breaking of rules are applied after the event, implying a lawful body able to administer adjudication of such rules and mete out punishment. In the global context, the closest parallel is the UN Security Council, which, because of its structure, the interests of its members and disagreement over the applicability of the UN Charter's sometimes conflicting requirements, has at best delivered incompletely on either securing peace or addressing conflict in a timely manner once it has occurred.

There is general agreement within the UN Security Council about the legitimacy of the R2P principle, although with a range of both general and specific qualifications, many of which preclude effective action in times of crisis. Moreover, the ancient rule of realpolitik in which interest and capacity determine outcomes more than legality and altruism has continued to apply. This has sometimes been under the guise of something approaching R2P or at least humanitarian intervention and at other times simply on the grounds of self-defence, preventative defence – a term that opens a whole new category of rationalisations for war – and other forms of national interest.

Underneath it all, there is a growing global consensus (even if around pre-existing codes), at least in principle, that war crimes and crimes against humanity should not be tolerated. The grounds for this are that they reflect a failure of sovereignty as manifested in the will of the people of which the state is but an instrument, that they contravene basic humanitarian principles of human rights, and that they constitute a threat to international peace, order and stability. From last to first, this is a standard requirement for a UN Security Council determination on action, that the various instruments contained within the UN's Charter and Conventions require a degree of adherence as balanced against competing claims (e.g. sovereignty) and that underpinning the whole notion of a global community is the fact that the states that comprise it are in turn made up of their citizens who implicitly have a range of rights in relation to those states. If the UN as the representative of the global community has any philosophical underpinning, it is in its universalist appeal on the basis of equity and justice. Thus, states that contravene such principles may expose themselves at least to international opprobrium, possible pressure and perhaps even one of a number of forms of diplomatic, economic or strategic intervention.

Further to this state-based consensus, there is also growing support among citizens of states for the idea of humanitarian intervention. Lyon and Malone (2010: 21) quote Jentleson and Briton as providing 'compelling evidence that the principle policy objective of an intervention has significant impact on public support for that intervention'. '[T]he public also views military missions with humanitarian goals quite favourably, Jentleson and Britton found that when humanitarian concerns triggered military interventions, Americans were strikingly supportive, with 75 percent in favour.' At foundation, the principle idea that informs R2P is that of reciprocal human rights; that all people deserve the right to be able to live free from fear of death, torture or undue imprisonment, and to be able to enjoy at least the basic necessities of life.

This dichotomy in favour of and against R2P reflects a competition between 'realist' and liberal approaches to international relations: moral and legal arguments and rule and consequence-oriented arguments. Further ethical divides on such issues include the distinction between naturalist and consensualist approaches, which correspond to natural rights or law or inherent norms and explicit rule-based norms. Other dichotomies that include but do not necessarily limit R2P responses include the object of moral concern being understood on the basis of its individual or group existence, and universalist approaches which assert that all people are the proper objects of moral concern as opposed to a particularist (or relativist) approach in which only some people are the proper source of moral concern (Holzgrefe 2003: 18–20).

Teson (2003: 100) argues against the relativist position by noting that relativists 'confuse the problem of the *origin* of a political theory with the problem of its *justification.* The truth (moral or empirical) of a proposition is logically independent of its origin'. '[T]he situations that warrant intervention – tyranny and anarchy – are morally abhorrent forms of political injustice', he notes.

> We are not dealing here with differences in conceptions of the good . . . We are confronting governments that perpetrate atrocities against people and situations of anarchy and breakdown of social order of such magnitude that no reasonable ethical or political theory could reasonably condone them.
>
> (Teson 2003: 101)

Teson's position tends to comply with the 'natural law' tradition, or the idea that there are certain inalienable laws that apply universally regardless of codification (positive law). Indeed, codification of law would not be possible without some acceptance of the idea of a pre-existing norm. Appeals to natural law can be found in most of the world's major traditions, indicating that its existence is a consequence of recognising a common humanity rather than a statist or other particularity. Amongst the world's religions, Islam appeals to reason as a God-given capacity to distinguish between good and evil, as noted by the Hanbali jurist Ibn Qayyim al-Jawzi, among others[2] (see Emon 2007).

The Aristotelian model also posited that (positive) law might differentiate, but that what was of nature was the same everywhere (Shellens 1959). Following Socrates and along with Plato, Aristotle developed a model of natural right or natural justice, from which the conception of natural law flows. This idea was resurrected in Christian thought by Thomas Aquinas, branching into a number of streams thereafter, though most importantly through John Locke and his influence on the liberal understanding of the state that followed. It was from this tradition that the US Constitution derived its fateful words: 'We hold these truths to be self-evident, that all men are created equal, that they are endowed by their Creator with certain unalienable rights.' This classical Romance appeal to natural law (see Cicero 1998) on the basis of a shared humanity was intended to apply to citizens of the state (initially to 'Romans', however broadly they might be construed) and was to varying degrees assumed by many states thereafter. The appeal, however, was not predicated upon an appeal to states but on an appeal to a natural law applying to people on the basis of their common humanity, regardless of state. One finds similar appeals to 'rights' in various religious and historical texts, the assumption being that if a 'right' exists it is predicated upon a protective mechanism which is, in either natural or positive form, a rule or law.

The appeal to rights, to positive benefits and from negative outcomes, underpins and goes to the heart of the claim to R2P. It is through rights that, in seeking them for oneself, one is logically obliged to acknowledge them also for others. The purpose of human rights is, or should be, about increasing human freedom as an intrinsic good (see Sen 1999a). This is not freedom in the sense of personal irresponsibility, or the model in which one is free to trample on the lives of others, but freedom from oppression and exploitation and, more positively, to explore one's personal capacities and human potential. Such freedom does not exist in only abstract terms, however, but on the political spectrum is at the opposite end to that other defining quality: power, or that capacity is not inherently limited other than by itself. Given that power of itself does not seek approval for its actions, a functional freedom requires certain guarantees in relation to power to be able to exist. These guarantees are usually referred to as civil and political rights.

In reference to the use, or abuse, of power, or in this case state capacity, Sri Lanka's 'state of emergency', which abrogates numerous basic human rights, has been in place almost continuously since 1971. According to Amnesty International in 2010:

> The emergency laws grant state authorities sweeping powers of detention and permit the use of secret prisons, a practice that encourages human rights abuses like enforced disappearances, torture and death in custody, which could constitute crimes under international law. In the last thirty years, thousands of Sri Lankans have spent years in detent years in detention without trial.
>
> Over the past year, the government has increasingly used these laws to crack down on journalists, political opponents, and trade unionists.
>
> (AI 2010)

This speaks directly to the type of political society that Sri Lanka has become and, as this was being written, remains.

By way of illustration, Sri Lanka's Secretary of the Ministry of Disaster Management and Human Rights, Rajiva Wijesinha, criticised a Human Rights Watch report stating that the Sri Lankan government had arrested a journalist because he criticised the government, which he refuted. 'The impression of that release is that Mr Tissainayagam has been arrested because he has criticized the government. This is not accurate.' Wijesinha then said: 'While it is conceivable that he was being used by other forces, there is little doubt that what he published was questionable . . . The passage is cited in the indictment' (Wijesinha 2008a). That is, Wijesinha claimed that the journalist in question had not been arrested because he had criticised the government but that he had been arrested because what he had written (which was critical of the government) was 'questionable'. Following such logic, it would be difficult to sustain any claim that journalists had not in fact been arrested for criticising the government.

None of this, however, was discussed by the first prime minister of Sri Lanka and an outspoken proponent of its formal independence, Don Stephen Senanayake, who employed the rhetoric of 'the achieving of freedom' (Rajasingham 2001). Such freedom was posited by Senanayake in contrast to Sri Lanka's then dominion status with the United Kingdom. It implies, however, the capacity and intention for the improvement of peoples' lives based on a wide-ranging sense of voluntary inclusion and participation through practical recognition of the validity and implementation of civil and political rights. Such political freedom implies the specific political freedom to which Senanayake referred. The key components of civil and political rights, as both rights 'to' and rights 'from', ensure the capacity for constituent members of a polity to communicate with each other without fear over matters of individual or mutual relevance and importance. Such rights have been demonstrated to apply not just to the West or other cultural constructs, and they have not been established as being immune from 'Asia'. The right to meet, to discuss, to express views and to disseminate those views amongst one's community is basic not just to political freedom, but also to the full and fair manifestation of the human condition.

It is not consistently possible, then, to claim either rights (to or from) or laws that give such rights substance without attributing such rights and laws to others. Short of distinguishing between humans on a hierarchical basis of race or ethnicity, elements of which appear to apply in Sri Lanka but which contradicts notions of rights and the equal and consistent application of law, logically that which applies to oneself must also apply to others, and vice versa. If it does not then a case may be made for legal discrimination on the basis of one's ethnicity. States may be the providers or guarantors of rights and laws (or they may be the opposite), but in this sense states are mechanism of social convenience for the expression of particular political bonds. Assuming that such bonds are not exclusively ethnic or racial (with the above noted problems), they must be regularised as civic law. The question then becomes not of the extent of application of such rights and laws in principle, which is theoretically universal, but the extent to which they are applied or denied in practice. In cases in which such freedoms are denied, in a wholesale malignant manner, as discussed the question becomes less one of choice of intervention and more one of moral compulsion.

As Farer has noted, notions of humanitarian intervention, which overlap with the sharp end of R2P, immediately raise issues in the wider debate over the circumstances in which 'legitimate violence' might be employed (Farer 2003: 58). The question of legitimate violence is in part answered within the context of the state as claiming a monopoly on the employment of legitimate violence. However, state violence can be and sometimes is illegitimate, depending on the defining criteria, while sub- or non-state violence, which is most often regarded as illegitimate because of its status, can also be argued to be legitimate in particular circumstances, for example in a defensive posture when the state is acting violently and without legitimacy against its own people. The question that is then raised is whether the state is the only site for the legitimate use of violence and, if so, how does this render, for example, the status and functions of the UN Security Council. On the other hand, if the state is but an actor among many within the wider international community and is governed by certain international rules (e.g. non-aggression against other sovereign states), what then of the authority of the international community, through its representative body, to similarly employ legitimate violence in cases in which the state employs illegitimate violence? No doubt the answer goes to the issue of what constitutes legitimacy, but sovereignty alone would be a poor and certainly incomplete answer

Employing a Kantian account of the state to identify its roles and responsibilities, Teson (2003: 96–7) argued that:

> The liberal state centrally includes a constitution that defines the powers of governments in a manner consistent with respect for individual autonomy . . . a solution to the dilemmas of anarchy and tyranny . . . the perpetuation of tyranny is not simply an obvious assault on the dignity of persons: it is a betrayal of the very purpose for which government exists . . . Humanitarian intervention is one tool to help move the quantum of political freedom in the continuum of political coercion to the Kantian center of that continuum away, on the one hand, from the extreme lack of order (anarchy), and, on the other, from the governmental suppression of individual freedom (tyranny).

Sovereignty as such reflects the single authority to rule and make law over a given territory, but it does not necessarily imply a normative or any other quality other than its fact. In its original incarnation, sovereignty was vested in the sovereign of the state, usually a king or similar position, either inherited or imposed. Neither inheritance of authority nor the arbitrary imposition of authority implies its legitimacy (Morris 1998: 45–6). For the purpose of this discussion, however, sovereignty can be characterised by two general streams, the first being juridical and the second empirical. Juridical sovereignty can be characterised as being based on equal and consistent rule of law, which finds common acceptance among the people to whom it pertains. That is, such sovereignty is also legitimate in that it complies with the etymology of the term. Empirical sovereignty is simply a statement of fact and does not necessarily imply legitimacy but it does require for its efficacy a claim to the monopoly on the use of violence. In the former instance, such a state is much less likely to engage in harmful acts against its own citizens and is similarly unlikely to become a target of R2P intervention. Conversely, a state's employment of or attempt to impose a monopoly on the use of violence, without recourse to law, implies grounds for R2P intervention.

Similarly, the employment of R2P principles as grounds for intervention in the affairs of a sovereign state, if they are to be consistent, requires due regard for equal and consistent application of law that has been agreed to by the community to which it applies (in this case the international community). Moreover, one might apply to such circumstances the Rawlsian test in which in a situation of absence of knowledge about how individuals in states might find themselves situated in relation to each other, what common rules would they agree to in order to protect their interests and freedoms vis-à-vis their states and, by extension, what guarantees might they seek beyond their states should there be a potential for it to turn malignant (see Rawls 1971).

The subject of what is and what is not legitimate and why is large and complex, but suffice it to say that there is no universal or standardised definition of the meaning of legitimacy or for being able to determine how and where it might apply. This then devolves to the question of standards (e.g. opposition to genocide) and principles (e.g. abhorrence of genocide on humanitarian as well as wider utilitarian grounds). In this respect, and insofar as legitimacy (*lex*) implies the application of the rule of law, the question is how international law is established, what it requires to function, on what grounds and by whom it is judged, and how such judgment is applied and by whom.

Notably, the idea of R2P would have struggled to take hold at a time other than when it did, acknowledging that even now it still has at least as many opponents as proponents. The internationalisation architecture within which R2P formally resides really only came into existence with the League of Nations, following the horrors of the Great War. In this, the principle purpose of the League of Nations was to prevent such a humanitarian catastrophe in the future. Yet the League and the architecture it represented at that time faltered because the world was not yet ready for it, nor perhaps was in a position to be able to accept and endorse its precepts, not least because of the 'unfinished business' of the Great War that was to erupt so disastrously in the 1930s. That the League's main protagonist, the United States, refused to join it perhaps alone spelled its death knell. But whatever its internationalist orientation, given that at this time 'internationalism' had radical leftist overtones that not even the Soviet Union was comfortable with, and whatever it might have ideally aspired to, it was first and foremost an organisation intended to ensure stability, not to promote an internationalist legal agenda. In this respect, the League had little capacity, for example, to stop late colonialist adventures by Italy and Japan, or to intervene in the bloody conflict that was the Spanish Civil War. Largely, it stood by wringing its metaphorical hands, protesting ineffectually and increasingly casting itself as irrelevant to the circumstances that confronted it. The institutional framework that could give rise to R2P had been established, if abandoned for a time, and R2P was a logical consequence of it. But R2P was still a long way off, in conceptual, much less practical, terms.

Similarly, the United Nations was born of the humanitarian catastrophe that was World War II and likewise its principle purpose was not to promote an internationalist legal agenda but to maintain stability in what was then and continued to be a fragile international environment. Not least, the purpose of the UN was to contain the Cold War in such a way that it did not become World War III, especially after the Soviet Union acquired a nuclear capability. Its purpose, then, was about maintaining equilibrium amongst the status quo, rather than to promote an adventurous internationalist agenda. This was and remains its strength as well as its ultimate weakness.

In particular, the UN came into being not only at a time when the world was engaging in a global ideological debate, and sometime proxy war, but also when the old order was in the process of falling apart. The empires of the past had begun to succumb, first to the Great War, in which the Ottoman empire, the Austro-Hungarian empire and the aspirant German overseas empire collapsed or were dismembered. The Wilsonian doctrine of self-determination was a key moment in establishing a normative international order, in which territorially defined nations had the 'right' to manifest themselves as states. World War II cemented the end of empire, notably of European states and the United Kingdom, but also Japan, in which their colonies asserted their 'right' also to statehood, if less on the basis of some pre-existing national identity then at least, in most cases, on the basis of a colonially defined territory. As the world – and the UN – came to accept these newer member states, born in many instances of very violent anti-colonial struggle, there was also an explicit acceptance that once such states existed they then continued to have the right to exist. The Westphalian notion of sovereign territorial integrity was held paramount, which continues to be reflected in Article 2.4 of the UN Charter, which endorses the legitimacy of the territorial integrity of states.

The overriding criteria for the global order were, in a time of a state of political flux, assertion and change, to retain as much stability as was conceivably possible. It was not the purpose of the international community, at this time, to intervene in the internal affairs of states. Indeed, although there were (and have continued to be) post- and neo-colonial interventions, the idea that formerly colonial states should again intervene in the affairs of former colonies was an anathema to the whole decolonisation ethos. It was only when the world increasingly settled, in geo-political terms, and in particular following the end of the global ideological contest that was the Cold War, that it was possible and sometimes even necessary for states or collections of states to intervene in the affairs of other sovereign states. The first rationale was and has always been to maintain order and peace where it could spill over into neighbouring countries. But increasingly there was the view that the horrors of the past not only could not be condoned or accepted, even with the benefit of historical distance, but also could not afford to be repeated. Key figures in the global community such as President Clinton said 'never again', and despite the continuation or repetition of 'again', and the all too often reluctance to act, that which is to never again be tolerated has firmed as a set of principles. How to address circumstances that might lead to 'again' has also increasingly been codified, if not in all cases as an international law then as a series of practical steps to be applied if necessary, if possible.

Universal rights?

If there is to be a claim to R2P, it is based upon the notion that all people are everywhere fundamentally equal and that all share the same rights, including the rights to 'protection from' (negative rights). Therefore, there is a clear link between notions of R2P and claims to universal human rights, in particular civil and political rights. In this sense, R2P acts as a theoretical guarantor of the right to life. However, claims to human rights remain contested, not least by individuals and institutions that benefit from their abrogation.

The claim that human rights generally and civil and political rights in particular are culturally specific or a neo-imperialist imposition precisely parallels rejection of the notion of R2P. Similarly, political leaders who object to civil and political rights and R2P – a normative consequence of their widespread, serious and systematic abuse – tend to be just those individuals and groups who can be mostly reasonably claimed to be potentially subject to scrutiny on those grounds. The claim for universal human rights, then, is deeply embedded in the logic of R2P; if one is to be accepted then so too, logically, is the other.

In the sciences generally, and mathematics in particular, there is a considerable body of universals, and where there remains debate about some theoretical applications this tends to be at the more arcane or 'fuzzy' fringes. The capacity to count, for example, is universal. Like mathematics, logic may not be universally employed, but it has a functional universal method. Similarly, although there are minor variations between people, human physiology is common as are its responses to external inputs. Intellectual capacities may vary from individual to individual, but it is the key marker of the human condition that people share intellectual capacity and a conscious awareness of self.

The question, then, is whether it is possible to extrapolate from such universals to establish a set of 'rights' that continue such universality or, if as claimed by some, cultural distinction – in the case being Sri Lanka – supersedes such claims. In this, there are two sets of issues, the first concerning the quality of being human, and the second concerning the logic of power. If human beings share a common physiology (accepting that beyond childbearing the principle difference between men and women is cultural), then all people have similar fundamental physical needs. This includes the basics of adequate nutrition and shelter, and the equal value of health care. But basic nutrition and shelter are, of themselves, adequate only to sustain life, potentially in constrained circumstances. As Filippino jurist Jose Diokno noted, food and shelter alone are not enough: 'many prisons do as much' (Diokno 1981: 54). For many of Sri Lanka's Tamils, even when they had or have food and shelter, other aspects of their condition more closely resembled a prison.

Beyond basic physiological needs, people have consistent physiological responses to negative stimuli (allowing for individual tolerance). Physical torture afflicts people equally and other forms of depravation have consistent negative effects. So too, all people respond similarly to imprisonment, isolation, death and loss, with consistency of response speaking more to social psychology than to individual psychology. There may be minor variations between individuals, but alienation, fear and trauma apply consistently in like circumstances. Not least, the intended effect of such conditions derives from a similarly common set of motives: compulsion, fear, hatred, ignorance, greed and psychosis. These are the handmaidens of unrestrained power.

Again, if language varies but a capacity for speech is inherent, and speech is the principle mechanism by which people communicate needs, desires and emotions, then limitations upon speech constitute a restriction upon a basic expression of the quality of being human, rather than, for instance, being Sinhalese or Tamil (or Burgher or Muslim). The next question then arises as to acculturated acceptance of imposition. If acculturation is a consequence of resolving social dissonance, for example by accepting a situation because of a lack of capacity to change it, this does not legitimise the situation but rather just explains why it is unchallenged. If that lack of capacity is a consequence of unequal power relations, then the situation is not one of culture as such but one of politics. This is not to deny the capacity for the acculturation of political methods and values, but that its explanatory method is primarily political and not cultural. Nor is it to deny the subtlety and impact of interplay between culture and politics and the deeply rooted forms of acculturation that might exist despite the objective interests of the respective parties. But acknowledging that a hegemonic framework exists does not then exculpate the actors within it. Rather, it acts as an analytic tool for understanding that framework.

The claim to human rights – civil and political rights in particular – is based upon assumptions about universal political values. These values were initially expressed in universalist terms during the period of the European Enlightenment, although their antecedents derive from antiquity, and across a range of cultures. Contrary to some claims, conceptions of human rights (of which civil and political rights are seen as the 'first generation'[3]) are neither culturally specific nor especially recent. Moreover, although the codification of human rights ensures that there is a specific set of criteria by which they can be measured and applied, human rights do not necessarily rely on codification to retain validity. The conception of 'natural rights' applies here, parallel to natural law (e.g. see Hobbes 1962; Locke 1960; Rousseau 1973), as those rights that pertain in a range of circumstances in which each are interpretations of the same or a similar original first principle. Such rights are claimed to exist as a consequence of freedom in a state of nature. This implies a natural moral order (sometimes said to be under God) in which humans are equal in a state of nature, as the application to others of self-regard (moral coherence and consistency) or, most forcefully and without reference to God, as a practical consequence of a capacity for ethical reason (e.g. see Kant 1997; Locke 1960).

Following the gross humanitarian abuses of World War II, these values were formally endorsed in the Universal Declaration of Human Rights (UN 1948a), a document supported by 48 member states, with no votes against and eight abstentions (the Soviet Bloc states, South Africa and Saudi Arabia). Since then, the declaration has been endorsed by almost all member states, with critical Islamic states adopting the conceptually similar Cairo Declaration on Human Rights in Islam (CDHRI 1990), which sought to establish Islamic law as the basis for such rights (and which constrained rights within Islamic law). In this, there is now close to a universal rhetorical agreement that human rights exist, or should do so, and that they are or should be universal in application. This universality, including the universality of an obligation to protect rights, then begins to provide a basis for moving on towards R2P.

Despite some observations that the UN declaration contains conceptual flaws (such as those addressed in the CDHRI), it remains the key human rights document. There is broad agreement that any effort to address perceived flaws in the document would diminish it in other respects, recognising that its strength is its protection for the plurality of views that might criticise it. It is, then, nothing if not implicitly reflexive. It has thus been left intact. There has, however, been similar recognition of a broader range of human rights, including the right to development (UN 1986). The addition of rights does not contradict or diminish the quality or scope of the original declaration, but rather enhances it. This being the case, all people consequently share an equal right to protection from human rights abuses, with a reciprocal responsibility on the part of others to ensure that protection.

The exceptionalist claim

Not all people, or states, agree, however, to the assertion or applicability of rights or to the protection that such rights imply. By way of illustration, since the 1980s, claims to universal human rights have been countered by an 'exceptionalist' assertion, often coming under what has been termed the 'Asian values' paradigm or in opposition to 'imperialism' or 'neo-imperialism', as claimed by some Sinhalese advocates in Sri Lanka (e.g. Mahindapala 2009). Somewhat separately, a post-structural analysis has also favoured the relativisation of values over universal assumptions. This latter group includes academics who wish to defend the cultural particularities of their site of interest from a more generalized absorption into Western or global culture (the *authentic* local as opposed to the presumed neo-imperial global). The former main group comprises political figures who use culturally relativist arguments about rights to sustain unequal power relationships or to rationalise otherwise inexcusable abuses. Such individuals or groups may draw on pre-existing conceptions of power relations that may be 'reified' (see Pemberton 1994) or 'naturalised' so as to preclude the conception that another possibility could exist (e.g. see Lukes 1974). Within this, the proposition of 'Asian values' reflects particular power relationships. In either case, R2P is inimical to such a position and is opposed by it. Portrayed as cultural rather than political, such 'Asian values' have in some cases attracted the implied support of academic relativists, who also tend to see R2P in cultural imperialist terms.

These overlapping positions reject the universal claims of human rights and consequently R2P, instead positing that political values are relative to the cultures (world views) in which they arise. This in turn rests on a claimed category of linguistic distinction around the embeddedness of culture in language, and the fact that languages are different and not immediately or sometimes at all mutually intelligible. According to this position, at base there is a point of untranslatability, and so too cultures and forms of social organisation that arise from such cultures are mutually and fundamentally unintelligible and untranslatable (Whorf 1956; Sapir 1955).

As such, this varied body of linguistic thought, and in particular its post-structuralist elements, broadly agreed on the epistemological position that knowledge is always contingent on the perspective of the observer and as such is always subjective. Hence, one could only know one's own thoughts and never truly those of another. In some cases, this took the form of one's own thoughts even being the sole product of a range of other influences and capacities and, as such, one might not even truly know oneself. Indeed, for many who accepted this premise, the whole notion of 'truth' became at best problematic and at worst ceased to exist altogether. The 'truth' was certainly a victim of the last months of the Sri Lankan government's war against the LTTE and arguably had been so for years before. The appeal, however, was based less on the more sophisticated argument that often underpinned its claims and more on simple assertion, denial or claiming that the source of comments other than supportive reflected neo-imperialist ambitions, were in league with terrorism or, at best, were the foolish comments of LTTE dupes.

As such, claims to universal civil and political rights are rather a reflection of a particular world view, in this case one dominated by a specific form of Western thinking, and did not apply in non-Western, in this case 'Asian', contexts. *Ipso facto*, assertions of particular values, in this case 'Asian values', could not be countered on the grounds of unsustainable claims to an impossible universality. An assertion of 'Asian values' by an 'Asian', then, was self-legitimising (on relativism and human rights see, for example, Tilley 2000; Milner 1999; Heard 1997; Ayton-Shenker 1995; Renteln 1985).

From a less power-centric and more intellectually engaged perspective, a relative conception of rights thus assumes that what is understood by one might not (or cannot) be understood by another, and that neither understanding is privileged over the other. More disconcertingly, though, the deferrals of meaning implied in relativism can also be adopted to support 'negative relativism'. Negative relativism positions people according to a subjective cultural or physiological scale, at the far end of which blurs the categories of value of existence. This can manifest as, for example, institutional racism, and is able to be applied in gross numbers as part of a specific programme, the Holocaust and apartheid being cases in point. But beyond a rationalization for amoral power, negative relatism still suffers from arbitrary categories of victims that can, logically, turn upon itself or elements of itself (e.g. Stalin's USSR, China's purges in the 1950s and again during the Cultural Revolution, Nazi Germany and Cambodia's Khmer Rouge). Perhaps the internal conflicts of the Sri Lankan government in the period after the ending of the war against the LTTE did not reflect such theoretical considerations. However, when one 'victor' of the war against the LTTE, General Sarath Fonseka, ran for president against the incumbent Mahinda Rajapksa, he was quickly charged with nominal crimes, duly found guilty and jailed. The political space in Sri Lanka, already shrinking, closed even further as the supposedly one true version of the Sinhalese-dominated state increasingly took hold.

Post-colonial responses

At approximately the same time as the shift towards post-structuralism in which relativism featured so strongly, Western hegemony was being challenged by the rise of a number of post-colonial states, notably in East Asia. In the immediate post-colonial period, many decolonised states had opted for a plural democratic or other 'liberating' system as a method of government in which civil and political rights were implied. However, the post-colonial experience was commonly beset by a series of similar problems. The first problem was that the removal of the colonial yoke did not automatically produce all or in most cases even many of the benefits that liberation was supposed to guarantee. In this, expectations grossly exceeded capacity, which was often reduced rather than enhanced by the act of independence.

The common post-colonial experience was of political failure, especially in cases in which plural democratic structures that had taken decades or even centuries to formulate and refine in Western countries were expected to take immediate hold in post-colonial countries. The emphasis within human rights on claims to free expression and assembly are seen in some political environments to not just challenge the status quo but also create an unstable political and economic environment and incite already restive populations to undertake illegal activity. In circumstances in which the state struggled to construct basic institutions, to provide services and to head down one consistent development path, such political distractions were often unwelcome. Set against often arbitrary and increasingly fractured polities fighting increasingly desperate internal battles, it became both a convenience and arguably a necessity for political elites controlling the levers of power to abandon or violently repress plural democratic or other emancipatory processes in exchange for the 'stability' of one party or person authoritarian rule. The functional claims of plural democracy or other forms of actual liberation, and the civil and political rights that are inherent in them, were thus discarded as impeding changing expedient political practice.

Combined with and rationalizing the imposition of authoritarianism, many critics of human rights, especially in developing countries, opposed universal conceptions of human rights as being specific rather than universal and as reflecting a type of cultural imperialism (e.g. see World Conference on Human Rights 1993: 3). These critics claimed that, rather than being universal, claims to human rights were a reflection of specific cultural values and, as such, amounted to the imposition of an alien culture. This argument was usually advanced in association with claims to other forms of imperialism or neo-imperialism, such as economic or strategic relations that favoured former colonial or Western powers over post-colonial states. Notably, the issue of perceived or claimed imposition of an alien culture led to rejection on the grounds of imposition. However, arguments about the imposition of human rights, as with the imposition of democracy, contradict their liberating principles so that such imposition, if it existed, would contradict the principles it was trying to support. It would further call forth rejection based on the fact of the imposition, rather than for the inherent quality of the rights in question. Such rejection would itself be couched in terms of 'rights', in this case the 'right to resist imposition'.

Beyond the above, there is the further problem that there is an inherent egalitarian assertion underpinning attempts to delegitimise conceptions of universally valid human rights. That is, detractors of universal civil and political rights argue that their view is of equal validity to views expressed in support of such rights. Yet implicitly, a relativised understanding should logically not accept such equality of the value of assertions. To accept such equality accepts the equal legitimacy of the right to express it as a freely held value and the universality of such equality. This in turn implicitly supports the underlying principle in favour of universal civil and political rights and hence their protection.

The only circumstances under which claims to relativisation that propose an inequality of values can be sustained are where there is the aforementioned hierarchy of value claims, for example that the individual is less important than the community, or that some individuals have less value than others (which could be argued to be the underlying agenda in Sri Lanka). Although hierarchical ordering has the potential to separate and privilege particular value claims, and thus avoid the egalitarian principles that underpin universal claims, there is nothing in this which presupposes that claims against universal civil and political rights would be privileged or sustained. That is, cultural relativism opens the door not just to difference, but also to persecution rationalized by such difference. The argument of a particular ordering of human value based on cultural exceptionalism thus lays the grounds for intervention on the basis of stopping or limiting such persecution.

Claims to the relativism of rights continue, if decreasingly at an official level. Like claims to democracy, the widespread acceptance of the terminology around civil and political rights has on the one hand tended to be devalued, as in the case of Sri Lanka, and has on the other hand been all too often observed in the breach. But despite such rhetorical if not actual acceptance of civil and political rights, there continue to be moments when arguments are put to 'explain' the special circumstances of particular cases. Atrocities against civilians in conflict zones are a principle example of 'explaining' such 'special circumstances', often accompanied by dissembling rhetoric such as the 'necessity' of torture in the 'war on terror', or the flat denial of mass deaths and a culture of disappearances and intimidation.

Assuming the claim for the relativisation of civil and political rights overcomes these hurdles, this claim then implicitly raises the question of different sets of rights for different people in different circumstances. That is, it assumes cultural- or state-specific rights, rather than rights predicated upon the universal quality of existing as a human being. Yet the universalist claim of civil and political rights pertains not to the specificity of one's circumstances but to the quality of being human, which is commonality (*consensus gentium*) (see Geertz 1993: 43, 50, 60, 350–1; Geertz 1989: 15, 70; Todorov 1986: 374). Assuming such commonality there is, then, not just a claim but an ethical necessity to protect others in dire circumstances.

'Tiger' values?

In some cases, and for a variety of often similar reasons, some post-colonial states that adopted authoritarian or dictatorial political models succeeded in economic terms; in East Asia these states are known as the 'Asian Tigers'. South Korea built a strong economy under military rule as did Taiwan, while Singapore flourished under quasi-authoritarian one-party rule and the colonial anomaly of Hong Kong similarly flourished with access to plural democratic processes. It was but a short step from such economic success to a conclusion that it was not just linked to but was a direct product of a particular 'Asian' way of doing things. Sri Lanka has, since the end of the war against the LTTE, also claimed that its economy has boomed (Asian Tribune 2010a), in significant part as a way of undermining complaints that its democratic processes have become a sham.

As well as guaranteed political stability, the main contributing factors to economic success among what came to be termed the 'Asian Tigers' included substantial economic input from the United States through its involvement in the Korean and Vietnam Wars and its and the West's massive consumer purchasing thereafter. This was bolstered by a legacy of Japanese economic infrastructure in both South Korea and Taiwan, Singapore and Hong Kong's histories as key free ports in a global trading network and, importantly, Japan's economic leadership, in which regional economies picked up discarded Japanese industries, often with Japanese finance, as Japan moved higher up the technology scale. In Sri Lanka, infrastructure construction led economic growth, followed by higher farm outputs and growth in tourism (Williams 2010).

Regardless of the varied reasons for these specific economic successes, it was relatively easy for governments presiding over economic prosperity to accord it to political style, in this case the 'can do' leadership of President Rajapaksa. The logic of such claims was that such political style reflected cultural values that did not accord with Western ideals of plural democracy and civil and political rights. In this, Sri Lanka could assert a 'national' pride based on economic success that countered the cultural ignominy that was a product of colonial imposition. Thus, an exceptionalist claim became an assertion of the legitimacy of an authoritarian political model. Indeed, for many post-colonial one-party states, rejecting plural democracy and civil and political rights became a further method of asserting a non-colonial state identity. For such states, the common claim of economic efficiency took precedence over civil and political rights. If the 'luxury' of civil and political rights was to be granted, or returned, it would be only after the establishment of prerequisite economic success.

The assumption by some states that democratisation was contingent upon economic development ('full bellies thesis') or, in the case of Sri Lanka, that economic development was contingent on militarily defeating the LTTE was undermined by many post-colonial states having neither 'rice' nor 'rights', with Sri Lanka in particular increasingly closing rather than opening public political space. The assumption of structural determinism between economic development and democratisation has since been contradicted by economically successful Singapore failing to democratise while Indonesia and the Philippines both returned to democratisation despite being in the depths of economic crisis. As Sen (1999a,b) has noted, there is no necessary link between political forms and economic development (see also Przeworski *et al.* 2000; Barro 1996; Przeworski 1995). Moreover, political freedoms, as implied in a representative, transparent and accountable political system that not only allows but also encourages a high degree of public participation, have helped ensure that no democratic state has ever suffered a famine, which, he claims, is due to the accountability of governments (Sen 1999a; see also D'Souza 1990; Dr'eze and Sen 1987; Human Rights Watch 1992; RC 1994). Corruption, too, appears to be significantly more prevalent in states in which there is no or little accountability. Economic development may actually go backwards as a consequence of a lack of political openness as implied in plural democracy and civil and political rights (see Sen 1999b).

Tensions within rights

It has been a basic assumption of democratic government, in which the interests of the majority prevail (if not at the overwhelming expense of the minority), that it should pursue policies that produce the most favourable outcome for the greatest number of people. This utilitarian position of pursuit of broadly favourable outcomes, or 'public good', assumes the existence of an overarching political unity, usually understood as 'nation', which is intended to secure and preserve its interests (i.e. the 'national interest') within the context of a territorially bounded and institutionally capable territory (the 'state').

Such good can be construed in purely material terms, such as economic benefit, security of economic conditions, strategic (sovereign) security and access to the benefits of the state, such as a consistent and equitably applied law, infrastructure and social services. This good may also be construed in terms of security of political benefit, including political participation and representation, and the associated rights to freedom of speech and communication, and assembly, and from arbitrary arrest, detention, torture and so on. However, in a generally open society, the public good of rights that secure political goods may be in tension with the public good of rights that secure utilitarian goods, especially when those utilitarian rights are more narrowly conceived (e.g. by limited private interest). That is, political debate in favour of some economic redistribution might potentially limit absolute economic accumulation or growth. The two may coexist and, indeed, in most rights-based societies do so with relative equilibrium between them. But, in that they do so, it is only in an unending contest for supremacy based on orderings of individual and group interest.

The fundamental assumptions underpinning utilitarianism are that there is a political cohort to which its value applies and that the utility applies to most of the people in a given community most of the time. This in turn assumes a unity of purpose, which in a fully realised form may constitute a nation within the institutional context of a state. This is not to suggest that the nation, the state or the 'nation-state' is a political ideal or absolute political end in itself. Rather, it suggests that the fully realised form of a bonded political community may be called a 'nation', but may potentially be less or greater than contemporary conceptions, by being less than what is represented by a state (e.g. economic class) or by being spread across states (e.g. multilateral organisations). A nation may be a devolved or relatively evolved political community, either less or greater than the rather static interpretations of nation (and also state) that tend to apply. The general tendency has been for specific political unities to devolve to their constituent parts, while larger unities have tended to form as the result of perceived or actual economic or security benefits. The idea of nation, then, has tended to reflect a devolution, or largely a return to aspects of primordialism, rather than an evolution, and as such reflects vertical (ethnic, cultural) rather than horizontal (class, economic) interests. This can be seen in Sri Lanka with the class-based Janatha Vimukthi Peramuna (People's Liberation Front, or JVP) having been subsumed into the conventional political process by supporting President Rajapaksa's campaign in 2005 and, following a split in 2008, its breakaway Jathika Nidahas Peramuna (National Freedom Front, or JNP) joining the government in 2010 on an anti-LTTE platform.

Assuming a common bonded political identity, that is, a nation, the focus on the welfare of the community within an agreed sovereign territory supports the utilitarian proposition. However, the degree to which the community is bonded may not apply equally to all elements of the community. To ensure the good of the constituent members, the community must allow all individuals the opportunity to express their preferences (where there is no harm to others) and protect them from the potential imposition of a singular communitarian will. This could be understood in particular in the case of a post-colonial state in which none of language, economy or security is an absolute unifiers in itself, but which through sufficient proximity (colonial geo-spatial organisation) identify enough in common to maintain the value of the point of overlap. This could be said to imply a tendency towards vertical social integration, with the areas where there is no overlap comprising assertions of local identity or, potentially, vertical disintegration.

Alternatively, assuming that these interests are all economic, for example around sectors of capital, technology and labour, but with a common language and security focus, there might be greater common ground to form a single community, creating the horizontal conditions for national identity, but a particular point where unity of purpose is contested by specific economic interests. The points at which these respective interest groups do not overlap suggest a probable desire to preserve or promote specific interests, and the capacity to be able to do so. Given the tendency of the centre or middle ground to act as a median point of interest, utilitarianism assumes that the greatest number of people receive at least some benefit, while relatively few are disadvantaged. This implies mutual acceptance of legitimate plurality.

Assuming that each interest group will assert their primary interest, or at least assert a claim to what constitutes a fair balance of interests, the middle ground and definitions of 'greatest good' become contested. Even when there is agreement about the greatest good, there may be instances when the greatest common good remains deleterious to constituent members. That is, it may be necessary to sacrifice the interests of a few for the greater good of many. This then suggests an inconsistent application of agreed codes (law) or the expedient abrogation of the interests of some members of the community for the benefit of others. Because of either the inconsistency of this application, or the institutionalisation of expediency, abrogation of the rights of some is likely to lead to social discord, potentially at high and destabilising levels. Ensuring that both judicial inconsistency and institutionalised expediency are constrained therefore requires the institutionalisation of a counter-balance, that is, the rights of the constituent member to freedom from such impositions and the freedom to fully engage as an equal in the process of determination of the common good.

The contrary position to community rights and interests, then, is to assert the 'right' of the social constituent – the individual – against a presupposed uniformity of interest or the assumed overarching welfare of the community. This then sets up a competition between community rights and individual rights. In putting forward a claim to individual freedom, Bentham (e.g. Bentham 1781: ch. XVI) and Hobbes (1962: ch. 21) argued that every law diminished freedom, even if the purpose of such law was to prevent a greater loss of freedom. Yet recognising the practical value of majority claims, especially in a functioning democracy, the rights of an individual must on occasion be required to give way to wider social benefit. Rejection of this compromise of absolute individual rights neglects the reality that individuals live within communities, and the rights of all cannot be compromised, without exception, by the rights of one.

The balance between community necessity and individual claims, then, posits liberalism – a preference for freedom – against libertarianism, – an absolute freedom – particularly in the economic sphere, and recognises that the rights of one are bounded by their capacity to negatively impact on others. That is, freedom, which rights are supposed to make available, does not equate to freedom from law (see Larmore 1996: 108), but rather freedom for all under law. In this respect, the rights of a community are best preserved by guaranteeing the rights of its constituent members within the context of the rights of others, or the substance of liberalisation (O'Donnell and Schmitter 1986: 7). As noted by Berlin, in arguing for a balance between rights, 'every law curtails some liberty, although it may be a means to increasing another' (Berlin 1958: 123, n. 49). Similarly, the judicial theorist Rawls did not see freedom (or 'liberty') as an absolute, but as 'a certain pattern of social forms' (Rawls 1971: 63), or as what might be described as the positive right of rational individual autonomy along with freedom from domination or unnecessary interference as a result of the absolute rights of others. Indeed, not only is the idea of individual rights not contrary to a sense of community, and hence certain communitarian values, but, as Larmore suggests, the community is the safest place in which rights can reside. 'Take our fate out of the hands of individuals', he said, 'and give our immunity to interference an impersonal or collective basis' (Larmore 1996: 114). Such a collectivity, in this case, rests with the international community and not with the personalised political leadership of a particular state, such as Sri Lanka.

Legitimacy and rights

If the universal claims of human rights have a measurable basis, it is not so much in what people in common wish for, even though there is a high degree of commonality in basic aspirations. Rather, the most absolute point of consistency in human rights is in what people do not wish for or, more to the point, wish to avoid at all cost. If there are quibbles about some universal claims, one that stands up irrespective of time, place, culture or other circumstances is abhorrence of personal torture. That is, no one likes it, no one would willingly put up with it and everyone would wish that it did not exist should they be subject to it (see Singer 1979). Similarly, being jailed is for most people a negative experience and few people would willingly surrender themselves to incarceration. This is particularly so if incarceration is outside of the due process of law and if it does not include the relative comforts and security of some of the more enlightened prison systems, but is constructed around the bare minimum to sustain life, and perhaps then not for the long term. Since soon after independence, many Tamils in Sri Lanka had variously undergone these types of privations, while the population more generally was aware that this was the fate that could befall anyone who was 'troublesome' and sometimes individuals who were simply mistaken for being troublesome.

The question of normative forms of and respect for civil and political rights is best addressed by being directly tested against a specific universal set of criteria, and whether political rule meets the test of legitimacy (see Morris 1998: 24, 105–11). Broadly, 'legitimacy', in the positive sense, complies with the exercise of power in accordance with a broadly socially accepted set of principles, procedures or method of conferral of authority. As this is generally codified in order to achieve some standardisation of application, it implies the existence of law. In that 'legitimacy' was established in Sri Lanka at this time, it implied rule by law rather than rule of law. Indeed, the word 'legitimacy', like the word 'legal', derives from the Roman *lex* ('law'), and its original application did not distinguish between the legitimacy and legality of a regime; in order to be one it had to be the other, in contrast to arbitrary rule or tyranny. In later discussion, especially under the influence of Christian theology, the idea of legitimacy was linked to natural law, and through the Enlightenment gradually democratised. Weber's theory of legitimacy of rule canvassed different ideal models obtaining to different preconditions, but throughout asserted that legitimacy arose through acceptance of a precondition, imitation, rational belief in its value or its legality (Weber 1946: 130). Such was the case only in qualification in Sri Lanka, and largely if one was not Tamil.

Another set of criteria might construe legitimacy as comprising a normative natural order that translates as political order. For example, such criteria can be found in traditional forms of rule and elements of 'organic' political corporatism or in a liberal-minimalist model dependent upon a state's capacity to maintain peace under rule of law, characterised by the 'small state' approach of neo-liberalism. They can also be located in a democratic-proceduralist model of agreement between free and equal citizens, based on individual self-determination (as the only rational basis for morality) as outlined by Kant (1997) and as construed as social contract by Rousseau (1973). The 'natural' order of a people, linguistically and to a high degree territorially separate, is to seek legitimacy from a source that either guarantees law for all equally or reflects the needs of a particular group separate to another. In this, legitimacy not found in a multi-ethnic post-colonial state such as Sri Lanka, which is seen by many as actively illegitimate through its use of coercion and violence, finds itself expressed as the desire for a separate state.

In this, there is a parallel between the somewhat artificial separation of positive and negative rights, in the distinction between the individual and the community, and between freedom and equality. A community is no more than a collective of individuals, just as an individual is no more or less than a constituent member of a community. A conceptual differentiation of both may be required for theoretical purposes, but in practice the community and individuals overlap and live within each other. As the individual goes forward, within a framework of respect for the rights of others, so too does the community; when the community regresses and diminishes its access to rights, so to do the individuals who comprise it. In that the 'Asian values' position proposes a dichotomy, it is therefore a false one. Sri Lanka began life as an independent state in 1948, relatively free in the sense of rule of law applied equally, if with a significant class-based hierarchy and divisions between ethnic groups. As the state continued, however, these distinctions hardened, to the extent that laws employed by the colonial British were being used in an equally and sometimes more brutal manner to compel compliance with an inequitable economic and political environment. As the largest identifiable minority, Sri Lanka's Tamils were targeted for much of the discrimination, but it occurred more widely as well. Although new laws of arrest and detention were applied to separatist groups, they were also applied more generally, particularly in the case of the JVP's uprising in 1971 and again in the 1980s. Freedom of speech has been curtailed in Sri Lanka for all except those who agree with the general government position. Regression of the law in Sri Lanka and the rise of a dominant elite backed by force has had negative consequences far beyond, if commonly focused upon, the Tamil community.

There is, of course, a claimed paradox between conceptions of freedom and law: to the extent that freedom is understood as the absence of domination, just laws form its precondition (Larmore in Weinstock and Nadeau 2004: 105) Yet this 'sense of paradox is due to confusing the absence of domination with the absence of interference' (Larmore in Weinstock and Nadeau 2004: 106), which is most often associated with the utilitarianism of Bentham. Moreover, in ancient Greece, 'Demokratia was committed to the rule of law because it recognised that the rule of law protected the interests of the poor as well as the rich' (Ober 2000). This is, although law imposes some limitations upon freedom, normatively such restrictions are only to the freedom to restrict the freedom of others. In that law normatively guarantees protection from such arbitrary restrictions, it enhances real freedom. Under the 'Asian values' paradigm, law is itself a restriction upon freedom, marking the differentiation between a normative rule of law and, in the 'Asian values' context, rule by law.

Freedom from arbitrary arrest, detention and torture, which find themselves more commonly applied under 'rule by law', are among the first-generation civil and political rights, as legal protection from authoritarian excesses intended to quell challenges to the authority of an oppressive state. These freedoms 'from' are necessary rights alone, but are especially important as protective measures in concert with rights 'to' freedom of speech and assembly, and so on. Freedom from arbitrary arrest, detention and torture also implies the existence of the consistent and equal rule of law. Beyond that, strictures against the use of inhumane or degrading punishment, including torture, reflect the positive values of a society in relation to its own members, and imply a broadly benign approach and a degree of mutual respect as human beings, even for law breakers. Taken from a negative perspective, strictures on the use of torture or other cruel, degrading or inhumane forms of punishment also reflect an awareness that it is not possible to separate one aspect of a society's behaviour from others, and that what occurs in prisons, and the means by which citizens might get there, says much about how a society more generally treats itself, its capacity for empathy and its sensitivity or otherwise to human suffering.

Thus, when the issue of R2P is raised, it is done so either when the government of the state lacks the capacity or the will to secure the welfare of its citizens from the degradation of widespread and serious abuses of human rights or when it is the principle perpetrator of such abuses. Human rights are not culturally or politically specific; neither is the responsibility to protect them. There is, then, an implicit acknowledgment that, if human rights are indeed universal and acknowledging them is therefore obligatory, the responsibility to protect them is similarly universal and therefore obligatory.

Legitimate and illegitimate violence

At the bottom of concerns over R2P is the use by the state of illegitimate violence. This then raises questions as to the nature of state and non-state violence and the legitimacy of the use of violence in differing circumstances. If the goal of states is about creating a sense of security in which a broad sense of freedom becomes available to its citizens – the general basis of the legitimacy of states – then illegitimate violence is the greatest challenge to that freedom and the rule of states. Conversely, legitimate violence can be freedom's saviour. But because violence has such absolute consequences, questions of legitimacy around it use are profoundly contested.

Illegitimate violence can not only preclude political development, but also define the way in which development might take place by imposing through force a particular ideological outcome. More positively, through acting as a guardian, legitimate political violence can ensure and enhance political development through securing the state and the efficacy of its institutions. In its application, the point between potential and actual violence may only be marginal. Potential violence is experienced as actual violence not yet manifested, but always imminent and hence retaining its coercive quality.

There are four categories of political violence, the first being 'legitimate state violence', in which the state is manifested in its political regime. Such regimes retain the reserve power of the state as the legitimate manifestation of the collective will of its citizens to employ violence in support of state goals. 'Legitimate violence' is used to maintain the state's laws, and the state claims a monopoly upon the use of such violence, excluding all others from using violence. By contrast, the second category might be called 'legitimate non-state violence', in which violence or the capacity for coercion is employed by non-state actors in pursuit of legitimate goals, in particular when the state is regarded as acting illegitimately, for example when the state employs extra-judicial violence or otherwise behaves unlawfully. This is clearly a much more problematic category than 'legitimate state violence', not least because it does not enjoy the legitimising quality that the state brings to its coercive capacity. As the dominant claimant to legitimacy and to a monopoly on the use of violence, the state by definition characterises violent non-state actors as illegitimate, regardless of the validity of their claims. The third category is 'illegitimate non-state violence', which can range from simple criminal activity to political violence in pursuit of goals that do not accord with prevailing or even common minority views. Non-state actors may also employ particular methods that are held to be delegitimising, such as 'terrorism'. Violent non-state actors might claim their actions as legitimate, but as a consequence of the invariably formal non-representative structure of non-state actors their claim is less able to be substantiated on that basis. They are therefore beholden to establish their legitimacy through weight of other evidence. Finally, there is 'illegitimate state violence'. Although all states claim legitimacy on the basis of their statehood, they may still exercise violence illegitimately. Illegitimate state violence may be exercised outside a state's own codified legal structures, by ignoring conventional global standards on arbitrary arrest, detention and torture, or by assuming power through illegal or non-representative means. It may also be used to perpetuate a regime that is otherwise lacking in legitimacy, which in turn abrogates the generally agreed terms of the social contract under which the nation coheres as an agreed political unit.

Legitimate state violence

Traditionally, violence, its threat or its unstated presence has been the primary method by which state interests have been asserted and by which order has been maintained. In such cases, the state as the sovereign authority over a territorially demarcated area claims a legitimate and exclusive right to use violence to compel compliance with its laws, protect its sovereignty and maintain order (see Weber 1948[4]). Assuming popular acceptance of state laws – that is, the establishment of legitimacy – state violence should exist only as a reserve power, in which the police or other state agents take action only against explicit challenges to, or contravention of, the law. Implicit in this is that law is an accurate reflection of the values of the society in question. This constitutes legitimate state violence, and as a guarantor of peace and order can be said to be a significant contributor to political development.

Illegitimate state violence

States can also and sometimes do employ violence to compel compliance, and their actions might not always conform to the full range of conceptions of legitimacy. Indeed, the methods employed by the state can resemble non-state methods, particularly in pursuit of narrowly conceived political goals, and may include assassinations, bombings, and so on. Assuming that the state normatively claims to protect all its citizens under an equitably applied law (a basic criterion of state legitimacy), the extra-legal use of violence by the state in the form of torture, murder, rape and other methods that violate basic human rights, not to mention more standard forms of state violence such as conventional warfare (e.g. bombing from a distance), offers privileged opportunities for illegitimate state violence (see, for example, Anderson 2001).

More problematically, governments may not be widely perceived as legitimate and lack strong popular support. Alternatively, they may be legitimately elected or otherwise initially accepted as legitimate, but come to act illegitimately or introduce and enact laws that do not represent popular wishes, which may in turn reflect a non-representative and non-participatory political process (e.g. presidential decree), or which may run contrary to broadly accepted social and moral codes. Indeed, governments may use state force to control their citizens in a manner that is predatory (see Evans 1994 regarding sub-Saharan Africa) in order to serve the interests of an oligarchic elite (see Hutchcroft 1991 regarding the Philippines). Alternatively, political dictates may be carried out by state institutions regardless of, or despite, the rule of law, or where the law is so poorly codified or enforced that it is inconsistent and incoherent and therefore open to extensive interpretation or disregard (such as in Burma, or in Indonesia under Suharto). Such violation or reinterpretation of laws may run contrary to the popular will, but can be maintained and indeed further developed by employing mechanisms that support more popular or conventional law, being the reserve use of violence. In cases in which social dissent is deep, governments may employ a range of methods to achieve compliance, including not only conventional police but also political police, intelligence operatives and informers, and military and paramilitary organisations, in widely focused political oppression. This in turn further weakens the legitimacy of the government and possibly the state in the eyes of its citizens. Although such actions are invariably justified by the wielders of power on the basis of order, national cohesion or other claims, they are almost invariably a consequence of a non-representative and non-accountable form of government and, as such, cannot be tested. That is, in the competition between structure and agency, or economics and politics, although a middle ground can be accommodated via social contract, without active political participation, communication and organisation, political development (and its popular manifestation as democratisation) cannot progress. The subsequent tensions that arise from this blockage may manifest as conflict, or the illegitimate (i.e. politicised) application of state violence.

Within the above is the role of the militaries, civil–military relations and military transitions (both to and from democracy). States that have achieved independence by military means, or in which a government has come to power through such means, are more likely to retain a prominent role for the military in political affairs. The military, in such cases, will often see or portray itself as the 'guardian of the state', and will reserve its right to intervene militarily in civil affairs if and when it believes that state interests are being threatened; hence, the propensity to *coups d'état* in a number of developing countries.

There are a number of problems with military intervention in political affairs. The first is that the military is rarely the best judge of when or if such intervention is necessary. This is particularly so given the institutional cultures of militaries, which are necessarily strongly hierarchical and driven by an absolute authority rather than a participatory and representative decision-making framework (Huntington 1957). Although the military is an institution of state, its engagement in anti-regime activity may exist partially outside state structures or state constitutional paradigms. Thus, the military may pose more of a threat to the state than 'threats' to the state that they sometimes seek to contain, as demonstrated by the political and often economic failure of military coups.

Militaries in many developing countries further suffer from conflicts of interest, in which political power assists them in maintaining institutional or extra-state power. Conflicting interests could also revolve around economic interests, such as military businesses and criminal enterprises (e.g. throughout Latin America, South-East and Central Asia and sub-Saharan Africa). The extent to which militaries are subordinate to, or outside, civilian authority and their ability to protect and enhance their own interests is a direct indicator of the political health of a state, and a primary marker of political development.

Legitimate non-state violence

The use or threat of violence is commonplace by states, and indeed the legitimate and sole use of violence is widely seen to be one criterion of successful statehood. The critical issues, and over which the debate becomes more divided, revolve around the legitimacy of state and non-state actors. States claim a monopoly on the legitimate use of violence as a primary capacity; *ipso facto* states deny the use of violence to non-state actors, and are obliged to regard such use of violence as *prima facie* illegitimate. This delegitimising of non-state violence is sometimes assisted by the methods used by non-state actors, usually as a consequence of their limited capacities. As a leader of the armed separatist Algerian National Liberation Front (FLN) said: 'Give us your bombers [planes] and you can have our [bomb] baskets' (Pontecorvo 1966). Personally delivered bombs and other methods of non-state violence may be effective but are not conventional state methods, which further distinguishes non-state from state actors in a negative sense.

Just as states claim legitimacy on the basis of their statehood, non-state actors can also have claims that they regard as legitimate. In asserting these claims in response to state or state-associated violence, non-state actors can claim to legitimately employ reciprocal violence (see, for example, Fanon 1970). For example, the formation of the Liberation Tigers of Tamil Eelam in Sri Lanka and like organisations elsewhere reflects the claim to legitimacy of reciprocal violence following discrimination by the Sri Lankan government and violence by groups that were seen to be aligned with and supported by government institutions (especially the police and army). Both the government of Sri Lanka and organisations associated with it have specifically targeted and used indiscriminate terror against the LTTE, along with more conventional military approaches to violence. The identification of the LTTE as a 'terrorist organisation', therefore, was inaccurate in that it applied only to the LTTE (although the LTTE also used terror as a tactic), and implied that the LTTE had no function other than as a terrorist organisation (within the territory it controlled, it fulfilled most state functions, including the application of rule of law).

The realm of non-state violence is perhaps the most controversial area within the field of political development in that it constitutes a direct challenge to the legitimacy of the state, to conventional forms of order and, not least, to those institutions and actors that hold state power (the government, military, police and so on). As noted, non-state violence will always be characterised as illegitimate by states and their representatives and supporters, not because of the legitimacy or otherwise of state violence, but because it is *prima facie* an attack against the legitimacy of the state. It may be claimed, with good reason, that much non-state violence is indeed illegitimate, and it is usually dangerous to defend cases in which non-state violence takes place, regardless of the arguments for or against it. This was especially so at the time of writing, when terrorism had gripped the imagination of the Western world and much of the non-Western world. As a consequence, actual or so defined 'terrorists' successfully achieved their first aim of bringing attention to their cause. The governments of many countries have not only defined themselves in opposition to such terrorism, but also redefined themselves in relation to their own citizens.

Even a cursory assessment of non-state violence, in particular in relation to domestic insurgencies, will quickly show that what are understood by less subjective audiences as rebellions, revolutions, claims to separate state identity and so on are almost always characterised by the government under attack as 'terrorism'. The use of the term 'terrorist' is clearly an emotive one, raising fear of attack outside conventional conflict environments, and, hence, lacking that element of predictability that conventional conflict is felt[5] to offer. The term 'terrorist' also constitutes an attempt to delegitimise the attacker and, more importantly, to delegitimise their motives. The term 'terrorist' also constructs the attacker as a violent sociopath who lacks a coherent agenda, and who is very much one of 'them' as opposed to the unifying qualities of 'us'. Yet the truth – and this is one of the more contested areas in which the term 'truth' can be used – is that non-state actors engage in violence for a range of reasons, many of which may seem perfectly rational within a particular political or economic context in which intolerable situations create little space for non-violent methods.

Assuming that 'common to all men is the strong desire for fair treatment and justice' (Angiolillo 1979: 5), or the fulfilment of basic elements of a social contract, there is a view that if the law is unjust then there is a moral obligation to not cooperate or to oppose it, usually through civil disobedience (Locke 1960: second treatise; Thoreau 1993 [1849]; Kurland and Lerner 1987: ch. 3). This perceived moral obligation necessarily establishes elements of society in direct opposition to the state and its guardians who are authorised to employ violence. The dispute over legitimate non-state violence versus illegitimate state violence tends to quickly devolve into a contest of violence between the opposing parties, with the result being either the suppression of the non-state 'uprising', or a change of government (or indeed change of the state). However, civil disobedience or political violence aimed against unjust laws or state actions may reflect or evolve into a paradigm that is itself of questionable moral validity, especially in cases in which social responses are commonly seen as out of balance with the 'evil' they seek to overturn (e.g. 'the Terror' of the French Revolution, or acts of indiscriminate terrorism). Although the claim that political violence is necessary to adequately institute desired change (e.g. Sorel 1970: ch. 6) does have an element of truth in it given capacities for resistance and reaction, it is dangerous to adopt standardised violence as a first response to a variety of situations (e.g. Cambodia's Khmer Rouge 1975–9). Beyond this, the primary intention of non-state violence might be not to overturn illegitimate state behaviour, but rather to overturn legitimate state action, such as through organised crime (illegitimate non-state violence).

2 The politics of ethnicity

The war in Sri Lanka between the state and Tamil separatists is, at one level, relatively easy to understand. A minority ethnic group unhappy with the distribution of opportunity and resources in a post-colonial state began to push for an independent state to represent its interests. This claim was, in effect, rejected by the central, ethnic majoritarian government and escalating conflict ensued. How this came about, however, and how it reflected particular interpretations or impositions of culture and ethnicity is more complex. In particular, the conflict in part has origins in and in part has exacerbated not just ethnic tensions but notions of ethnic exclusivity, up to and including who the original inhabitants of Sri Lanka were, who has a right to live there and in what circumstances.

The competing claims about the origins of the peoples of Sri Lanka, in particular about when the country's Tamils arrived and whether this should give them less claim to being authentically Sri Lankan or having equal civil and political rights, inform some of the more chauvinist Sinhalese contributions to the conflict. This, in effect, anchors more moderate Sinhalese to a racist paradigm. As Harris has noted:

> there are three main bastions of Sinhala nationalism. These are the government, the pro-government media, and the Buddhist clergy. Together, these groups present a mutually reinforcing (and indeed mutually benefiting, in terms of maintaining power and control) notion of Sri Lanka as essentially a historically Sinhala Buddhist country which tolerates other ethnicities, but whose national integrity has been under attack for the past three decades by the secessionist aspirations of the militant Liberation Tigers of Tamil Eelam (LTTE).
>
> (Harris 2010: 2)

As a result, any sense of unified 'nation' that might have existed in Sri Lanka has increasingly become predicated upon the notion that non-Sinhalese should either assimilate, by becoming literate in Sinhalese and adopting Buddhism, or at the very least remain inconspicuous as secondary citizens of what is functionally an ethnic Sinhalese state. As a result, one can refer to the Sri Lankan state with little conceptual concern, but it is much more problematic to refer to the 'Sri Lankan nation' or to Sri Lanka as a 'nation-state'.

'Nation' in Sri Lanka

The idea of a specific 'nation' may be contested, especially in cases of ethnic separatism such as that which has arisen in Sri Lanka. But there is broad agreement around the key conceptual components of 'nation', which corresponds to a group of people who cohere around and define their political interests in common. The idea of nation generally manifests as support for the creation, continuation or strengthening of an idea of a common bonded identity, an assertion of independent unity and, usually, self-determination (see Connor 1994; Anderson 1991; Smith 1986a,b, 2003; Gellner 1983). These criteria were those that helped inform Sri Lanka's bid for independence in 1948 and which informed many other post-war independence movements. However, self-determination can be double edged, implying as it does not just self-determination in relation to a distant coloniser but also self-determination from a more local dominant power.

In this latter sense, self-determination can be seen to apply to the Tamil areas of Sri Lanka (referred to here as Eelam), as well as to the peoples sharing a common political identity of numerous other ethnically specific territories who have claimed or continue to claim separate political status. Means of understanding and recognising or creating such a common political identity usually revolve around a common language, more broadly shared cultural values, world view (*weltanschauung*) or ideology, and sets of myths and history (Smith 1986b: 13–18, Gellner 1983: 44). This often involves a common hero or heroes as the national archetype and, not infrequently, develops in response to a commonly perceived threat or struggle for liberation. These criteria can be seen to apply to Eelam, through the Tamil language, elements of caste (if unpopular with the dominant egalitarian ideology of Tamil liberation), the Hindu religion (although allowing for other religious forms such as Christianity), a world view that identifies Tamils as conscientious and hard working as well as marginalised by the dominant Sinhalese culture, a further ideology of liberation or self-determination and a set of myths or history that not only valorises Tamil 'martyrs' and heroes but also draws on the status of Tamils under British colonial rule and pre-colonial Tamil kingdoms, notably the extensive 'golden era' of the Chola empire from the third but in particular the ninth century until the early thirteenth century (other Tamil dynasties followed for a further 200 years). Mythologising of the Chola era came to inform much of the self-understanding in particular of the LTTE.

Other qualities that contribute to the successful creation and maintenance of a nation can include having a reasonably compact territory and a capable and energetic intellectual class, each of which help but are not absolutely necessary (Gellner 1983: 46). In the case of the Eelam Tamils, the territory they occupied was relatively compact if partially divided by a central hill area. That the Tamils had a capable and energetic intellectual class was not only established but also the foundation of at least some of their grievances – that it had been arbitrarily excluded from numerous sources of opportunity in favour of often less-qualified ethnic Sinhalese.

As proposed by Sitrampalam, the development in Sri Lanka of nationalist sentiment during the colonial era was based:

> on the foundations of the society's traditional past. They saw the modern phase of nationalism, not as a novel, essentially different phenomenon, causing a break with the past, but rather as an extension of their past, a rebirth of the old society, its renaissance in a new form.
>
> (Sitrampalam n.d.)

If this assertion is correct, then Sri Lanka did not at any time experience a sense of national unity or purpose and its two main ethnic groups always saw each other in separate and sometimes oppositional terms.

Indrapala explicitly viewed the 'evolution' of Tamil and Sinhalese ethnic identity as separate, with distinct Tamil identity (*Damila* in Pali chronicles, *c.* 500 BCE) dating to the Mesolithic/iron age era, between 900 and 300 BCE (Indrapala 2007: 24, 38, 74). The region of Tamil Nadu in southern India and north-western Sri Lanka across the narrow Palk Straits shared a common culture, and remained close until the advent of modern states (Indrapala 2007: 82), as opposed to Sri Lankan Tamils having some closer bond with the southern Sinhalese. However, Indrapala identifies the establishment of the Sinhalese city of Tambapanni (Indrapala 2007: 97–101), later supplanted by the city of Anuradhapura, about half-way between the west and east coasts and about two-thirds of the way up the island, from south to north, as being culturally linked to the island's northern coast (Indrapala 2007: 88–9). Anuradhapura's significance lies in its longevity as the island's dominant city, from around the fourth century BCE[1] to around the eleventh century CE, and in it being the site of acceptance of Buddhism to the island. Regardless of the links that might have existed, from time to time, between Anuradhapura and the island's north coast, Tamils and Sinhalese were often at war, reflecting very different conceptions of control of their spheres of influence over their respective parts of the island and which might have contributed to Anuradhapura's ultimate decline.

The island that now constitutes the state of Sri Lanka was variously known as Ila in Prakrit (root language of the Sinhalese), Sihala in Pali, Taprobane to ancient Greeks (from the city of Tambapanni) and Salediba to Greco-Romans, probably from Ila and Dvipa, the former the chief progenitor of the lunar dynasty (one of three) in Hindu mythology and the latter a Sanscrit word for 'island' or 'land'. This in turn led to later Arab and Persian traders to know the island as Serendib. It is from this name that the term 'seredipity' is derived, which has come to imply good fortune or accidental sagacity and was originally drawn from a Persian fairy tale of three princes of the island and their accidental good fortune. The independent state has, however, enjoyed little of that quality since. The Portuguese name for the island, Ceilao, probably derives from the first part of the Greco-Roman Sela-diba, which was then passed to the British as Ceylon. Being close to the southern tip of India and about half way between the east coast of Africa and the Middle East and China, the island has long been both a destination for local, regional and international trade, as well as a stopping-off point for traders from further afield, hence the variety of names given to it by outsiders.

Based on linguistic patterns, commonalities between legends (e.g. see Indrapala 2007: 100–1, Appendix V) and scant few and, notably, later written records, it appears that the people or their leaders (Indrapala 2007: 101) who were to become the Sinhalese at least in part migrated from what is now northern India and Bangladesh, joining and mixing with the indigenous Vedda (Wanniyala-Aetto, or 'forest people') and probably other traders and migrants. It is likely, however, that the development of the Sinhalese language arose as a result of the acceptance of Buddhism (Indrapala 2007: 117). The unresolved debate about the relations between and origins of languages continue, often in a forceful manner, with no research to date proving to be conclusive (Indrapala 2007: 102–18).

The issue of region of origin of the Sinhalese and the Tamils is vexed, in large part as a result of racist claims to distinction between Indians and hence Sri Lankans of Aryan and Dravidian descent (see Indrapala 2007: ch. 3). This is in turn based in part on interpretations of ancient Indian scripts (Vedas) and in part on nineteenth-century European colonialism, which perpetrated racist theories based on skin tone. Regardless of the regional or linguistic origins of the Sinhalese and the Tamils, one finds strong echoes of such racism among some of the more outspoken Sinhalese, in turn informing official Sri Lankan language and religious policy, as well as less official forms of cultural chauvinism. This is then less a debate about from where languages or peoples originated and much more about claims to 'superiority' and 'inferiority'. It is worth noting, however, that there were various inter-linguistic alliances and considerable admixture between the peoples who occupied the island, so that claims to 'ethnic purity' by either Tamils or Sinhalese are nonsensical (Indrapala 2007: ch. 5); 'Out of the complex interplay of cultures, languages and religions, there emerged the modern ethnic groups' (Indrapala 2007: 296, see also 258–60). Despite this 'complex interplay', Sinhalese chauvinists have employed ethnic distinction ('*Para Demala*') as a way of delegitimising the status and indeed presence of Tamils in Sri Lanka.

But it is not only the Sinhalese who have adopted racial myths by way of justifying their various claims; so too have some of Sri Lanka's Tamils. Despite the fact that Tamils have been shown to have had a continuing presence in Sri Lanka from the first millennium BCE, it is notable that in constructing a formal armed opposition to Sinhalese hegemony the LTTE drew on myths of Chola warriorhood by way of reinventing Tamils as a fighting people (see Indrapala 2007: ch. 7, esp. 255–6). Indeed, the use of the term and symbolic tiger by the LTTE reflects Chola use of the tiger on coins: 'LTTE leader Pirapaharan [Velupillai Prabhakaran] selected Tiger as the Tamileelam national insignia to present an image rooted in Dravidian civilization symbolizing martial velour [sic] and the uniqueness of Tamil language and culture' (TamilNet 2005). The employment of the imperial Chola tiger emblem was in direct contrast to the Sinhalese lion and was a symbolic replacement for the traditional Jaffna symbol of a seated (passive) 'bull'. Quoting the LTTE's official organ Viduthali Pudigal (February 1991): 'The Tiger symbol illustrated the martial history (*veera varalaru*) and national upheaval of the Tamils. Our national flag is the symbol of the independent state of Tamileelam to be created, rooted in the martial traditions (*veera marapuhal*) of the Tamils' (Anon 1991).

The Chola empire lasted, in two phases, from 300 CE until the early thirteenth century CE and occupied the south and east of India and incorporated South-East

Asia's maritime states as vassals. The period of Chola unification in Sri Lanka, beginning *c.* 923 and concluding by 1070, was well over a thousand years after Tamils (or their forebears) had become firmly established in Sri Lanka. That is, the LTTE's appeal to Chola militarism might have helped resurrect the idea of the Tamils as a warrior nation at a time when it believed it was faced with direct assault, but it also fed into the opposing mythologising by inferring that the Tamils history in Sri Lanka began with or reached its high point with the Chola invasion from southern India, well after the peoples who were to become the Sinhalese had become well established. This then inadvertently delegitimised Tamil claims to equal ancestry with the Sinhalese (despite having a presence dating back, even defined by the Chola invasion, of more than a thousand years[2]), assuming ancestry was to be the basis of a claim to citizenship.

The assumption, however, on the part of both the Sinhalese and Tamils that legitimacy derived from a mythologised ancestry in a given location rather than fact of birth or equality of contemporary citizenship fed back into a reification that reconstructed both Sinhalese and Tamils as continuations of earlier warring states rather than as ethnic groups with equal citizenship within a common state.

At the outset of British colonialism in Sri Lanka (succeeding that of the Portuguese and then the Dutch), in June 1799, Sir Hugh Cleghorn, Sri Lanka's first British Colonial Secretary, wrote to the British government identifying the island's distinct ethnic groups:

> Two different nations from a very ancient period have divided between them the possession of the Island. First the Sinhalese, inhabiting the interior of the country in its Southern and Western parts, and secondly the Malabars [Tamils] who possess the Northern and Eastern Districts. These two nations differ entirely in their religion, language and manners.
>
> (Cleghorn 1799)

The critical aspect of the war in Sri Lanka, and its subsequent conclusion, was that the Sinhalese clearly defined themselves as ethnically distinct from and, in many cases, superior to their fellow Tamil (and Muslim) citizens. Sinhalese nationalism had been rising since independence, but took on an increasingly virulent form in response to the war with the LTTE. In return, the LTTE took on an exclusivist cast to its own features; the two parties to the war looked nothing so much like two ancient kingdoms locked in a struggle to the death, which, in some respects, they were.

Basis of separatist claims

In a case of colonial divide and rule policy, the British had favoured Ceylon's minority Tamil population, who were generally better educated than the Sinhalese majority and who were employed in government administrative positions. As with other multi-ethnic colonial states that favoured an ethnic minority over a majority, when colonialism ended in 1948 the ethnic minority lost their privileged position, often accompanied by majority bitterness and backlash (e.g. Ruanda, Uganda, Zimbabwe). As Tamils and Sinhalese began to divide, a 'traditional' or reified cultural nationalism that had not yet otherwise developed as a civic identity led to an attempted hegemony by the majority ethnic Sinhalese over the Tamil and Muslim minorities, which in turn generated conflict as these minorities sought to resist such hegemony.

In recognition of the process of decolonisation that was then beginning to sweep the world, on 4 February 1948, the United Kingdom acceded to united local pressure and granted Ceylon (later to become Sri Lanka) its independence. The United Kingdom established the independent Ceylon as a unitary state, choosing not to create the new state as a federation and in doing so ignoring the continuing influence of the island's separate ethnic identities that it had otherwise acknowledged (Wickramasinghe 1995: ch. 1). Sri Lanka's one large majority was the Sinhalese (c. 70 per cent), with two significant minorities, one being Muslim (c. 7 per cent) and the other Tamil (c. 15 per cent) (Gunasingham 2005: 12–32). As early as 1951, at the first national convention of the Federal Party, Tamils asserted that they constituted a distinct nation 'by every fundamental test of nationhood' (quoted in de Silva 1981: 513).

However, independence within a unitary state meant that, with the rise of the politics of ethnicity, ethnic Tamils would quickly lose out to the demographically dominant Sinhalese. As a result of the 1947 vote ahead of independence, leftist parties won around a third of the seats, with many of them in Tamil-dominated plantation areas. No sooner had independence been declared in 1948 than the Sinhalese-dominated United National Party (UNP) government introduced the Ceylon Citizenship Act, which deliberately discriminated against the county's 'plantation' or 'up-country' Tamils by making it all but impossible for them to obtain citizenship. Most of these Tamils had been brought to Sri Lanka to work on the tea plantations in the early 1800s and thus had in most cases been in Sri Lanka for several generations. Yet with this move, around 700,000 Tamils were made stateless, with some 300,000 eventually being deported to India. The perhaps 300,000 or so remaining Tamils of Indian origin were not granted Sri Lankan citizenship until 2003 (UNHCR 2004).

The Citizenship Act that deprived 'Indian' Tamils of citizenship was supported by 'Sri Lankan' Tamil leader and cabinet minister Ganapathipillai Ponnamblam, who was anti-leftist and who viewed 'Indian' Tamils as aliens, despite initially seeking equal government representation for non-Sinhalese groups. It was from this time, too, that the government began to support the transfer of people from densely populated areas in the south to the less heavily populated areas in the north and east, in what has been viewed as 'state-aided colonization' (Perera 2009: 116). Despite this initial agreement between Sinhalese political groups and some more reactionary Tamils, 'After independence in Ceylon, . . . Tamils found themselves systematically and insidiously marginalised from education and the public sector . . . Marginalisation nourished feelings of profound resentment among the Tamils, contributing to the emergence of a nationalist organisation with a separatist agenda' (Smith 2009: 91–2) Without the deep establishment of an equal civic national identity, the stage was set for almost inevitable conflict.

Following the colonial model and in keeping with a desire to overcome linguistic divisions, Ceylon initially used English as its administrative language. The leader of the UNP, John Kotelawala, visited Jaffna where he promised to give equal status to both the Sinhala and Tamil languages (Yogasundram 2006: 281). In response, Sinhalese Buddhist agitators spread false information that the Sinhalese would be forced to learn Tamil in order to get government jobs, leading to anti-government protests across the country. The leader of the breakaway Sri Lanka Freedom Party (SLFP), Solomon Bandaranaike, quickly capitalised on this fear and promised that, if elected, he would make Sinhala the country's sole official language. Seeing his support base desert to the SLFP, UNP leader Kotelawala did an abrupt about face and also jumped on the 'Sinhala only' bandwagon. However, it was too late for the UNP and the SLFP won the 1956 election, immediately introducing the 'Sinhala Only Act', making Sinhalese the sole official language, with English being abandoned. This move immediately marginalised Ceylon's minority Tamil, Muslim and Burgher populations, limiting educational and government employment opportunities, in which Tamils in particular had been prominent. It also cut them off from many government services and led to calls for the establishment of an autonomous Tamil region in the north and east of the country to adequately represent Tamil affairs. Sri Lanka's politics had always had an ethnic caste to it, but such moves polarised and cemented the development of ethnically specific political parties, and further fuelled rising ethnic tensions. Tamils protested, a notable case involving 300 Tamils protesting peacefully in Colombo, who were subsequently violently attacked by a much larger Sinhalese group while police stood by and did nothing. There were further demonstrations and these were also violently disrupted, with Tamils being killed in what were the first communal riots.

The political competition between the UNP and the SLFP to capture the Sinhala Buddhist vote and in a sense to be more extreme than one another, has, since that time, marked Sri Lankan politics, with the main parties trying 'to outdo each other in stoking the fires of racialism, religious intolerance and rabid nationalism' (Yogasundram 2006: 282). This has been the main reason why respective Sri Lankan governments have been unable or unwilling to seek a political solution to the Tamil issue. No sooner has one party sought to occupy a more moderate ground than it has been accused by the other side of selling out Sinhalese Buddhists to Tamil Hindus and Christians. As a result, neither side has since been able to make headway towards establishing a rational basis for adequately incorporating into the state its Tamil minority or to agree to some form of devolution of political authority.

Recognising the problems that were being caused by the Sinhala Only Act, in 1957 Prime Minister Bandaranaike oversaw the passage of a bill allowing the use of Tamil for administrative purposes, limiting the sponsored movement of Sinhalese into Tamil-dominated areas and devolving administrative authority to regional councils. However, 'Sinhala only' extremists in his own party opposed the settlement, forcing the prime minister to abrogate the act he had ushered through parliament. The following year, in May 1958, the pressures and counter-pressure generated by these movements back and forth spilled over into further anti-Tamil rioting across the island, with up to 300 people killed, and the violence in some places taking on the appearance of a pogrom. It was this event in May and the deaths that resulted from it that shattered what trust had remained between the Sinhalese and the Tamils, establishing a pattern of protests and state repression throughout the 1960s.

There had been attempts to negotiate how to manage linguistic difference within Sri Lanka's post-colonial unitary framework, with an agreement looking likely to replace colonial English with both Sinhalese and Tamil. However, the 1956 Sinhala Only Act signalled that ethnic pluralism and power sharing was no longer available to Sri Lanka's minorities, in particular its Tamils. The state became ethnocratic, with appointments to the civil service being based upon political patronage and the police becoming overwhelmingly Sinhalese (along with becoming increasingly harsh in their treatment of minorities) (Perera 2009: 116–17). Tamil political leaders protested against the Sinhala Only Act, on one occasion, 5 June 1956, in front of the parliament. In an effort to moderate a situation quickly getting out of control, the prime minister, Mr Bandaranaike, and the leader of the Tamil opposition, Samuel Chelvanayakam, signed a pact to create a series of regional councils that would devolve some political authority and, it was hoped, reduce tensions. The pact, however, was attacked by extremists on both sides. Militant *bhikkhus* (Buddhist monks) protested outside Bandaranaike's house and he finally abrogated the pact. Tamil protests at this move led to an outbreak of anti-Tamil riots. In a further bid to moderate tension, in 1958 Bandaranaike introduced the Tamil Language (Special Provisions) Act, which allowed the use of Tamil for education, public service entrance examinations and the administration of the north and east of the country. This was regarded as insufficient by Tamils and rejected out of hand by extremist Buddhists. On 25 September 1959, as he prayed, Bandaranaike was assassinated by a *bhikku*.

According to de Silva (1981: 512):

> the abandonment of the concept of a multi-racial polity was justified by laying stress on the notion of a democratic sanction deriving its validity from the clear numerical superiority of the Sinhalese-speaking group. At the same time, the focus continued to be an all-island one, and Sinhala nationalism was consciously or unconsciously treated as identical with Sri Lanka nationalism.

In democratic theory, this state of affairs is usually referred to not as majority rule but as the imposition of majority views on a minority, known as 'majoritarianism'. In democratic terms, it constitutes a procedural rather than substantive democracy, or a 'democracy' in name but not in substance and certainly not in spirit.

By 1958, anti-Tamil riots had begun. Interestingly, it was Bandaranaike as prime minister who presided over the Sinhala Only Act and the linguistic singularity of the state, yet in the mid-1920s, as leader of the Progressive Nationalist Party, he had advocated a federal model for the state (see de Silva 1981: 513). Like many Sri Lankan politicians after him, Bandaranaike became political hostage to extremist views, being vulnerable to accusations of betraying the Sinhalese majority if he adopted views that countenanced a degree of autonomy of non-Sinhala-dominated areas of the island.

Although the Sinhala Only Act, in which Sinhala replaced English as Ceylon's national language, was intended to increase Sinhalese employment in the Tamil-dominated public service, it also excluded non-Sinhalese-speaking Tamils from education (exacerbated by the 1971 Universities Act[3]) and the judicial process as well as from a range of other economic opportunities. The 'claim to separate Tamil lands is a very recent phenomenon, brought about by the growing racism of the state . . . Racism is now becoming institutionalised at every level' (Pereira 1983).

One consequence of the Sinhalese-only language policy was that Tamils were effectively denied access to the legal process, which was conducted exclusively in Sinhalese, which in turn functionally reduced their status as citizens with equal access to the law. As a foundation quality of both citizenship and statehood, this single act spelled the end of Sinhalese and Tamils being able to coexist within a unitary state. Similarly, the compromise of the civil service and the judiciary ended the notion of separation of powers (*trias politica*), which is fundamental to the democratic and otherwise effective functioning of a state.

In a belated attempt to limit the damage caused by this policy, in 1977 Tamil was made a 'national language' (along with the dropping of the Universities Act) and ten years later it was made an 'official language'. However, by then, Sri Lanka's ethnic divide had become all but irreparable. Other forms of official discrimination against the Sri Lankan Tamils included the state-sponsored colonisation of traditional Tamil areas by Sinhalese peasants and the banning of the import of Tamil language media.

Throughout the 1960s and 1970s, Tamil political parties negotiated with government. Every time agreement was reached, the Sinhalese-dominated government came under pressure from Sinhalese extremists and broke the agreement. In 1971, the Sri Lankan United Front government introduced a quota system to increase the number of Sinhalese attending university. This was widely seen among Tamils as a further discriminatory policy aimed at reducing the proportion of Tamils in higher education as opposed to Sinhalese. Tamils now required a qualifying entry mark of 250 out of 400, whereas Sinhalese required only 229, even if they were sitting for qualifying examinations in the common language of English. Among Tamils, the policy was:

> Believed to be a virulent effort on the part of the Sinhalese Government to disadvantage the Tamils, it permanently changed the face of ethnic politics in Sri Lanka. The extent of Tamil bitterness at standardisation induced the government to modify the scheme by 1975, but the psychological damage had already been done.
>
> (Perera 2009: 120–1)

In response to this increasing structural marginalisation and alienation of Sri Lanka's Tamils and especially in response to the violence with which it was accompanied, many Tamils became increasingly radicalised and looked for extra-judicial answers to what were increasingly seen as otherwise unsolvable problems.

Not only were many Tamils being radicalised at this time, so too were many Sinhalese. In 1971, the JVP led a Marxist uprising in the south of the country, which was forcefully and often brutally suppressed by government forces, with up to 16,000 people more or less arbitrarily killed (Yogasundram 2006: 296). The state was under attack from the far left, under constant pressure from chauvinist Buddhists and increasingly pressured by dissatisfied Tamils. Its responses were to increasingly oppress the left, notably in the form of the JVP, and to marginalise the Tamils, while growing closer to chauvinist Buddhists.

Having crushed the JVP uprising, the following year, in 1972, the parliament voted for a change of constitution from secular (Section 29(2) of the constitution) parliamentary democracy to become a socialist (communal) republic, along with the formal changing of Ceylon's name to the Sanscritic (preferred by the Sinhalese) Sri Lanka, meaning 'auspicious' Lanka,[4] while Buddhism became the official state religion, further marginalising Hindu Tamils. The upper house was abolished, the presidency was established as a more powerful institution in relation to the parliament and the judiciary was subordinated to the National Assembly (Yogasundram 2006: 296–7).

According to da Silva:

> By 1977, the issue of university admissions had become a focal point of the conflict between the government and Tamil leaders. Tamil youth, embittered by what they considered discrimination against them, formed the radical wing of the Tamil United Liberation Front. Many advocated the use of violence to establish a separate Tamil state of Eelam. It was an object lesson of how inept policy measures and insensitivity to minority interests can exacerbate ethnic tensions.
>
> (C. R. da Silva, quoted in Wilson 1989: 131)

The Tamils increasingly came to see non-violence and peaceful negotiations as not helping them achieve civic equality with the Sinhalese. As a result, by 1972, radicalised Tamils resorted to violence in support of their claims, with the precursor group to the LTTE being formed.

Ethnic redistribution and then monopolisation of political and increasingly economic power added to this growing resentment and the beginning of calls for an autonomous Tamil region in the traditionally Tamil-dominated north and north-east of the country. As a result, several Tamil groups, including the three Tamil parties – the Federal Party, the Tamil Congress and the Ceylon Workers Congress – came together as the Tamil United Front (TUF), campaigning for linguistic, ethnic and religious equality. The government refused this claim, and embarked on a further anti-Tamil campaign, banning the importation of Tamil language books and films from Tamil Nadu in India. In response to government refusals to meet TUF's demands, long-standing Tamil parliamentarian and pro-peace and unity campaigner Samuel Chelvanayakam resigned his seat, forcing a by-election as a test of the popularity among Tamils of the government's policies. Chelvanayakam overwhelmingly won. Having worked for so long with Sinhalese-dominated governments and having promoted national unity, at this point he changed his position, saying: 'I consider the verdict as a mandate that the Tamil Eelam nation should . . . become free' (Swamy 2006: 18). In 1976 the TUF reorganised as the Tamil United Liberation Front (TULF), contesting the 1977 elections on a platform of independence for the Tamil state of Eeelam in the north and east of the country. At its first national convention at Vaddukoddai on 14 May 1976, the TULF resolved:

> that restoration and reconstitution of the Free, Sovereign, Secular, Socialist State of Tamil Eelam, based on the right of self determination inherent to every nation, has become inevitable in order to safeguard the very existence of the Tamil Nation in this Country.
>
> (Tamil United Liberation Front 1976)

This 'Vaddukoddai Resolution' formed the basis of future Tamil claims, principally concerning the right to self-determination.

At the same time, in 1976, more than 40 radical Tamil organisations formed to press for armed struggle against the government, from which five became prominent, with the Tamil New Tigers (TNT) quickly taking a lead in militancy that quickly devolved into a series of attacks reasonably described as 'terrorism'. In 1976, the TNT's leader Chetti Thanabalasignham was arrested, with his place being taken by Velupillai Prabhkaran who renamed the TNT the Liberation Tigers of Tamil Eelam.

Within the Sinhalese majority there was a tendency towards a national chauvinism (De Votta 2004a), underpinned by the dominant religion of Buddhism, which still occupies the state's 'foremost place'. This was based on the development of Buddhism as a Sinhalese nationalist counter to British colonialism from the late nineteenth century, gaining momentum into the twentieth century as a nationalist ideological force, including among its clergy those who are prone to not distinguishing between their religion and claims to ethnic majoritarianism.

In this, the view is that the country of Sri Lanka is a global repository of Buddhist values and hence must be maintained as wholly Buddhist. Within this world view, Hindu Tamils and Muslims (also mostly of Tamil descent) are an unwanted intrusion and should preferably convert to Buddhism or otherwise subsume their sense of difference. The framework for Buddhist chauvinist unity is the state; the intention is that the unitary quality of the state reflects the unifying quality of Buddhism, hence (religious or political) plurality within the state constitutes the diminution of Buddhism, which its adherents have opposed, often in very strong and indeed extreme terms.

Following independence, the status of Buddhism was established as pre-eminent, with even the minimalist Sinhalese position of having Buddhism elevated to its 'rightful place in the country' (Bond 1992: 112) following the re-establishment of Buddhism as a site of resistance to British colonialism in the nineteenth century (de Silva 1981: 339–42, 434–7, 351). At the same time, however, a sense of Tamil national identity also arose (Rasaratnam 2009: 253). '[T]he focus on Sri Lanka as the land of the Sinhalese and the country in which Buddhism stood forth in its purest form carried an emotional appeal compared with which a multi-racial polity was a meaningless abstraction' (de Silva 1981: 512).

Recognising Buddhism as the religion of Sri Lanka's majority Sinhalese population and acceding to its assertive ideological orientation, the government of Sri Lanka has since established two state institutions to promote Buddhism: the Ministry of Buddhist Sasana[5] and Religious Affairs, principally to foster and protect Buddhism, and, under the president, the Department of Buddhist Affairs (alongside departments of Christian Religious Affairs, Muslim Religious and Cultural Affairs and Hindu Religious and Cultural Affairs). The Mahasangha [Great (Buddhist) Monastery] is defined 'foremost' as not being in 'a position of mere equality with others' (*The Island*, 11 November 1988, quoted in Perera 2009: 143).

Although some Buddhist clergy and leaders have worked for peace efforts, others from its monastic order have been religiously assertive and in some cases combative. In particular, the Jathika Hela Urumaya (National Heritage Party or JHU) is very closely associated with the Buddhist clergy. All JHU candidates in the 2004 elections were Buddhist monks, although it has since distanced monks from electoral politics, instead relying on lay Buddhists as candidates. It has a strong, almost extreme, Sinhala nationalist ideology and advocated the military destruction of the LTTE, along with limiting political concessions to Tamils. The patterns of riots that had characterised the late 1950s and afterwards resumed in 1977 upon the United National Party coming to power, and in 1981 the army and police participated in burning down Jaffna public library, which was widely viewed by Tamils as constituting an attempt to destroy Tamil identity.

In response to this broad shift towards Sinhalese domination, Tamil separatist militant organisations were formed in the early 1970s, including the Liberation Tigers of Tamil Eelam in 1976. In 1977, the pro-separatist political party, Tamil United Liberation Front, won elections in Tamil-dominated areas, sparking further anti-Tamil rioting and more clearly demarcating the geographic and political distinction between Tamils and Sinhalese. President J. R. Jayawardene came to power promising to root out corruption, but instead oversaw the introduction of more brutal rule and political thuggery. With opposition political parties and newspapers banned, dissidents imprisoned and parliamentary elections suspended for six years, the president had created what was effectively a dictatorship, if by 'constitutional' means. What started off as a 'minority' problem increasingly became a problem of human rights for all Sri Lankans (Pereira 1983).

The congruence between Sinhalese nationalism, Buddhism and the state was nowhere more evident than in the constitutional changes in 1978, which fundamentally altered the nature of governance in the island state. More than 80 per cent of the parliament, led by the Sri Lanka Freedom Party, voted to introduce a political system closely resembling the French Fifth Republic, which created a directly elected executive presidency with even more authority than under the French model, with the prime minister as deputy executive. Election based on proportional representation was increased to a 12.5 per cent cut-off instead of the usual 5 per cent, which marginalised smaller parties, including those from the left and representing ethnic groups. The new presidential electoral system was based on 'first past the post', meaning that in a multi-cornered contest a president could be elected with an absolute minority of votes (but with more than other candidates), and the state structure was confirmed as unitary and hence disallowed the type of devolution that could have eased ethnic tensions, ensuring a continuing lack of guarantees for minorities. All of this contributed to supporting a Sinhalese political order able to pursue ethnocentric policies, supported by Sinhalese associations that benefited from the diminution of the Tamil community. The outcome was ethnic majoritarian democracy (De Votta 2004b: 303).

The changes to the constitution also allowed the parliament to supersede the supreme court, demolishing its independence. The new constitution made a number of allowances for Tamil sensitivities, in particular engaging the parliamentary TULF in talks, easing Tamil entry requirements into university and offering a number of senior civil servant positions to ethnic Tamils. However, a large number of Tamil judges and lawyers, trained in English, were at this time forced to resign. The LTTE responded to these changes with renewed attacks, leading to the introduction of the Prevention of Terrorism Act in 1979.

Although initially conceived of as a temporary measure, this widely condemned authoritarian measure was to become permanent legislation. The Prevention of Terrorism Act continues to allow security forces to 'arrest, imprison and leave incommunicado for 18 months without trial anyone suspected of unlawful activity'. Confessions to police, including under duress, were admissible in court while deaths in custody were not investigated. The act was also used against the Marxist JVP between 1987 and 1990, before that organisation reconstructed itself and joined parliamentary politics.

In 1983, an LTTE ambush on a military convoy led to an anti-Tamil Sinhalese riot, known as 'Black July', in which it is believed that up to 3,000 Tamils were killed in especially brutal circumstances and in some cases with the complicity of state officials and the organisation of Sinhalese activists. The response to this organised anti-Tamil rioting swelled the ranks of the LTTE and, along with covert training from India and later (sometimes brutally compelled) consolidation of militant Tamil groups under the banner of the LTTE, led to the formation of a highly developed military organisation. By the mid-1980s, the LTTE was engaged in full-scale conflict with the government of Sri Lanka, occupying the Jaffna Peninsula. Indian intervention in 1987 eventually led to conflict between the LTTE and the Indian army, concluding with the Indian army withdrawing in 1990. Conflict has continued, with pauses, since that time.

In 1987, Tamil was nominally made an official language, if still having effective minor language status, while Sinhalese was retained as the functionally dominant language for all ethnic groups. The 1987 changes also merged the northern and eastern provinces ahead of a vote on acceptance or rejection of the merger, which was an LTTE demand and which was a precondition of a degree of limited autonomy. However, the vote was never held and in October 2006 the Supreme Court ruled that the merger was unconstitutional.

Sri Lanka's Tamils face day-to-day ethnic discrimination, by government departments that employ Sinhalese as their sole language, the judiciary that is predominantly in Sinhalese, Sinhalese-speaking police and soldiers and so on. This reflects a deeper sense of ethnic exclusion, characterised by some as Sinhalese chauvinism or, in cases of religion, as Buddhist chauvinism. Many Sinhalese believe that Sri Lanka is 'the island destined to preserve and propagate the Buddha's doctrine' (Kearney 1967: 41), with no room for non-Buddhists or anyone who might in some way diminish or dilute their faith. When Tamils speak up they are routinely shouted down. By way of illustration, when Australian newspaper correspondent Matt Wade wrote of the repression of the media in Sri Lanka (Wade 2010), he received a barrage of personal criticism, which was a common tactic employed against anyone who dared speak of the problems of Sri Lanka. Interestingly, though, some of his critics illustrated the oppressive ethnic divide that characterises Sri Lanka (The National Times 2010). One commentator referred favourably to the 'Buddhist Sinhalese government', while another said of the subject under discussion: 'The asylum convention is designed to protect people from systemic persecution, not to guarantee their rights to free speech or to protect them from their own stupid mouthing off'.

Although such comments were not, of course, official government policy, they were all too common and did find resonance in the government's policy of increasing restrictions on the freedom of expression of the news media, as well as its institutionalised racism. Such racism was reflected in comments by President Mahinda Rajapaksa when he told a rally in Jaffa: 'Yes, we are Sinhala. The country is also Sinhala. Therefore, you Demala (Tamils) listen to me. If you cannot listen without trying to be too smart, then leave' (Lanka News Web 2010). What was official government policy was that, in October 2010, Tamils living in Colombo were again singled out on the basis of their ethnicity and were required to be registered with the police. Despite having already been required to be registered, the police issued a statement requiring all Tamils to register with their local police. This requirement applied to all households with Tamil residents. This was despite the state of emergency under which such draconian measures had been initiated having been repealed by the parliament and, at that time, the war having been ended for a year and a half. One of the concerns about the requirement for registration of a specific ethnic group was that it was just such forms of registration that had been used by other regimes to identify and eventually arrest and deport or murder ethnic minorities. The registration of Jews and Roma ('Gypsies) by Nazis before and during World War II led directly to their mass murder. Similarly, the registration of Roma people in some European states in 2010 was used as the basis for their deportation.

In its usually austere judgment about reasons why people seek refuge, Australian Refugee Review Tribunal member Christine Long said that a Tamil applicant 'has a well-founded fear of being persecuted for reasons of her imputed political opinion and her race if she returns to her country now or in the reasonably foreseeable future' (Barns 2010).

In 2002, the government and the LTTE agreed to a Norwegian-brokered ceasefire, which established lines across which each other could not pass. The territory controlled by the LTTE was significantly less than they claimed as representing 'Eelam', but it was a start at demonstrating that the Tamil people could administer themselves. By establishing a *de facto* state, a model existed for Tamil Eelam, with a civil administration that included police, a judicial system, transport, tax, economic planning and development, rehabilitation for internally displaced people, and health and welfare services. The *de facto* state, which lasted for six years until 2008, created a sense of pride in being Tamil, after having felt like – and been – second-class citizens in the country of their own birth for the previous 20 years or longer. The creation of the *de facto* state also enhanced a sense of Tamil national identity, proclaimed a quarter of a century previously. Finally, it gave back to the Tamil people that which they had lacked since just after independence, which was a sense of individual and community dignity. With the ending of the ceasefire, the loss of the *de facto* state and the military defeat of the LTTE, Tamils again felt alienated, second-class citizens in Sri Lanka, experiencing systematic discrimination, in many cases on the basis that all Tamils were presumed to be LTTE supporters and hence were terrorists.

According to one Tamil activist:

> For three and half decades politically and militarily the Sri Lankan Tamils have failed to regain their rights as equals citizens. Although the militant struggle for self determination was crushed in May 2009 real factors to address grievances have not been addressed. The euphoric mind of the chauvinistic forces set today only contributes to further oppression and divisiveness in the society. In ostracising and marginalising of all minorities a Buddhist supremacist psychosis prevails in the country today. Tamils in Sri Lanka remain voiceless, subjugated by an oppressive racist regime [and] lacking bold and undeterred representation.[6]

As noted by one dismayed Sinhalese:

> Each and every Government which held office from 1948 till the present bear culpability for the failure to achieve good governance, national unity and a framework of peace, stability and economic development in which all ethnic, religious and other groups could live in security and equality. Our inability to manage our own internal affairs has led to foreign intervention but more seriously has led to the taking of arms by a desperate group of our citizens.
>
> (Dhanapala 2010)

Although the frustration, indeed desperation, of many Tamils is easy to understand, the slide into the desperate act of violent conflict and in particular often indiscriminate attacks against civilians is difficult, if not impossible, to justify. Yet unless all communities in Sri Lanka can again feel that they can live in safety and dignity, with equality of respect for human rights, on the one hand Tamils will continue to leave as refugees, and on the other there is a high likelihood that the conflict will arise again.

3 The war in Sri Lanka

The war for a separate Tamil state in Sri Lanka was ended in May 2009, if perhaps only for the time being. Understanding how the war progressed and in particular the bitterness and brutality with which it was conducted is fundamental to understanding the circumstances in which the minority Tamils found themselves towards the war's end and following its conclusion. The circumstances that led to the war, the actions of the government and the LTTE during and their status since the war are central to determining whether or not there were or remain grounds for external intervention in Sri Lanka.

What leads a people to war against the state they are formally a part of is a compelling question, given that the reasons for going to war usually contain the seeds of its potential resolution. There are a number of theories about the causes of war but, based on the evidence on the ground and working back from that on a deductive basis, it would appear that the following holds true in the case of Sri Lanka, as well as a number of other conflicts.

According to Toft, writing about former Soviet states:

> For ethnic groups, territory is often a defining attribute of their identity, inseparable from their past and vital to their continued existence as a distinct group. States are defined by borders and therefore tend to view challenges to those borders as threats to their very existence.
>
> (Toft 2003: 19)

Much the same could be claimed about Sri Lanka, with the Tamil people identifying primarily with specific geographic regions in the north and north-east of the island, despite a significant minority also residing in the capital, Colombo. The territory of the state of Sri Lanka is defined by it being an island, with its shores (and territorial waters) determining its geographic reach. Although it does not suffer under threat of invasion, its geographic proximity to India and in particular to the state of Tamil Nadu has left some Sinhalese in particular feeling insecure about the integrity of the state. Moreover, some Sinhalese believe that the whole of the island is home to them as an ethnic (and religious) group, with Tamils being unwelcome interlopers, despite their shared history dating back millennia. For Tamils, retaining territorial integrity was critical to their continued existence as an identifiable group; for the Sinhalese, territorial integrity, if extended beyond their traditional homelands, was similarly critical to their continued existence as an identifiable group. Where these claims overlapped constituted the basis for conflict (see also Toft 2003: 30).

However, the claim for a separate Tamil state within the island had not always existed and came about as a consequence of deteriorating circumstances. According to Horowitz (2000: 230): 'Whether and when a secessionist movement will emerge is determined mainly by domestic politics, by the relations of groups and regions within the state'. Further, as noted by Toft (2003: 21): 'Ethnic groups will demand sovereignty when two conditions hold. First, their capabilities must give them a reasonable chance of gaining control of the territory they desire. Second, they must believe their cause is legitimate'.

Discussing the rationality of war, even when groups face likely defeat they may still engage in warfare for the following reasons: it may not be certain that a secessionist movement will lose, the group might be compelled to violence by the state, fear of waiting could expose the group to an even worse outcome, leaders may provoke a crackdown to consolidate support, or conditions have deteriorated to the point where the group believes it has nothing to lose (Toft 2003: 31). Each of these conditions could be said to apply to the Tamil claim for an independent state: there was a genuine belief that a military victory was possible, the events leading up to and following 'Black July' 1983 made many believe that the situation would only deteriorate further if they did not act, there was a consolidation of support for the Tamil separatist agenda in response to a government crackdown and conditions continued to deteriorate for many Tamils to the point where they believed they had nothing left to lose. In sum, it was almost inevitable that the belligerence of the Sinhalese majority set against a distinct Tamil identity and geography would produce conflict, and it has been Sinhalese blindness to or refusal to accept the inequity of the circumstances of Tamils in Sri Lanka that made conflict inevitable.

The brutality that increasingly came to mark the conduct of the war was a consequence of the breakdown of the political order. As Kalyvas (2006: 55) has noted: 'When belligerency and lawlessness extend to the entire society, barbarism is a predictable and unescapable outcome'. It can be argued that the breakdown of the political order was not immediate but was a gradual process, if with marked bursts of state-sanctioned lawlessness and reciprocal and often unrestrained LTTE violence. The final months of the war were a culmination of this barbarism, with the government prosecuting the war against the LTTE, and, it appeared, against the Tamil people, with unrestrained ferocity and barbarity. The rules of war that would have been expected to apply to an interstate conflict, in which domestic populations are not as directly impacted, might have had some greater opportunity to be respected. But the Sri Lankan government's war with the LTTE impacted upon all of Sri Lankan society, with all citizens becoming viable (if not legitimate) targets. 'Unremitting exposure to violence, removal of social controls, decline of the cost of violent activity, rise in prominence of people with a propensity to violence, and the unlearning of peaceful skills and the learning of new violent skills' produced the brutalisation of Sri Lankan society and 'the creation of vested interests in the use of violence' (Kalyvas 2006: 55–6).

There is no precise date to mark the start of the Eelam separatist war; there was no formal declaration of hostilities or announcement of intent. It was just that a series of injustices built up to the point where they were regarded, by many Tamils, as no longer tolerable and thus requiring a militant response. Broadly, the war – or its first phase – is generally regarded to have started in 1983. There had been riots before this time and in some cases Sinhalese were their victims, even if usually it was Sinhalese perpetrating anti-Tamil rioting. Militant unrest was beginning to foment as early as 1970 with a young Tamil, Ponnuthurai Sivakumaran, attempting to assassinate a Sri Lankan government minister visiting Jaffna. In 1974, he then attempted to kill the conservative mayor of Jaffna, Alfred Duraiappah, whom he held responsible for a police attack on the World Tamil Research Conference in which seven people died. After being surrounded by police during a bank raid in 1974, Sivakumaran committed suicide by swallowing a cyanide capsule. His gesture established a precedent to be adopted by the LTTE. Although Sivakumaran had established his own gang, he had earlier associated with Nadarajah Thangathurai, who went on to co-found the Tamil Eelam Liberation Organisation (TELO).

This early period saw the formation of a number of Tamil activist organisations, such as the Tamil Students League and the Tamil Youth League, and more radical groups that later evolved into armed separatist organisations. There were local anti-government protests and the destruction of government property. By 1975, radical young Tamils had conducted their first killing of a government official, the mayor of Jaffna, Alfred Duraiappah. Duraiappah was elected as a conservative independent but joined the Sri Lanka Freedom Party and supported language standardisation. He was thus branded as a traitor by many Tamils and assassinated by members of a young radical group. One of those involved in the assassination, allegedly the person who pulled the trigger (Swamy 2006: 18) and who had been involved in other anti-government actions, was Velupillai Prabhakaran, later to become the undisputed leader of the LTTE and of the Tamil resistance.

The LTTE eventually became the sole Tamil militant movement, but initially militant Tamil opposition to Sinhalese discrimination came from a number of disparate organisations. The Tamil Students League and Tamil Youth League both had factions and offshoots that sought to address Tamil grievances through militant means from the late 1960s, with loosely formed groups of like-minded young Tamils staging attacks on government property. Prabhakaran had already been involved with a small militant gang originating in the west of the Tamil area and had been involved in a number of small but increasingly visible operations, including a series of bombings. In 1972, aged 18, his gang had been formalised as the Tamil New Tigers, being at the forefront of militant organisation.

Following the establishment of the TNT, an eastern districts-based militant Tamil student organisation, the Eelam Revolutionary Organisation of Students (EROS), was founded in 1975. EROS was based on a Marxist student discussion group and, with a distinct ideological focus, quickly established links with other liberation organisations, in particular the Palestine Liberation Organization (PLO) and Abu Jihad, from whom its members received training. Being better organised, EROS invited the TNT, renamed as the LTTE in 1976, to train at its camps. From the outset, the LTTE and other militant Tamil groups had as their sole goal the establishment of an independent Tamil state. As with the other organisations, the LTTE was established as a socialist revolutionary organisation but which retained a strict sense of formal hierarchy, claimed to be in response to its war footing.[1]

EROS also organised the training of Tamil militants from TELO (established in 1979), the Eelam People's Revolutionary Liberation Front (EPRLF, founded in 1980 as a faction of EROS) and the People's Liberation Organisation of Tamil Eelam (PLOTE, founded in 1980 as an LTTE breakaway group). TELO had grown out of a radical student group that had been engaged in protests since the late 1960s and quickly became a highly effective militant organisation. However, following the arrest of its two leaders in 1981, its activity declined, with its leaders being murdered in jail.

At the forefront of militant activities, the LTTE staged attacks against police officers and local politicians and robbed banks. In response, in 1979, the government passed the draconian Prevention of Terrorism Act and stationed a full Sri Lankan army (SLA) brigade in Jaffna, the main Tamil city of the north. The LTTE was proscribed as a terrorist organisation. The identification of the LTTE as a terrorist organisation is at one level subjective and pejorative. It is a cliché that one person's terrorist is another person's freedom fighter. However, it is correct to note that the term implies not just the methods employed but also whether or not the organisation is a state or non-state actor and the legitimacy or illegitimacy that might be argued to flow from such status. There is no doubt that the LTTE from the outset employed methods that fall under the conventional heading of 'terrorism', including assassinations, generalised bombings and attacking uninvolved civilians in a number of highly publicised cases. It also employed considerable violence against its political rivals in the Tamil camp, showing little or no mercy when political competition became fierce. It was such acts that alienated some Tamils from the LTTE cause and divided some of the Tamil community, even after the LTTE was destroyed as a military organisation. Similarly, the Sri Lankan state could similarly be accused of employing terrorism, notably in relation to mass killings of civilians, presiding over the 'disappearances' of suspected activists and indiscriminate attacks against civilian populated areas. 'When terrorists killed soldiers the Sri Lanka Army retaliated by going on a rampage and massacred civilians, burning and looting their properties' (Yogasundram 2006: 313), which simply drove more Tamils into the arms of the LTTE. At another level, however, identifying the LTTE as a terrorist organisation assisted the government of Sri Lanka in bringing international pressure to bear on its increasingly sophisticated international operations. It also helped to delegitimise the goals of the LTTE and of Tamils more generally and was eventually used to internationally isolate the organisation.

LTTE attacks escalated, in response to which police and soldiers arrested suspected LTTE members and arbitrarily executed them. On 23 July 1983 the LTTE hit back, ambushing an SLA jeep and truck near Jaffna, killing 13 soldiers with two dying later. In response, soldiers killed 51 people in Jaffna and, following the funeral for the soldiers, anti-Tamil rioting broke out across the country, leading to many deaths – the toll was somewhere between a conservative 400 (Yogasundram 2006: 310) and a more probable 3,000. The rioting was the worst that had ever been seen in Sri Lanka, and it served to drive many Tamils living in the south of the country to the north or overseas, helping to establish what would become the LTTE's international network. The LTTE's July 1983 attack is generally regarded as marking the beginning of the Eelam war, although in reality it had been under way for some years previously. The increased polarisation caused by the events of 'Black July' pushed many young Tamils into the arms of the LTTE and other militant organisations, increasing their numbers so that they became formidable fighting forces. These events also effectively ended Tamil representation in the parliament, meaning that if the government was to seek a negotiated solution to the Tamils' claims it would henceforth have to deal with the militant groups, which had begun to coalesce. The events also caused considerable international concern, nowhere more so than in India, with its own large and sympathetic Tamil population. Moreover, Tamil militants had for some years been receiving training and support in the Indian state of Tamil Nadu and increasingly from India's external intelligence agency, the Research and Analysis Wing (RAW). RAW's interest in the Tamil groups was in part based on their ethnic links to Tamils in India but was also a counter-measure to the government of Sri Lanka, which had allowed Pakistan to use Sri Lankan facilities to refuel its ships in the Indo-Pakistani War of 1971, which ultimately led to the creation of Bangladesh from East Pakistan. Pakistan, along with Israel, also provided military aid to the government of Sri Lanka, which India saw as a potentially threatening alliance. India therefore supported Tamil separatists in small part because of some Indian sympathy for their situation, but primarily as a counter to what was perceived to be an unfriendly regional government.

The separation between pro-independence Tamil groups necessarily limited their operational effectiveness and, as early as September 1982, Prabhakaran had called for a united front, which was rejected by the other organisations. Despite this initial reluctance, following the events of 'Black July', in February 1984 TELO and the EPRLF joined forces to establish the Eelam National Liberation Front (ENLF) and, following the advice of Anton Balasigngham to Prabhakaran on the necessity of a united front in the face of Indian ambivalence, the LTTE joined in April. Prabhakaran retained reservations about the new united force, believing it to be excessively influenced by India and that it created an equality between its constituent members that did not exist in the field. However, the alliance was formed, with an initial agreement to have a single political objective, to combine military forces and eventually to combine finances (Balasingham 2003: 98–9). The new combined force did act, destroying the main police station in Jaffna and attacking military convoys, leading to the collapse of government authority in Jaffna. This period marked a high point in separatist violence. But, having evolved separately, there were also divisions between the organisations that comprised the ENLF.

Following the murder of the two jailed TELO leaders, TELO tended to lose direction, with some of the cadres viewed as throwing their weight around. TELO's military effectiveness was also limited by relying on India for weapons. The LTTE was concerned about TELO's close relationship with India, which LTTE leader Prabhakaran believed was being used to shape the conflict to suit India's strategic interests rather than those of the Tamil people. As a result of his concerns Prabhakaran believed that TELO could be used to murder him. Dissent within TELO had also developed, leading to the murder of one of the factional leaders in 1985, which led to an internal split the following year. When two prominent and respected Tamil politicians were murdered in Jaffna, both the LTTE and TELO blamed each other. In February 1986 the LTTE withdrew from the ENLF and, following the murder of one of Prabhakaran's bodyguards during a tense meeting with TELO, in April the LTTE launched a full-scale attack on TELO bases. No quarter was given to TELO cadres, including those who surrendered. A few TELO members found refuge with the EPRLF and EROS, but more than 400 members were killed, in some cases unarmed and trying to surrender, and the organisation was effectively destroyed.

Although responsible for bombings in 1984 and 1985 and the kidnapping of a British journalist, EROS itself was never a major actor in the struggle for a Tamil state, in part because its leadership was based in London and had little direct contact with its supporters. EROS worked closely with the LTTE, but internal disputes over support for military activity led to its effective disbanding in 1990, with a majority of members joining the LTTE. Other remnants of EROS moved to Colombo and established themselves as a pro-government, anti-LTTE paramilitary group and political party. Because the EPRLF had sheltered TELO cadres, the LTTE also attacked it, with most of its members either killed or taken prisoner. The remnants of this organisation then split into two factions in 1986, with one faction reforming as the Eelam National Democratic Revolutionary Front (ENDRF), and a further breakaway group contributing to PLOTE, later transformed into the Eelam People's Democratic Party.

PLOTE had strong international links, notably to other revolutionary organisations, and in 1998 was involved in sending mercenaries to overthrow the government of the Maldives, which was thwarted by Indian intervention. Given the bitter rivalry between PLOTE founder Uma Maheswaran and Prabhakaran, it was not surprising that the two organisations fell to fighting from 1982. Maheswaran was assassinated in Colombo in 1989, allegedly by a PLOTE splinter group. Members of PLOTE later formed a minor political party and pro-government paramilitary group operating in the north and east of Sri Lanka.

In one sense, the manner in which the LTTE either absorbed or dispensed with other organisations constructed it as intolerant of political or military competition in its representation of the Tamil cause. There has even been a case that the LTTE committed war crimes or crimes against humanity and, although evidence for this is more difficult to obtain, it is probably a correct assessment. Much has been made of the brutality of the LTTE in this regard and there have no doubt been some Tamils associated with organisations that it has destroyed who have remained bitter about it, in some cases remaining loyal to the Tamil cause but rejecting the LTTE or in other cases preferring a Sinhalese government in Colombo to an LTTE-dominated independence movement. Given the polarisation caused by the conflict, there was little room for half measures and those who chose to oppose the LTTE often took the extreme step of going over to the other side. However, the LTTE did consolidate its military and political authority in a way that was probably necessary for possible success in prosecuting the war for independence. What many, perhaps most, Tamils quickly came to realise was that, even though they sometimes did not approve of the methods employed by the LTTE, they believed there was no other organisation capable of protecting or representing their interests. In that the LTTE's brutality was itself a cause for external intervention or the invocation of R2P, there may have been some grounds for this, particularly in a mediating function. However, R2P applies primarily to states that themselves have a responsibility to protect their own citizens and not to non-state organisations, the LTTE's aspirations in that regard notwithstanding.

Following an escalation of fighting, peace talks held between six Tamil groups and the government of Sri Lanka in Thimpu, Bhutan in July 1985 failed to reach any agreement. Government talks with TULF continued through 1986, with India acting as an intermediary, although still without success. The LTTE consolidated its power over other separatist organisations and continued to launch attacks against the government, with the government responding with increasingly overt military measures. It had become clear that any peace agreement, if it was to be meaningful, would need to be made with the now-dominant militant group, the LTTE.

What is now referred to as Eelam War I is regarded as having run from 1983 until 1987, with a break in 1985 to allow for the peace talks in Bhutan. By 1987, the SLA had cornered the LTTE in the Jaffna Peninsula and was preparing for a final assault. However, under pressure from its own ethnic Tamil population, the Indian government called for a halt to the offensive and, faced with rejection by the government of Sri Lanka, Indian prime minister Rajiv Ghandi attempted to send supply boats to relieve the LTTE. These boats were blocked by the Sri Lankan navy, so India supplied the LTTE with an air drop in what was known as Operation Poomalai (Garland). Following this intervention, the Sri Lankan president Junius Jayewardene entered talks with the government of India, which led two months later to the signing of the Indo-Sri Lankan Accord, the lifting of the siege of Jaffna and an agreement to send an Indian Peace Keeping Force (IPKF) to the island, bringing to a conclusion the first stage of the conflict. The introduction of the IPKF could perhaps be termed an early use of R2P, even if it did ultimately go horribly wrong.

Despite the ostensible peacekeeping role of the IPKF, when the LTTE was required to disarm and refused to do so, fighting quickly broke out between the

LTTE and the IPKF (with the LTTE in part being supported by the anti-Indian Sri Lankan government). In response to the unpopular Indian presence, the JVP again launched an uprising, principally in the south, in which there were general strikes and attacks against the government and civil society organisations. The government initially reeled from this rebellion and, in the face of popular anti-Indian sentiment, assisted the LTTE in its own fighting with the IPKF. In suppressing the JVP uprising, by 1989 perhaps 50,000 were killed, inuring the government to the idea that its first duty was to protect lives. Meanwhile, the IPKF, unprepared for a guerrilla war, only lightly armed and equipped and inadequately supplied, was unable to control the military environment. Having become a participant in the conflict rather than helping to end it, the Indian government ordered the withdrawal of the IPKF in 1990.

Following the withdrawal of the IPKF and the failure of peace talks between the government of Sri Lanka and the LTTE in June 1990, more than 100 Tamil and Muslim police in the north-east who surrendered to the LTTE were massacred. Differing accounts have this as the police being ordered to surrender or otherwise being surrounded and deciding to surrender. The reports of numbers involved vary from 30 to up to 600. In any case, there is little dispute that upon surrender the officers were lined up and summarily executed. This then resulted in a retaliatory massacre of Tamil civilians in the town of Kalmunai, in which between 160 and 250 people were murdered and a further 1,000 disappeared. Two weeks later there was a further massacre of some 70 Tamil civilians. In all, around 7,000 were killed in June 1990, marking one of the more brutal periods of the war and initiating the second phase of the conflict, known as Eelam War II. Similar massacres of civilians continued throughout the rest of 1990, with more than 50 civilians being murdered by the LTTE in Gonagala near Ampara and 184 civilians being murdered by soldiers near the village of Sathurukondan in the east of Sri Lanka in September. A somewhat hagiographic biographer of LTTE leader Prabhakaran described the LTTE's employment of massacres as 'Perfecting the Jimmy Malone Offense', in which a police character in a crime movie advised his senior to always respond to violence by increasing the retaliatory stakes (Kantha 2005: 49). Unfortunately, if this was the source of such behaviour, it seemed that both the government forces as well as the LTTE had watched and learned the lessons of retaliatory escalation from this movie. The mass slaughter of civilians by both the army and the LTTE became one of the hallmarks of the war, continuing regularly until 2002 and then again in the most brutal and wide-scale fashion towards it end.

Following the return to war in 1990, the following year, 1991, an LTTE suicide bomber assassinated the former Indian prime minister, Rajiv Gandhi, over India's handling of its intervention, as closely implied by chief LTTE strategist Anton Balasingham (NDTV 2006). The assassination of Gandhi effectively ended sympathy for the LTTE in India, including among India's 80 million strong ethnic Tamil community. In 1993, an LTTE suicide bomber assassinated Sri Lankan president Ranasinghe Premadasa at a political rally.

Following a three-month ceasefire, Eelam War III began in April 1995, and quickly led to a number of major clashes. After seven weeks of heavy fighting and the use of air attacks that led to high numbers of civilian casualties and around 2,500 SLA and LTTE troops being killed, following a decade of LTTE control, the SLA retook the Jaffna Peninsula. However, despite this significant victory, the SLA also faced setbacks, with the LTTE using suicide bombers – the so-called 'Black Tigers – to overrun the SLA base at Mullaitivu in July 1996, consolidating its position in the north of the country and establishing strong bases in the east.

The LTTE has been credited with inventing suicide bombings as a means of specific targeting, and often engaged in attacks well outside its principle geographic area of concern, notably in Colombo. Its attacks were so successful that Colombo's business district was effectively shut down in 1996. Its general justification was that such attacks were a legitimate response to government attacks within its claimed homeland and that it could not afford to limit its operational capacity over concerns about how it was externally viewed. In August 1996, the SLA retook Kilinochche from the LTTE. But in February 1998, the LTTE pressed an attack and overran what had become the SLA's heavily fortified Kilinochche base. In March 1999, the SLA attacked the LTTE in the Vanni area around Kilinochche from the south, making limited gains, but that November the LTTE counter-attacked and retook the regions it had lost. In 2000, the LTTE pressed its growing advantage in the north, capturing the SLA's twin major bases of Iyakachchi and Elephant Pass, which remained in LTTE hands until 2008. Whereas the LTTE used commandos to overrun Iyakichchi, in the case of Elephant Pass, rather than using suicide bombers or commandos, it employed heavy artillery, forcing the SLA's retreat. The SLA's loss of the Elephant Pass base was a significant strategic blow as it controlled access to the Jaffna Peninsula and gave the LTTE a forward northern defence line to protect its new capital at Kilinochche from attack from the north. However, an LTTE attempt to press its advantage by moving on Jaffna was blocked by the SLA. An angry attempt to take back the Elephant Pass base in April 2000 was repulsed by the LTTE. By 2000, it has been estimated that 64,000 people, mostly civilians, had been killed in the conflict.

The United National Front under Ranil Wickremasighe had campaigned on a pro-peace platform. As a consequence of what amounted to a strategic stalemate and a practical end to hostilities, some weeks before the elections on 22 February 2002 the LTTE and government signed a Norwegian-brokered ceasefire agreement (CFA), introducing the Norwegian-led Sri Lanka Monitoring Mission (SLMM). This was a muted version of R2P of which type the Norwegians have been particularly engaged, both in Sri Lanka and elsewhere, if with little success. Part of the text of the agreement read as follows:

> Responding to a proposal by the leadership of the LTTE, the parties agree to explore a political solution founded on the principle of internal self-determination in areas of historical habitation of the Tamil-speaking peoples, based on a federal structure within a united Sri Lanka. The parties acknowledge that the solution has to be acceptable to all communities.
>
> (GoSL/LTTE 2002)

As claimed by an LTTE negotiator:

> Identifying Tamils of Sri Lanka as a nation of people is not a matter of linguistic scholarship – reiterating the Tamil identity is a reflection of our nationhood as a distinct people. Even by merely identifying ourselves as Tamils, we continue our journey to free our people and our homelands; we commit ourselves to fight the forces that seek to marginalise us and stigmatise us into a second class status.[2]

The CFA allowed the combatant forces to withdraw to their respective zones behind technical control lines, which quickly morphed into 'borders', complete with immigration checks, visas and customs and tax (see Stokke 2005; Gopalakrishnan 2006).[3] The CFA also saw the opening of the A9 Highway through the LTTE-controlled area to Jaffna in the north and the lifting of an embargo on goods to the LTTE-controlled Vanni. Despite the LTTE pulling out of further peace talks the following year, the ceasefire continued to hold, with the LTTE establishing what amounted to a *de facto* state within a state in a northern area of Sri Lanka known as the 'Vanni'. From 2002 in particular and following the ideological origins of the Tamil separatist organisations, the LTTE tended towards establishing a state socialist model, although blended with a high proportion of small business activity and an, in principle, acceptance of free market capitalism (Stokke 2005).

After walking away from peace talks in April 2003, the LTTE followed up on the CFA by proposing to the government the establishment of an Interim Self-Governing Authority, which was immediately rejected. 'Although the outright rejection of the Interim Self-Governing Authority was predictable enough, the political backlash in Colombo was disproportionate' (Smith 2009: 98) Tensions between President Chandrika Kumaratunga and Prime Minister Wickremasignhe over what were claimed by the former and other nationalist groups to have been too many concessions to the LTTE meant that further progress on finding a political solution to the problem was effectively no longer available. Kumaratunga then declared a state of emergency, suspending parliament, taking control of the mass media and Interior and Defence portfolios and calling new elections for April 2004. The People's Freedom Alliance in coalition with the JVP won the elections, with Mahinda Rajapaksa becoming prime minister. From the outset, despite formally acknowledging the 2002 ceasefire agreement, Rajapaksa intended to seek a military victory over the LTTE. In what was to be a critical blow to the LTTE, in early 2004, the LTTE's eastern military commander, Colonel Vinayagamoorthy Muralitharan, better known as 'Karuna', defected to the government after being called to account for alleged misallocated funds (Karuna claimed the defection was caused by northern Tamil high-handedness), which almost certainly meant going to his death. On Karuna's part, he claimed that the northern LTTE was economically exploiting the culturally differentiated eastern branch without giving it due recognition for its successes. The LTTE attacked the Karuna group just south of Trincomalee on April 2004 and effectively disbanded it, with remnants and more recent recruits seeking the protection of the SLA and effectively working as its key militia. Although many of the 5,000 cadres under Karuna's command returned to the LTTE, this defection fatally weakened the LTTE's hold on two eastern provinces, and confined the LTTE's military capacity to a relatively small area in the north.

At the end of 2004, Sri Lanka was hit by the Boxing Day tsunami. This event was a catalyst for peace for the separatist conflict in Aceh, Indonesia. But in Sri Lanka, disputes over the division of funds and responsibility for their allocation created new tensions between the government of Sri Lanka and the LTTE; the perspectives of both sides of the cause of these renewed tensions will be considered here. In reality, both the LTTE and the government had been using the period since the ceasefire agreement to build up stockpiles of weapons and by the end of 2004 it appeared that the two parties were ready to resume fighting. The government in particular was using remaining Karuna group defectors and assistance from India's Research and Analysis Wing to conduct what amounted to an insurgency campaign against the LTTE. What sympathy there had been for the LTTE in India was diminished by LTTE attacks against Indian peacekeepers between 1987 and 1990 and effectively ended by the LTTE's suicide assassination of former Indian prime minister Rajiv Gandhi in May 1991. Although initially denied by the LTTE, the suicide bomber who killed Gandhi was identified as LTTE member Thenmozhi Rajaratnam, admitted to by LTTE chief ideologue Anton Balasignham in 2006. The tsunami of 26 December 2004 prevented the two parties from returning to full-scale war at that time. This natural disaster left some 30,000 people dead and vastly more homeless. But disputes over the allocation and distribution of relief funds, based on claimed areas of territorial control, further exacerbated already profound divisions between the two parties. It was one more issue over which the government and the LTTE bitterly disagreed and which fuelled animosity between them.

In November 2005 Mahinda Rajapaksa was elected as president with a clear mandate to militarily defeat the LTTE. The LTTE refused to allow Tamils under its control to vote in the election, which Rajapaksa won with the slimmest margin of just 1.8 per cent over his rival Wickremasignhe, who would have otherwise received Tamil support. Refusing Tamils under LTTE control permission to vote in the election handed power to Rajapakse, guaranteeing that there would be no further peace negotiations and that a return to war would be almost inevitable. This refusal was the LTTE's single greatest strategic error and spelled the beginning of its end.

Although the CFA held in formal terms between 2002 and 2006, it was undermined by both sides almost from the beginning. The LTTE used the period of relative peace to open 'political offices' in non-LTTE-controlled Tamil areas to raise funds and control dissent, to recruit new fighters (including those underage) and to stockpile weapons. Notably, the LTTE was widely held responsible for the assassination of Sri Lankan foreign minister Lakshman Kadirgamar on 12 August 2005. Similarly, the government or front groups engaged in extra-judicial killings of public Tamil figures and political activists and also stockpiled weapons.

The CFA held until early 2006 when it began to fray, in particular following the abduction and murder of Tamil civilians, initiating escalating LTTE responses. The A9 Highway that runs through Kilinochche between Jaffna and Kandy (and then to Colombo), which had been closed between 1994 and 2002, was again closed in August 2006 in a bid to limit supplies to the LTTE and to stop it from collecting 'taxes' from vehicles passing through. But the closure of the road, which had been regarded by many as a symbol of the renewed peace, also cut off Jaffna from supplies and led to significant hardship among civilians in Jaffna. The road was reopened the following October.

By July 2006, following full-scale government attacks in both the north and east, the CFA existed only on paper and what was commonly becoming referred to as Eelam War IV had begun. Although there were a number of factors that led to the return to conflict, two in particular were important. The first was the 2004 tsunami, which had a serious impact on Sri Lanka, with some 30,000 people being killed. It did not draw in foreigners relative to the local population to the extent of other affected regions nor did it act as a catalyst for a negotiated peace (as opposed to that which was achieved in Aceh, Indonesia). Rather, the tsunami and the aid flows associated with its relief acted to further entrench divisions within the state, especially over the allocation and control of the flow of aid. These disputes over aid fed into increasing antagonism on the part of the LTTE, leading to it imposing a boycott in areas it controlled of the 2005 presidential elections, which was the second important factor by contributing to the creation of conditions for a return to war. This boycott assisted in the defeat of the pro-peace presidential candidate Ranil Wickramasinghe and election of the more belligerent Mahinda Rajapaksa. Following Rajapakse's election as president and the appointment of his brother to the head of the defence ministry, the Sri Lanka government took a significantly more aggressive attitude towards the LTTE, escalating its attacks via proxy 'militia', and engaging in direct kidnappings, murders and assaults, and eventually full-scale military confrontation. Notably, since the breakdown of the CFA, the GoSL again picked up on its efforts from 1998 to have the LTTE listed as a terrorist organisation by a number of governments, including those of the United States, Canada and the states of the European Union. The purpose of this listing was principally to limit the raising of funds for the LTTE by expatriate Tamils, thereby denying it an important source of foreign income.

Beyond the escalation in fighting and the limited prospects of a return to meaningful peace talks, since the ceasefire of 2002, both sides had also upgraded and stockpiled weapons ahead of what was acknowledged as expected by the LTTE would be a new round of fighting. In this, the LTTE's responses to increasing GoSL belligerence demonstrated a similar level of belligerence. There were no reliable data on the LTTE's military capacity, but it was estimated that it could field a conventional SLA of perhaps up to 25,000,[4] was well trained, relatively heavily armed (with field artillery but few armoured vehicles) and possessed a small functional naval unit (Kadul Puli, or 'Sea Tigers'). It even developed a small 'Sangkar Air Wing', which it used to symbolic effect in air strikes on military bases in Colombo and the north of the country in March and April 2007. By comparison, the then recently expanded Sri Lanka Armed Forces had perhaps 158,000 personnel whose training was generally no better and perhaps less than that of the LTTE, who lacked motivation and, although better equipped with conventional weapons, ships and planes, until 2007–8 did not enjoy a consistent advantage in conventional combat.[5]

Although there were significant expressions of concern over a return to conflict from Tamil civil society groups, there also remained profound impediments to returning to peace. From the perspective of the LTTE, there was a clear lack of trust in the intentions of the Sri Lankan government to genuinely pursue peace.[6] This lack of trust in a negotiated outcome was supported by the announcement at the beginning of January that the government intended to seek a military solution to the LTTE issue (Balachandran 2007). Moreover, Sri Lanka appeared to be moving away from open democratic processes and towards a type of bureaucratic authoritarianism. Sri Lanka had shifted from a parliamentary to a presidential-led system (akin to the French model) in 1978. Since then, executive authority had been increasingly located in the hands of the president, who appoints ministers as well as the Supreme Court judges who decide on constitutional issues. The role of the prime minister, in contrast, had become increasingly ceremonial. The president appoints, among others, the defence minister, who was from late 2005 an SLA brigadier-general and brother of the president. This has been accompanied by increasing failure of the judicial system (ICG 2007: 4), which has granted effective impunity to extra-judicial killings and other grave human rights violations. Parliamentary politics continued in Sri Lanka, although the use of SLA-linked death squads (see Human Rights Watch 2007), torture and denial of *habeus corpus* contributed to an increasingly constrained political climate (USAID 2006). Although an outcome that promoted democratisation and political devolution could have theoretically worked, it appeared to have little real hope due to the organisation of Sri Lanka's political parties and the voting patterns of its citizens, which continued to ensure that ethnic Sinhalese parties dominated the parliament, if not always in mutual agreement. This has also meant that the executive president has, to date and by default, been ethnic Sinhalese, and the extensive powers of that executive president.

Another factor militating against a resolution to the conflict prior to its last brutal phase was the growing capacity of 'state' institutions in the LTTE-controlled area. The 'capital' of Eelam, Kilinochche, was the LTTE's administrative centre, and hosted a range of institutions such as a police force, three levels of courts and a detailed legal code (LTTE 2004). Other signs of administration included departments of works, public transport and fuel, hospitals, asylums, clinics, children's homes, rehabilitation centres, primary and secondary schools and the construction of a proposed university.[7] Related to the LTTE's state capacity was its military capacity, which challenged that of the Sri Lanka military in various military operations. Although it was always unlikely that the LTTE could win a war outright against the Sri Lankan government, it had demonstrated a capacity to take and hold significant territories, although the LTTE's territorial control was reduced by mid-2007, with the loss of military bases in the eastern area following a sustained onslaught by the SLA. If the LTTE felt pressure, then it was pressure of a similar type to that felt by the Sri Lankan government and its military (e.g. in October 2006, the LTTE defeated a sustained SLA attack, killing 129 government troops). The relatively even matching of the two sides until 2008, if not in numbers then in capacities, did not introduce the disequilibrium that could have pushed one side into a position of seeking a negotiated settlement. The LTTE had offered a negotiated settlement around a federated state model, but this was not engaged with by the government of Sri Lanka. In 2006, this offer was effectively withdrawn as intended talks failed to start.

The capacity of the LTTE to negotiate was severely limited by the serious illness (and, in December 2006, the death) of its chief negotiator and ideological strategist, Anton Balasingham. It was his illness and inability to attend negotiations in 2006, aimed at de-escalating violence, that could in significant part be held responsible for their failure. It was around this time that the LTTE's earlier offer of a federal solution, based on unified northern and eastern provinces, was withdrawn and it again called for a completely independent state (Pirapaharan 2006, i.e. Prabhakaran). The small, unarmed and, in terms of human rights violation monitoring, poorly trained (ICG 2007: 6) Sri Lanka Monitoring Mission, established to oversee the 2002 CFA, was unable to prevent Sri Lanka's slide back into conflict. Although all such agreements require the active support of all combatant parties,[8] the SLMM lacked the resources or political capacity to impose its will on the combatant parties.

Similarly, any serious option of negotiation from the LTTE's perspective had to include control over at least some of the eastern provinces and in particular the strategically important deep-water port at Trincomalee, which it intended to make the capital of an independent Eelam state. Any prospect of talks aimed at ending the conflict was made more difficult by the LTTE seeking to control all of the territory of the state before, rather than as a result of, such negotiations. Indeed, the reduction of Tamil preponderance in areas they had previously dominated was one of the reasons for the return to war after 2006. The LTTE had believed it could militarily conquer especially important parts of its claimed area, including the deep-water harbour at Trincomalee, and then negotiate for peace from a position of strength.[9] This overreaching was one of three important factors in the LTTE's strategic undoing.[10]

For its own part, the government of Sri Lanka was prepared to re-enter negotiations towards a peaceful settlement to the conflict, but only from a position of strength, in which the LTTE came to the table as a supplicant. As such, the GoSL's claims to continuing support for the 2002 ceasefire were rendered meaningless by events in 2006 and 2007. In the period from November 2005 to February 2007, it had been estimated that more than 4,000 people had been killed in the renewed fighting, with more than 250,000 made homeless (SLMM 2007; ICG 2007: i, 1). Perhaps a further 1,000 or more were killed between February and August 2007 and a further 1,000 had disappeared and remained unaccounted for. Comments by influential figures in Colombo appear to confirm that it no longer seeks a genuinely negotiated settlement, but rather that it wishes to impose its own interpretation of what constitutes a settlement, which is control of all of the territory of the state. Similarly, in 2006, the LTTE sought to expand its territorial control, as indicated by renewed attacks near Trincomalee and in the southern Jaffna area, both of which are areas claimed as Tamil homeland. In this respect, as previously noted, the LTTE also hoped to be able to negotiate its claims from a position of relative strength.[11] That is, both sides resumed and escalated the conflict and both were seeking an effective military victory, or to be able to negotiate from a position of strength. In either case, the positions of the two parties appeared, within this framework, to be mutually exclusive and, as such, irreconcilable.

There was never any likelihood that the government would willingly accede control of Trincomalee to the LTTE and the LTTE understood this. To that end, it had made a conscious decision to capture Trincomalee and, based on its fairly impressive conventional military record to date, believed it could do so. This self-belief in the military capacity of the LTTE was in large part born of hubris; that the LTTE had survived for 30 years against all that the government of Sri Lanka could throw against it and had come out intact as the sole functional representative of Tamil aspirations for independence. But in large part the LTTE's aspirations to the trappings of statehood were its undoing. Having evolved from a highly mobile if heavily armed and highly skilled guerrilla organisation, the LTTE had become a conventional army fighting a largely conventional rather than asymmetric guerrilla war. In the final analysis, if the government put into the war as much determination as the LTTE had demonstrated, its overwhelming size and access to funds and military hardware meant that it would ultimately be successful. The LTTE had become a captive to its own dream and, along with its increasing international isolation, in particular from India, entered into the final phase of a conventional war that it could not possibly win.

Perhaps as part of a divide and conquer strategy and somewhat in contrast to the more belligerent approach that characterised the government position following the election of Rajapaksa, in early 2006 Rajapaksa formed an 'all party' conference (but not including the LTTE) to try to develop a political formula that could be used as a basis for negotiations with the LTTE. The work of this conference did not advance. The prospects of advance were limited by the fact that one of the two main protagonists, the LTTE, did not regard any talks that did not include it as legitimate, and few Tamils were willing to speak without the inclusion or direct support of the LTTE. This was either through their regard for the LTTE as the sole legitimate representative of the Tamil people or because of fear of reprisal from the LTTE for attempting to engage in negotiations without consent.

The renewal of fighting in 2006 marked the beginning of the end of the overall Eelam war. Despite initial signs of LTTE strength, notably an artillery attack on Muttur that was eventually repulsed by the SLA, as was a later assault on an airbase at Muhamalai, there was a series of increasingly successful SLA campaigns. The first was to push the LTTE out of the eastern provinces, including an LTTE artillery sight near Trincomaleee, followed by the capture or destruction of LTTE-owned ships carrying weapons and supplies. The LTTE resumed its bombing campaign, with one suicide attack at Habaraba killing around 100 sailors in the single deadliest attack of the war. By 2007 the SLA felt ready to launch an assault on the LTTE's northern bases, initially targeting the LTTE's leadership with air strikes. In November 2007, the LTTE's political leader, Thamilchevan, and five others senior leaders were killed in a claimed air strike. Despite these setbacks, LTTE forces on the ground put up a stiff defence against continuing SLA assaults. In a somewhat odd statement after the fact, the government formally withdrew from the 2002 ceasefire agreement in January 2008. After a number of setbacks, from August 2008 the SLA eventually advanced, taking Mannar in the west and then assaulting the LTTE's 'capital' of Kilinochche from three sides, beginning its attack on Kilinochche in November 2008 and capturing it in January 2009. With the loss of its 'capital', the LTTE retreated to Mullataivu where it underwent a sustained air attack, including against civilians sheltering with or being held by the LTTE. Again overwhelmed, by the end of January 2009 the remaining LTTE forces retreated further. Throughout this period is was clear that a humanitarian disaster was unfolding and, despite LTTE overtures that it was willing to talk, the government pressed the SLA's attack while foreign governments refused to intervene.

The last months of the war were marked by unremitting brutality against civilians with consequently rapidly mounting civilian casualties. Human Rights Watch accused the SLA of 'slaughtering' civilians through indiscriminate air and artillery attacks against positions where large numbers of civilians were known to be sheltering, making a mockery of President Rajapaksa's 'zero civilian casualties' policy (Nelson 2009) and the SLA's claim that the area being shelled was a 'no fire zone'. The report also called on the government and the LTTE to release civilians being held by them, in particular some 200,000 who were pushed into a narrow 14-kilometre strip of beach near Mullataivu, which was the LTTE's last refuge. A UN confidential report estimated that 20,000 civilians were killed in the 'no fire zone' in the last weeks of the war, at a rate of about 1,000 a day (AFP 2009). The Sri Lankan High Commissioner in London rejected claims that any civilians had been killed, and then qualified this by saying that: 'If civilians had been killed, then that is because of the actions of the LTTE who were shooting and killing people when they tried to escape' (AFP 2009). The question, then, was not whether civilians were being killed, but in what circumstances. There is no doubt that the LTTE held many of the Tamils against their will and used them, in effect, as human shields. It is also clear from subsequent reports that civilians trying to escape the LTTE stronghold were shot by LTTE cadres. This forced holding of civilians resulting in their deaths could be considered as a crime against humanity and was itself perhaps grounds for R2P. Having said that, it is also clear that many civilians feared the SLA and remained in proximity to the LTTE for what they perceived to be its protection. Again, however, the focus of R2P concerns the responsibility of states to protect their own citizens and at this stage the LTTE's last claims to statehood had very much disappeared, while those of the government of Sri Lanka had grown very much stronger.

Government denials of the killings were common but increasingly unsustainable with mounting evidence showing that the denials were at best a cover-up for the mass deaths. The government also routinely accused anyone who raised such allegations of either being duped by LTTE propaganda or actively working for the LTTE. This dissembling created a degree of possible doubt about events in Sri Lanka within the UN Security Council and allowed China to thwart any moves by it towards sanctions or intervention. It did express, however, 'deep concern at the reports of continued use of heavy calibre weapons in areas with high concentrations of civilians, and expected the Government of Sri Lanka to fulfil its commitment in this regard' (UN News Centre 2009). This 'deep concern' and 'expectation' may have been thought to have saved face for some UN Security Council members, but it did nothing to halt the mass killings in Sri Lanka. US president Barack Obama ineffectually urged Sri Lanka to stop the 'indiscriminate shelling' of civilians and urged Tamil Tiger rebels to lay down their arms (BBC 2009). The 'never again' of President Obama's predecessor President Clinton was happening again.

In response to the humanitarian catastrophe and because of its conduct of the war, the United States said that it would block Sri Lanka's application for a $1.9 billion emergency loan from the International Monetary Fund. The United Kingdom also said that it would not support the loan and called for an investigation into allegations that Sri Lankan forces committed war crimes by shelling and bombing civilian targets, including hospitals (Page 2009). The UN Security Council, however, remained deadlocked, with Russia and especially China ensuring that discussion about Sri Lanka remained muted and that invoking R2P was never seriously considered.

The issue of ethnicity in Sri Lanka had gone from being problematic to catastrophic, with the options that once potentially existed for compromise now destroyed. That Sri Lanka was constructed as a unitary state, when a federal state would have more usefully accommodated its different national interests, was an error of late colonial administration. However, attempts to move away from a unitary model, which would probably be a necessary condition for an agreement to long-term peace by the LTTE, have to date foundered on the requirement to change the constitution and the implications that this would have for a common Sinhalese desire for geographic unity and hegemony.

Beyond this considerable problem with establishing a negotiated settlement to the Sri Lankan conflict, there was little doubt that there would continue to be a Tamil resistance and that Sri Lanka would not experience long-term peace without giving substantive recognition to the separate political identity of its Tamil people. To that end, and despite the constitutional and political impediments, there needed to be an acceptance by all parties in Colombo that any meaningful answer to Sri Lanka's conflict lay in acceptance of a compromise, including the broad principles of self-determination, which in application implied a version of a two-state policy in which the people of the north and east voted on unity of their provinces ahead of an interim self-governing administration. This would create the possibility of a further vote on simple federalism or confederation under a limited uniting structure within the context of agreement on establishing a plural democratic framework in Sinhala Sri Lanka and Tamil Eelam. Such an overarching structure could have responsibility for immigration, customs, external affairs and key infrastructure, but devolve authority in most other areas to the self-governing states. The question of external defence would need to be carefully handled, probably on the basis of separate forces for an interim period and only later a united force based on recognition of its separate origins.

A resolution to the Sri Lankan conflict would had not been likely, or possible, without significant international pressure to adopt measures that reflected a fundamental compromise on the part of both parties, and support for such measures once adopted. This would have implied, among other measures, a more substantial version of the SLMM, the promise of extra aid and the threat of sanctions on either party should they break the agreement. Equally important, Sri Lanka needed to return to being a more substantive democracy, working gradually back towards a notion of civic nationalism in which equity under rule of law rather than ethnicity was the effective basis for a sense of inclusion and participation, or at least the equitable management of different interest claims. After perhaps generations, a sense of normalcy and unity might have returned to Sri Lanka, but not before and not without deep and far-reaching changes. Following the end of the war, such an outcome appeared to be further away than ever, and such a potential path appeared littered with almost insurmountable obstacles.

In a practical sense, the LTTE's creation of a state within a state was a concrete step towards the realisation of its aims, and its functional acceptance by the Sri Lankan government by way of the 2002 ceasefire agreement confirmed that there was a starting point for some sort of mediated arrangement. But perhaps more than anything, the return to conflict from 2006 demonstrated that there was little taste for sustaining, much less pursuing, long-term and sincere compromise in Sri Lanka, and little interest in coming to any sort of compromise other than through absolute material necessity.

In the face of humanitarian catastrophe, the manner in which the Sri Lankan civil war ended highlights the failure of R2P, for at least 20,000 and perhaps 40,000 people were killed during the last phase of the war, often targeted deliberately. Deeply disturbingly, a further 10,000–15,000 people were 'disappeared' from internment camps in the months following the war, with 'disappearances' and extra-judicial killings again becoming a common aspect of life for Tamils under the Rajapaksa government (JDS 2011). Although most of the internees from the last phases of the war were released during 2009 and into 2010, there remained claims that thousands of Tamils were unaccounted for, that mass graves of dozens of bodies had been discovered and that there were still occasional extra-judicial executions of individual Tamils.[12] This, however, was more difficult to substantiate and constituted a less compelling case for R2P as such, although probably a stronger case for action from the international community on simple human rights grounds.

In principle if not in practice, given its competing positions on the UN Security Council, the world had a clear opportunity and, in terms of civilian deaths, a moral obligation to bring R2P principles to bear in the Sri Lankan war. It was clear to anyone who bothered to look that Sri Lanka was returning to war in 2006 and that there would, by any estimation, be serious civilian casualties. Instead, tens of thousands of people were killed in a relentless and barbaric act of warfare that finds parallel only with the mass killings of Bosnia and Kosovo, Rwanda and Darfur. Indeed, it is probably inappropriate to try to compare acts of barbarity and inhumanity, as though there was some sliding scale by which some could be deemed more or less cruel and inhuman than others. All have the same intent and malignant lack of regard for human life; it was and remains only the efficacy of application that differentiates them.

4 Cultural dominance, genocide and crimes against humanity

The term 'genocide' is, like the term 'terrorism', a highly emotive term that is loaded with meaning, some of which does not correspond to its formal definition. Among all the terms that can describe the worst aspects of human behaviour, genocide is perhaps the most negative. It also constitutes clear and incontestable grounds for R2P: 'there can be no neutrality', according to the UN, 'in the face of genocide' (UN 1999: 33).

There are well-known examples of undisputed genocides, such as in Rwanda, in Cambodia and among Jews and Romani people during World War II, in which the intention was to kill all of a particular group of people. There have also been many other very serious losses of life or attempts to extinguish entire cultures that probably fall into the category of genocide. The question is whether the events that have unfolded in Sri Lanka been among them. If so, the further question is how have events in Sri Lanka conformed to the definition of genocide and, if not, how can they be characterised and what does this then mean. Given the disputes over the meaning of the term 'genocide', it may even be that employing this term is unhelpful, given that anything that can be technically excluded from such a definition can then more easily be dismissed as somehow of more marginal importance, despite the gross human rights abuses, mass loss of life and very serious crimes against humanity that can still be implied.

Within the context of extinguishing a culture, there is the further question as to whether the ethnically specific and Sinhalese-privileging policies of the government of Sri Lanka, including the methods employed in its war against the LTTE, constitute the deliberate and systematic destruction, in whole or in part, of Sri Lanka's Tamils as an ethnic, racial, religious and, as perhaps most Sri Lankan Tamils claim, national group. That is, the question has been and will continue to be asked if the government of Sri Lanka has engaged in all or part of a policy of genocide or of regional ethnic cleansing. If not, there remains a serious set of charges that the government would ordinarily be obliged, under international law, to answer. These include whether it committed war crimes and crimes against humanity. It does appear that a compelling, if not absolute, case can be made to sustain the claim that the policies of the government of Sri Lanka were and continue to be aimed at the deliberate and systematic destruction of Sri Lanka's

Tamils as an ethnically distinct people. This discussion then needs to take the criteria that constitute genocide and examine them against the evidence that is currently available. This may then form the basis as to whether the implementation of R2P would, under its own terms, be warranted.

What is genocide?

The term 'genocide', first coined in 1944 by the Polish Jewish lawyer Raphael Lemkin, derives from the combination of two words. The first is the Greek word '*genos*', meaning race, stock or kin, which derives from the same root word that means 'genus', which characterises all humans as of the same genus (generically the same). In this case, however, the 'genus' in question is not the whole of humanity, but specifically identified component parts of it. The suffix 'cide' derives from the Latin word '*caedere*', which means to cut or kill, as in 'homicide', 'fratricide', etc. Genocide is therefore literally understood to mean to cut or kill a 'race' or ethnic group. The notion that genocide can apply to a 'race' raises a series of questions about the definition of 'race', its changing meaning and application over time and space, whether it is or can be physically determined and the social and political constructs that apply to understandings of its meaning.

Insofar as 'race' has any meaning, it can apply to broad classifications of people according to genetically divergent physical characteristics, for example the ways in which sub-Saharan Africans are physically distinct from Europeans who are distinct from inhabitants of South Asia who are in turn distinct from inhabitants of North-East Asia. However, each of these groups has blurred or fuzzy racial 'boundaries', in which groups segue into each other, as well as lesser distinctions within the broader groups, so that specificities start to lose other than a broad meaning. The use of the term 'race' to denote ethnic or language groups is, however, more problematic, given the sometimes arbitrary inclusion or exclusion from such groups and the derivation of such groups, for example claims to a British 'race' were undermined by the complexity of British origins as well as the close genetic and linguistic relationship between many British and northern German and Scandinavian people. Basing genocide on 'race', then, implies the killing of vast populations. Genocide can apply to 'race', for example the genocide perpetrated against indigenous populations by colonists. But more usefully, the term 'genocide' applies not to a people by 'race' but to a people by ethnicity, culture, language or heritage or other self-identifying groups of peoples.

The United Nations' definition of 'genocide' is that which is most commonly employed, giving as it does a standardised understanding to the term. In response to the ethnically focused mass killings of World War II, the UN Convention on the Prevention and Punishment of the Crime of Genocide was adopted by the UN General Assembly in December 1948 as Resolution 260, coming into effect in January 1951. Article 2 of the Convention states that:

> genocide means any of the following acts committed with intent to destroy, in whole or in part, a national, ethnical, racial or religious group, as such:

(a) Killing members of the group;
(b) Causing serious bodily or mental harm to members of the group;
(c) Deliberately inflicting on the group conditions of life calculated to bring about its physical destruction in whole or in part;
(d) Imposing measures intended to prevent births within the group;
(e) Forcibly transferring children of the group to another group.

(UN 1948b)

Taking sections (a) and (b) as criteria, the killing of or serious harm to ethnic Tamils in Sri Lanka conforms to these meanings of genocide. However, killing or harming members of a group is so broad in application that it could be applied to a vast range of circumstances that are otherwise not understood as genocide. Section (c) is perhaps closer to a conventional understanding, assuming the 'in part' element is deleted, and again could be said to apply to Sri Lanka's Tamils, although sections (d) and (e) probably do not, at least on a mass scale. Building on the intellectual and legal foundation laid by the Streicher decision in the post-World War II Nuremburg trails,[1] Article III (c) of the Genocide Convention declares that 'direct and public incitement to commit genocide' is also a crime (UN 1948b).

According to a study on the claim of genocide in West Papua, Indonesia, the crime of genocide requires both the prohibited act (*actus reus*) and the requisite intent (*mens rea*), with proof of the act required in cases of killing, causing serious bodily or mental harm and the forcible transference of children. In these cases, it is not necessary to establish a relationship between cause and effect, but may be based on showing harm and intent to cause harm, for example when a senior officer or other official with the capacity to stop an event by subordinates omits to do so (e.g. see ICTR 1998). The other two acts, deliberately inflicting conditions calculated to bring about the physical destruction of the group or imposing measures to prevent birth, do not require proof but do require evidence of intent (Brundage *et al.* 2004).

Of major concern in Sri Lanka, and which has come to receive greater international recognition as a war crime, is enforced 'disappearance', in which people have been unlawfully deprived of the right to bodily integrity and in most cases either tortured or otherwise treated in a cruel and inhumane way and/or murdered. In simple terms, 'enforced disappearance' means the abduction and murder of individuals by agents of the state.

In 1980, the UN Human Rights Committee established the Working Group on Enforced or Involuntary Disappearances, from which developed a body of international human rights law on the issue of enforced disappearances, to complement the existing humanitarian law on missing persons (OUNHCHR 2010). International human rights law places obligations on states to guarantee certain rights to their citizens and prohibit the arbitrary deprivation of liberty, torture, murder, and refusal to provide information regarding the status of missing persons. This was given a more specific focus in relation to 'disappearances' with the introduction of the 2006 Convention for the Protection of All Persons from Enforced Disappearance (UNGA 2006), which codified international human rights law, humanitarian practice and international criminal law in relation to 'disappeared' persons. At the time of writing, 19 of the 20 countries required to ratify the convention had done so, with a total of 87 countries signing a document saying that they would ratify the convention. Article 2 of the convention defines enforced disappearance as the deprivation of liberty by agents of the state, or persons acting with the support or knowledge of the state, followed by a concealment of the fate or whereabouts of the disappeared person. Unsurprisingly given its rejection of the status of the International Court of Justice (ICJ), Sri Lanka has not ratified the convention and is not a signatory to it.

The further element of international law that could apply in the case of Sri Lanka in relation to disappeared persons and which could contribute to establishing a case for R2P is based on Article 5 of the Convention. This focuses on individual criminal responsibility rather than focusing responsibility on states or armed groups and makes possible to bring to justice perpetrators of war crimes and human rights violations so serious as to constitute crimes against humanity. Enforced disappearances – state murder of its citizens – may constitute a crime against humanity if it occurs within the context of 'a widespread or systematic attack directed against any civilian population' of which the perpetrators had knowledge (ICC 1999: Article 7(1)(i)).

A major question that arises in determining whether genocide has been committed and which distinguishes it from an ordinary crime is, according to the International Criminal Tribunal of Yugoslavia, the *mens rea* or criminal intent (lit. 'guilty mind') behind the crime (Klip and Sluiter 2001: 294, 296, 562, 770). That is, the act (*actus reus*) determines that a crime has been committed, but it is the intent of the crime that characterises it as genocide.

In the period following the Cold War there has been a significant increase in the prosecution of crimes against humanity, including genocide. In 1993, in response to the atrocities occurring in Bosnia, the UN Security Council passed Resolution 827, establishing the International Criminal Tribunal for the former Yugoslavia (ICTY) in The Hague. This was the first international criminal tribunal since Nuremberg and prosecuted grave breaches of the 1949 Geneva Conventions, violations of the laws or customs of war, genocide, and crimes against humanity. The following year, in October 1994, the UN Security Council extended the International Criminal Tribunal for Rwanda (ICTR), located in Arusha, Tanzania. In September 1998, this resulted in the first conviction for genocide, of Jean-Paul Akavesu, for his role in the Rwandan killings. That it took four years to convict Akavesu and that many others charged with genocide have not yet faced court indicates that bringing to court and convicting people charged with genocide remains a difficult task. Moreover, not only is it difficult to prosecute perpetrators of genocide but also acts of genocide have continued despite the possibility of punishment. The war in Darfur, in western Sudan, has been referred to generally and by the US government in particular as genocide since 2004. Despite the issuing of several arrest warrants, no one from Sudan charged with crimes against humanity or war crimes has faced the International Criminal Court.

On the question of whether genocide has been committed in Sri Lanka or whether there has been an attempted genocide or incitement to genocide, it is clear that there have been mass killings that have been orchestrated by senior government officials. This refers not just to the events of late 2008 and 2009, but dates back to the threats of 1980 and the killings of 'Black July' 1983. In 1980, Sri Lanka's first executive president, Junius Jayawardene, said, regarding the Tamils: 'If you want a fight, let there be a fight' (comment in reply to a question in Sri Lanka parliament, 18 August 1977). In 1983 he added further fuel to a growing fire by saying:

> I am not worried about the opinion of the Tamil people . . . now we cannot think of them, not about their lives or their opinion . . . the more you put pressure in the north, the happier the Sinhalese people will be here . . . Really if I starve the Tamils out, the Sinhalese people will be happy.
>
> (Ward 1983, quoted in Perera 1983)

Jayawardene's statement was made just two weeks before the unleashing of the anti-Tamil pogrom known as 'Black July', which, under the Streicher judgment, could qualify as incitement to murder and which even more clearly could be seen as an act of omission, a distinct failure to prevent murder.

Although laying charges of genocide against the government of Sri Lanka would be difficult for technical reasons, in 2009 former US Associate Deputy Attorney General and lawyer for the LTTE, Bruce Fein, submitted to US Attorney General, Eric Holder, a grand jury indictment for genocide against US citizen and Sri Lankan Defence Minister Gotabaya Rajapaksa, and for genocide, war crimes and torture against Tamils in Sri Lanka against US green card holder, former military commander General Sarath Fonseka. Fein urged the Department of Justice to open a grand jury investigation based on evidence amassed in a three-volume, 1,000-page document, which he said 'amply satisfies the Department's threshold for commencing a criminal investigation' (Fein 2009).

In an attached letter headed 'RE: Investigation of U.S. citizen and U.S. green card holder for genocide, war crimes, and torture against Tamils in Sri Lanka' and submitted with the indictment, Fein said that, under the US 2007 Genocide Accountability Act (GAA), Rajapaksa and Fonseka should be charged with 12 counts of genocide based on 'command responsibility for genocidal acts perpetrated by their subordinates in the Sri Lankan security forces' (Fein 2009). According to Fein, the GAA applies to genocide 'irrespective of the place of its occurrence and irrespective of whether the accused is a U.S. national', although he noted that Rajapaksa was a US citizen and Fonseka was a green card holder. The indictment charged Rajapaksa and Fonseka with genocide of Tamils in 12 geographic areas between 6 December 2005, when both assumed their government positions, and February 2009. The indictment detailed over 3,750 extra-judicial killings, a further approximately 30,000 Tamils suffering serious bodily injury and more than 1.3 million displacements, which Fein noted far exceeded displacements in Kosovo, which led to genocide charges before the International Criminal Court (ICC).

In Fein's indictment, he noted that the final count of genocide:

> is indistinguishable from the genocide of 7,000 Bosnian Muslim males in Srebrenica, which had been declared a safe zone by Bosnian Serbs. Count

> twelve charges Rajapaksa and Fonseka of bombing and shelling 350,000 Tamil civilians into one large 'safe area,' and, since January 21, 2009, killing and maiming the Tamils who had amassed there by aerial bombing and artillery. In the month of January, according to the model indictment, 750 Tamils have been massacred and more than 2,250 have been seriously injured. On the BBC, on Feb. 2, *Rajapaksa declared that nothing should live or breathe* outside the Orwellian 'safe area.' Thus, one hospital outside the area has been bombed three times, including by cluster bombs. More than 1,000 Tamils are in detention camps, and reports of rape have already emerged.
>
> (Fein 2009, author's emphasis)

As noted elsewhere, evidence was later presented to indicate that about 40,000 people were killed in the above-noted event, with hundreds and probably thousands more 'disappearing' from internment camps in the following months. Following his visit to internment camps, UN Secretary-General Ban Ki-moon said: 'I have travelled around the world and visited similar places, but this is by far the most appalling scenes I have seen'. Ban also contradicted the Sri Lankan military's claim that not many civilians had died in the last period of fighting (CNN 2009).

Fein's letter noted as 'exemplary genocidal events' the murder of five Tamil students and 17 Action Against Hunger aid workers in 2006, the discovery of mass graves, and the regular and frequent 'disappearances' of Tamils into white vans without identification (Fein 2009).

In identifying the ethnic or 'racial' quality of the charges, Fein noted that:

> Every member of the Sri Lankan security forces is Sinhalese. There are no Tamils. No member of the security forces since Rajapaksa and Fonseka assumed their respective positions has ever been prosecuted or punished for atrocities against Tamils, including torture or murder. Indeed, in more than 60 years, only one prosecution has been pursued for rape, murder, torture, or other crimes against Tamils, and that one isolated exception was for peculiar reasons.
>
> (Fein 2009)

Fein said that the evidence for the indictment was based on:

> affidavits, court documents, and contemporaneous eye-witness reporting from media sources, for example, the BBC . . . If Rajapaksa and Fonseka are indicted, Sri Lanka would be obligated to extradite them to the United States under the Genocide Convention of 1948 and implementing legislation.
>
> (Fein 2009)

This would thus overcome the hurdle of Sri Lanka not being a signatory to the Rome Statute.

Applying its formal definition, it could be argued that the term 'genocide' did and continues to find application in Sri Lanka, especially within the sense of it being the causing of serious harm to members of a group or the destruction of a people 'in whole or in part'. However, applying the common definition, which limits genocide to an attempt to destroy a whole people, means that relevant crimes against humanity are diminished in popular understanding. This diminution of genocide is exacerbated by the popular media, which tends to focus on the more 'newsworthy' sudden bursts of mass killing but to overlook longer-term or more chronic rather than acute killings. This then refers to what former US Secretary of State and President Obama advisor Madeleine Albright called a 'rolling genocide' (with reference to Darfur) (Albright 2010). If the idea of a 'rolling genocide' or an extended genocide is accepted rather than a sudden burst of genocide, and particularly if the formal as opposed to the popular definition of genocide is also accepted, then there is little doubt that events in Sri Lanka, in particular since 1983, meet the criteria.

There is little doubt that successive Sri Lankan governments have also engaged in the cultural destruction of the Tamil people, from the infamous burning of the Jaffna library to the wholesale displacement of Tamil people from areas where they have legally lived. However, rather than let them return, the state has both declared some areas as 'high security zones' and permanently displaced Tamils and in other cases sponsored usually landless Sinhalese peasants to occupy these formerly Tamil lands. The Sri Lankan state officially displaced Tamils by forcing them to leave their lands as a result of warfare (IASC 2007). In part, the purpose of this policy of displacement has been to provide land for landless Sinhalese peasants. However, the main purpose of this relocation was to break up Tamil domination of specific areas and thereby reduce their capacity to vote as a geographic block. This meant that the chance of having Tamil officials elected as local representatives was reduced, in turn lessening overall Tamil representation. This policy not only led to the widespread displacement of Tamils but also changed the demographic map of Sri Lanka:

> We conceived and implemented a plan which we thought would secure the territorial integrity of Sri Lanka for a long time. We moved a large group of 45,000 land-hungry (Sinhale) peasants into the Batticaloa and Pollanaruwa districts of the Madhuru Oya delta. By settling Sinhala peasants people in the Madhuru Oya, we were seeking in the Batticaloa zone a mass of people opposed to a separate [Tamil] state.
>
> (Herman Guneratna, quoted in Fontgalland 2009: 304)

This policy of displacement and of turning Tamils into refugees in their own country further fuelled the Tamil sense of resentment towards Sri Lanka's Sinhala majority.

A report by a Colombo-based think tank highlighted the gaps and shortcomings in several areas concerning the displacement of Tamils, including the constitutional, legal and policy context, the practical challenges to accessing, owning and controlling land, and land disputes and conflicts, as well as boundary issues between administrative divisions. It also considered initiatives intended to address landlessness and compensation for people who had lost land (see Fonseka and

Raheem 2010). Among the report's recommendations were that the constitution and law need to be fully recognised and implemented, implying that the loss of land was both unconstitutional and illegal.

The categories that give rise to claims of genocide are wide and disputed, despite its official interpretation, raising doubt and hence debate about whether it has existed and, as a consequence, if this then implies external intervention. What is also debatable, if less so in definitional terms and more in terms of availability of evidence, is whether war crimes and crimes against humanity were committed in Sri Lanka's war with the LTTE. Ascertaining whether this was the case was impeded, unsurprisingly, by the government of Sri Lanka. According to the International Crisis Group (ICG), there were:

> repeated violations of international law by both the Sri Lankan security forces and the Liberation Tigers of Tamil Eelam (LTTE) during thc last five months of their 30-year civil war. That evidence suggests that the period of January to May 2009 saw tens of thousands of Tamil civilian men, women, children and the elderly killed, countless more wounded, and hundreds of thousands deprived of adequate food and medical care, resulting in more deaths.
>
> (ICG 2010a)

The ICG claimed that the Sri Lanka government 'has conclusively demonstrated its unwillingness to undertake genuine investigations of security force abuses and continues to deny any responsibility for civilian casualties'. This made an international investigation 'essential' (ICG 2010a). ICG president Louise Arbour said: 'The scale of civilian deaths and suffering demands a response . . . Future generations will demand to know what happened, and future peace in Sri Lanka requires some measure of justice' (ICG 2010a). 'Evidence gathered by Crisis Group provides reasonable grounds to believe that government security forces repeatedly and intentionally violated the law by attacking civilians, hospitals and humanitarian operations' (ICG 2010a).

According to one report based on first-hand evidence from a senior Sri Lankan army commander and frontline soldier, point-blank executions of Tamils at the end of the Sri Lankan civil war were carried out under orders. This evidence showing the point-blank execution of Tamils by Sri Lanka soldiers was authenticated by the United Nations. 'Yes, our commander ordered us to kill everyone', one soldier said. 'We killed everyone' (Miller 2010). A senior Sri Lankan army commander corroborated this account by saying:

> Definitely, the order would have been to kill everybody and finish them off . . . I don't think we wanted to keep any hardcore elements, so they were done away with. It is clear that such orders were, in fact, received from the top.
>
> (Miller 2010)

Confirming this claimed order, photographs released by Al Jazeera showed Tamil civilians and unarmed fighters after they had been executed, with many blindfolded and having their hands tied, some being dumped in shallow graves (Al Jazeera 2010). The broadcast said that the photos had been taken in the final days of the government offensives against the LTTE, but noted that it was unable to authenticate the photos. If authentic, which the photos appeared to be, they showed that the Sri Lankan military engaged in an orgy of violence against unarmed Tamil prisoners. Further footage was obtained and screened, but with some elements edited due to it being 'too gruesome to broadcast'. This footage also showed nine bound and blindfolded people who had been executed (Channel 4 2010). The Sri Lankan government said that the tape was a fake; however, 'the conclusion', according to former UN special rapporteur Philip Alston, 'is clearly that the videotape is authentic' (Alston, in Channel 4 2010). Channel 4 said that it had received hundreds of further photos and further video footage showing summary executions and rape by Sri Lanka soldiers.

Within this context, this deliberate murder of civilians and others who had surrendered or been taken prisoner constituted war crimes and on the face of it also came under the formal definition of genocide, although such crimes are more commonly covered by international humanitarian law and thereby constitute crimes against humanity. Within this definition is that these acts were not sporadic or random but were undertaken as part of a deliberate government policy. Crimes against humanity:

> are not isolated or sporadic events, but are part either of a government policy . . . or of a wide practice of atrocities tolerated or condoned by a government or a *de facto* authority. Murder; extermination; torture; rape, political, racial, or religious persecution and other inhumane acts reach the threshold of crimes against humanity only if they are part of a widespread or systematic practice.
>
> (UN 2002)

Once a state enters into this realm of behaviour, whether it has committed genocide or has committed crimes against humanity starts to beg the theoretical distinction between these crimes, even if the International Criminal Court recognises and tries them as distinct items. However, for the purpose of international intervention, each is reprehensible in a way that does not suffer a comparative understanding and which requires a comprehensive international response.

Given its history of state violence, it is unsurprising that Sri Lanka is not a signatory to the Rome Statute and this then limits the capacity for the ICC to invoke Sri Lanka's responsibilities under that statute. Moreover, although it is possible for the UN Security Council to refer a matter to the ICC and thereby compel Sri Lanka to comply with its orders, the continuing support for Sri Lanka from Russia and especially China and their veto powers in the Security Council ensured that this was not likely to happen. This then meant that the Security Council Resolution 1674, which 'reaffirms the provisions of paragraphs 138 and 139 of the 2005 World Summit Outcome Document regarding the responsibility to protect populations from genocide, war crimes, ethnic cleansing and crimes against humanity' (UNSC 2006a) – that is, the responsibility to protect – would fail, not because of a lack of grounds for its implementation but on the simple, expedient and morally barren grounds of realpolitik, as identified by the government of Sri Lanka itself.

Tellingly, rather than claim that the Rome Statute would not apply to Sri Lanka's recent history because its actions do not fall under the ICC's provisions, the government of Sri Lanka adopted a self-congratulatory position that it was wise not to have signed the Rome Statute so as not to be vulnerable to the ICC's charges. An article congratulating the government on not signing the Rome Statute but advocating further steps to protect Sri Lanka's political and military leaders from possible prosecution or the tarnishing of Sri Lanka's international reputation was published in a newspaper, which was in turn reproduced on the government of Sri Lanka's official website, which would seem to imply official endorsement for its views (Senaratna 2009). Regardless of the ICC's provisions and Sri Lanka's 'wisdom' in not having signed the Rome Statute, its leaders may still be held responsible for genocide:

> As the ICTR held in *Prosecutor v. Akayesu*, 'it is possible to deduce the genocidal intent inherent in a particular act charged from the general context of the perpetration of other culpable acts systematically directed against that same group, whether these acts were committed by the same offender or by others.' It is also possible to infer intent when genocidal acts are committed in connection with a separate objective with a non-genocidal motive.
>
> (Brundage *et al.* 2004: 53)

That is, even when a state is a non-signatory to the Rome Statute, individuals can still be charged with genocide on the basis of intent within the context of other culpable acts directed at the Tamil people, regardless of the claimed motive of the over-arching action (in this case the destruction of the LTTE).

Beyond this, a fixation with genocide and its definitions as a necessary (although not exclusive) trigger for implementing R2P perhaps misses the point that the international community has a 'responsibility to protect' not on the basis of legal argument around definitions of what has happened; it has a collective responsibility on the basis that gross collective crimes have been or are about to be committed against an identifiable people. This may comply with the formal and popular definitions of genocide and it may, in the longer term, comply with the idea of a 'rolling genocide', that is, a drawn-out rather than a sudden genocidal act. It almost certainly also complies with the wider definitions of 'war crimes' and 'crimes against humanity'.

According to the Nuremburg Tribunal Principles, war crimes are:

> violations of the laws or customs of war which include, but are not limited to, murder, ill-treatment or deportation for slave labour or for any other purpose of the civilian population of or in occupied territory; murder or ill-treatment of prisoners of war or persons on the seas, killing of hostages, plunder of

> public or private property, wanton destruction of cities, towns, or villages, or devastation not justified by military necessity.
>
> (Nuremburg Tribunal 1950: No. 6, b)

On this basis, it could be reasonably argued that continued systematic attacks against Tamil civilians included murder, ill-treatment and deportation, the murder and ill-treatment of prisoners of war, the plunder of public and private property, the wanton destruction of towns and villages and devastation not justified by military necessity. Indeed, it could be shown that these acts were a consequence of an intentional policy to break the back of a unified Tamil political identity and to cow the Tamil population into submission.

The same principles identify crimes against humanity as involving the persecution of individuals or groups in a widespread and systematic fashion, including:

> murder, extermination, enslavement, deportation, and other inhumane acts committed against any civilian population, before or during the war, or persecutions on political, racial, or religious grounds in execution of or in connection with any crime within the jurisdiction of the Tribunal, whether or not in violation of the domestic law of the country where perpetrated. Crimes against humanity do not necessarily require a connection to war or armed conflict.
>
> (Nuremburg Tribunal 1950: No. 6, c)

Again, it could be shown that these criteria were met by official government policy targeted against Tamils on political and racial grounds, both during periods of what might be agreed to be war, as well as at times other than war.

Although specific intent is a requirement for determining whether genocide has been perpetrated, according to the International Criminal Tribunal on Rwanda, in most cases genocidal intent can be inferred from the general context of the act systematically directed against the same group (Prosecutor *v.* Akayesu, in Boot 2001: 414).

> [I]ntent may be inferred from a number of facts such as words or deeds or a pattern of purposeful action that deliberately, consistently, and systematically targets victims on account of their membership in a particular group while excluding the members of other groups.
>
> (Kriangsak Kittichaisaree, in Brundage *et al.* 2004: 71)

No single act or set of acts in Sri Lanka can be said to have constituted genocide as such, and the required intent cannot be as obviously and overwhelmingly inferred as it was in the case of the Holocaust or the Rwandan genocide. But there can be little doubt that the Sri Lankan government has engaged in a systematic pattern of acts that has resulted in harm to and the destruction of a substantial part of Sri Lanka's Tamil population (with apologies to Brundage *et al.* 2004: 71).

Although the prosecution of such crimes by the ICC can occur only if the state in question is a signatory to the Rome Statute, when crimes such as crimes against humanity, like the crime of genocide, are equal, in that they may be held criminally accountable under international law, they similarly equally constitute grounds for the implementation of R2P. That is, if a state perpetrates war crimes or crimes against humanity against its own people, even when genocide is not found to have been perpetrated, these other crimes hold equivalence under international law and hence hold an in-principle equivalence as grounds for applying R2P. The 'rolling genocide' in Sri Lanka and the brutal mass killings of 2008–9 formally constitute genocide and hence grounds for applying R2P. But beyond this, the specific application of war crimes and crimes against humanity that can also be demonstrated should similarly be regarded as not just legitimate but also compelling grounds for invoking R2P. The international community should not require a specific number of people to have been killed to say that genocide has occurred or is occurring, nor should it claim that somehow genocide is unacceptable but war crimes and crimes against humanity are less so; in international law they are not.

Finally, although the ICC may hear cases concerning the breach of international law concerning only signatories to the Rome Statute, it makes little sense to have international law on such critical matters but have it discretionary as to whether one is or is not willingly subject to such a law. It may be a weakness of the international system that continues to formally allow some states to opt out of what are otherwise universal provisions and requirements. But it is much more a weakness of logic to have a law that, given the same circumstances, is discretionary in application. Like the basic concept of R2P, the purpose of law is not for it to apply only in those circumstances in which the perpetrator of a gross crime allows it, but for it to be imposed as a judgment by the international community on the fundamental unacceptability of perpetrating such crimes.

5 Sri Lanka and international law

The idea that it could become necessary to directly intervene in the affairs of a sovereign state implies that a situation has become so parlous for a specific group of its people and the state in question has moved so far beyond the bounds of internationally acceptable behaviour, defined by international law, that the international community has no choice but to take direct action. This chapter will identify those elements of international law that appear to have been breached by the government of Sri Lanka in the orientation of its state policies and in the prosecution of its war against the Liberation Tigers of Tamil Eelam. It will identify particular examples of such breaches and then consider the range of responses by the international community to states, and responsible individuals, that breach such laws.

In particular, this chapter will consider allegations of the perpetration, as a matter of official policy, of war crimes, including extra-judicial killings, the ill-treatment and murder of prisoners, intentional (or easily preventable) large-scale deaths (e.g. a claimed 7,000 civilians killed in the closing days of the war), and the use of torture and rape as instruments of war. It will also examine the difficulty in establishing the facts of war crimes as a result of the government's closure of large areas to access by independent media and humanitarian organisations.

Similarly, the LTTE has long been condemned for breaching a number of international human rights conventions, as well as for its widespread use of suicide bombers (the LTTE pioneered this mode of attack, even if it does have considerable precedent in other forms of warfare including the Malay 'amok' and Japanese 'kamikazi') against civilians as well as military and political targets. In particular, the LTTE has admitted that it recruited underage (child) soldiers, although it claimed that it had ended this practice by 2006. The LTTE also engaged in the forced relocation of people and, as the war came to a conclusion, used people as human shields. The LTTE defended itself on other charges of abuse of human rights and international humanitarian law, although its reputation among many Tamils both within and outside Sri Lanka suggested that it continued to breach basic conventions until its final defeat.

This chapter will therefore also consider the extent to which the actions of the LTTE itself required international intervention under the rubric of R2P, and the role played by India, later the Norwegian-led ceasefire monitoring program, and independent aid agencies in addressing such issues. The chapter will conclude by discussing whether and how such responses might be applied in the case of Sri Lanka.

The question arises as to the conduct of states under international law, both when states act internally in ways that contravene international laws and when states act in relation to each other in ways that contravene international laws. R2P is a norm, or set of principles in relation to which there is an obligation, rather than a law in its own right. There is no sharp distinction between that which is law and that which is a norm, notably in relation to natural law (that which is regarded as existing regardless of whether it is written or otherwise) from which R2P derives, and especially when that norm is codified. Legal scholars across the full range of laws, including constitutional law, tort law, contract law and criminal law, have commonly looked to norms as a means of addressing significant legal problems or gaps (see Massaro 1999).

Deriving in order from political philosophy, laws are a reflection of social norms, with the framework to the debate resting on a Hobbesian approach to law. As a basis for rational social order, Hobbes presumed that such order was built on a social contract deriving from natural law, articulated as civil (positive) law (see Hobbes 1962: 199–200). Law, according to Hobbes, was required to be enforceable in order to ensure its writ (Hobbes 1962: 200). As an extrapolation, a political philosophy that privileges peace over war and humanity over barbarism gives rise to global norms that are agreed to by the international community as international law. Following the Socratic approach to social contract,[1] one is obliged to accept such law even in cases in which one is subject to it but disagrees with its findings, and further, one is subject to such law even when one does not accept it as pertaining. Yet despite Hobbes' insistence that natural and civil law were necessary elements of each other, the literature employing social norms as a basis for legal theory tends to imply that a careful and more nuanced public policy should probably apply somewhere between enthusiasm for the application of natural law (e.g. Sunstein 1997; Sunstein and Thaler 2003) and a more reserved approach to applying natural law in favour of positive law (e.g. Posner, 1998, 2000, 2001; Posner and Rasmusen 1999).

A century or so after Hobbes, in arguing in favour of the rule of such an international law, Bentham admitted that its time – the late eighteenth century – was not yet ripe (Bentham 1843: Essay IV). It was to be, however, soon after, with British opposition to the international slave trade in 1807 (followed by the United States in 1808) and its intervention in the struggle for Greek independence. By 1815, the signatories to the Treaty of Vienna declared:

> the commerce, known by the name of the African Slave Trade has been viewed, by just and enlightened men in all ages, as repugnant to the principles of humanity and universal morality; . . . at length the public voice, in all civilized countries, calls aloud that it should be suppressed as soon as possible . . . [and] several European Governments have adopted the resolution of putting a stop to it.
>
> (Baines 1818: 532)

As this agreement became more firmly established and widely enforced (through a series of subsequent treaties, notably the League of Nations Slavery Convention of 1925), it gained credence to the point that by current standards no one would seriously challenge its validity or implementation beyond the writ of sovereign states. It is an example of both how international law is established and extends its reach over time, and the limits of the type of sovereignty claimed by some states. In particular, the outlawing of trade in slaves by the United Kingdom and the United States, initially only in their own markets, was eventually extended to combating the slave trade operated by African states, extending to the Middle East and India.

According to Putney (1908: section 2), the basis for international law is consent to be bound by such law, customs that arise around the application of that law, and continued acquiescence to that law. To illustrate this, being subject to the jurisdiction of the International Criminal Court applies only to member states that have signed the Rome Statute and thus agreed to be bound by the provisions of the court. However, whereas the ICC is bound by membership rules, the International Criminal Tribunals for Rwanda and Yugoslavia were established by the UN Security Council and apply regardless of voluntary membership.

Further, Putney (1908) outlined two perspectives on international law that appear to continue to hold. The first is the philosophical principle in which law is established as the rules and principles that ought to be observed in interstate relations. This might be regarded as the normative or 'idealist' position. The second, or more 'realist', perspective pertains to the rules and principles that are generally observed in interstate relations. At this time, Putney observed that international law existed, but had no system of penalties or mechanism for enforcement:

> In form . . . law is a body of rules and principles in accord with which phenomena take place. If these rules are not followed as enunciated by the state in case of statute law, certain penalties are inflicted. The nature of the penalty must, to a great extent, depend upon the source. International law is the body of rules and principles, in accord with which, interstate phenomena take place. Violations of international law do not meet the same penalties as those of statute law, as they do not have the same source nor an established tribunal for their enforcement. International law is, however, in form law and in practice so regarded.
>
> (Putney 1908: section 2)

The issue, then, that Putney raised was not the validity of international law but the capacity to adjudicate upon it and apply penalties for its breach. That is, the question was not whether international law existed or should exist, but specifically what laws exist or should exist and how to compel compliance with such law. The First Geneva Convention of 1864 on the treatment of prisoners, the wounded and sick, civilians and medical and religious personnel was the first such international agreement, followed by three further conventions respectively addressing issues of armed forces members at sea, the treatment of prisoners of war and the protection of civilians, in 1906, 1929 and 1949. These were supplemented by the Hague Conventions of 1899 and 1907 on the rules of war and the peaceful resolution of international disputes.

The Great War interrupted such discussions but, at its conclusion, made their resumption all the more compelling. The establishment of the League of Nations in 1919 was the first serious attempt to compel compliance with international law, specifically around the issues of non-aggression. Its powers of compulsion were to have included economic sanctions and military intervention; however, the League foundered through lack of commitment by member states and the non-inclusion of the United States, which was, ironically, its main protagonist.[2]

The League's inability to control the resumption of militarism, the belligerent invasion of numerous weak states, the outbreak of civil war and the persecution of minorities meant that it was an almost total practical failure. The outbreak of World War II spelled the death knell of the League and the practice of international law on the one hand, but only strengthened the case for the imposition of an international rule of law on the other. The conclusion of World War II saw the establishment of international war crimes courts and the trying of war criminals. The international community felt compelled to redouble its efforts at establishing both an international adjudicating body and a set of international laws that it had the authority to oversee. The question thus became not one of whether international law obtained, but of its detail, the extent of its writ and who would be its adjudicating authority.

In a federal state, if a provincial army or militia commits atrocities against an ethnic group and is prepared to resist the federal army, non-interventionists will generally not object to federal intervention. Yet they will object if troops cross an international border for the same purpose: a 'national border mysteriously operates a *change in the description* of the act of humanitarian rescue: it is no longer a humanitarian rescue but a war' (Teson 2003: 103, emphasis in original). However, there is a series of positive international laws (which are specific in their codification and intent), the breaching of which can act as a trigger for R2P. These laws include the conventions on genocide, crimes against humanity and war crimes, each of which can be said to have occurred in Sri Lanka against the Tamil people, as discussed in the previous chapter.

The Preamble to the UN Charter clearly spells out its intent that the world should live in equitable peace, including within as well as between states. This preamble could reasonably be interpreted as implying R2P, particularly in relation to the second and third points acknowledging 'fundamental human rights' and 'to establish conditions under which justice and respect for the obligations arising from treaties and other sources of international law can be maintained'. However, taking the charter as an agreement for international norms and behaviour, the preamble to any such agreement has no binding force, but rather simply states the purpose and spirit of the agreement to which parties are expected to comply. Compliance with the agreement is determined by the detail of the agreement or, in this case, the charter, the willingness to submit to its criteria and the capacity for other parties to enforce the conditions outlined in the agreement or charter. 'The

UN Charter is, at once, a freeze-frame of historically validated norms and also the foundation for a dynamic political and administrative institution' (Franck 2003: 205). At the center of this freeze-frame is Article II.4: 'All Members shall refrain in their international relations from the threat or use of force against the territorial integrity or political independence of any state, or in any other manner inconsistent with the Purposes of the United Nations' (UN 1945). And, importantly in relation to R2P:

> Nothing contained in the present Charter shall authorize the United Nations to intervene in matters which are essentially within the domestic jurisdiction of any state or shall require the Members to submit such matters to settlement under the present Charter; but this principle shall not prejudice the application of enforcement measures under Chapter VII.
>
> (UN 1945: II.7)

Yet Chapter VII concerns threats to and breaches of the peace and acts of aggression. In particular, it notes that:

> Should the Security Council consider that measures provided for in Article 41 would be inadequate or have proved to be inadequate, it may take such action by air, sea, or land forces as may be necessary to maintain or restore international peace and security. Such action may include demonstrations, blockade, and other operations by air, sea, or land forces of Members of the United Nations.
>
> (UN 1945: VII:42)

Other provisions of Chapter VII also deal with circumstances and conditions to avoid but which might warrant such action, while Chapter VIII addresses circumstances in which regional bodies may act under the authority of the Security Council. However, a number of states coalesced to protect Sri Lanka from full international scrutiny, with, in particular, Security Council members employing their power of veto to ensure that sanctions placed on Sri Lanka were retained at a minimum.

The International Court of Justice was established by the Charter of the United Nations, which provides that all member states of the United Nations are *ipso facto* parties to the Court's Statute. The composition and functioning of the Court are organised by this Statute, and by the Rules of the Court, which are drawn up by the Court itself. Part 2, Article 5 on 'Jurisdiction, Admissibility and Applicable Law, Crimes within the jurisdiction of the Court' says that:

> 1 The jurisdiction of the Court shall be limited to the most serious crimes of concern to the international community as a whole. The Court has jurisdiction in accordance with this Statute with respect to the following crimes:
>
> (a) The crime of genocide;

(b) Crimes against humanity;
(c) War crimes;
(d) The crime of aggression.

(UN 2002)

There can be no reasonable doubt that, under the terms of these articles, while protecting the general sovereign integrity of states from unwarranted external aggression, the UN endorses the use of compulsion, including military force (warranted external aggression), in cases in which states act in ways that breach regional peace or stability or which contravene the provisions of the International Criminal Court in relation to genocide, crimes against humanity or war crimes. Once a state engages in any of these activities, it is clear that such a state has abrogated its right to the protections otherwise guaranteed by the UN. Moreover, should they engage in such activities, they become vulnerable, as a matter of principle, to international intervention as determined by the UN Security Council. Under the terms of the UN articles, the Security Council can adjudicate on what does and does not constitute grounds for intervention. However, the ICJ can also make determinations, based on evidence brought before it, which can then be used as grounds for Security Council decisions, including intervention.

It can be clearly argued that, in cases that correspond to the ICJ's adjudicatory mandate, the Security Council has the authority to intervene to compel compliance or change. What is much less clear is whether, and to what extent, such authority exists outside the Security Council's own mandate. It may be argued that the issues that the ICJ addresses have been raised but the Security Council refuses or fails to act. This has occurred on numerous occasions, not least because of ideological or strategic preferences for one party or another to a conflict, for reasons of global one-upmanship or because Security Council members have other vested interests in particular outcomes. Even since the end of the Cold War, when relatively simple ideological consideration has declined relative to outcomes, the members of the Security Council continue to retain significant international interests in parts of the world, are parties to alliances or blocs, or are positioned counter to another's particular regional interests. There are, it is said, no friends in international relations; there are only interests.

This, then, raises the prospect of states or groups of states acting in concert outside the Security Council's remit, yet still doing so within the spirit, if not the entirety of the structure, of international law. If there is commonly debate within the Security Council over the circumstances in which it should authorise intervention, the debate over non-Security Council intervention is very much greater and more problematic. This is no more so than in terms of the formal legality of such actions, in which an act designed to address a wrong, without appropriate formal authority, may itself constitute a wrong.

There is no doubt that, under international law, sovereign integrity is the first condition of member states of the international community (UN 1945). Were this not the case, few, if any, states would have signed up to the UN Charter in the first instance. The underlying and, in some circumstances deeply problematic, concept of sovereignty is that it is indivisible, which finds its formally enunciated origins in sixteenth-century France (see Bodin 1992: 1–88) but which was more widely understood in claims by monarchs to be the supreme authority of the state. This claim to absolutist authority was frequently tested, not least by civil wars and the occasional diminution of the power of the monarch by powerful elites, the compelled signing of the Magna Carta being but one notable example. It is also tested by the somewhat arbitrary formation of states by means of previously compelled colonisation, often of incoherent origin, which have then claimed Westphalian sovereignty as a consequence of their existence as an administrative fact. That is, the absolutist claims of Westphalian sovereignty are often overstated, not least by more recently formed states that have a somewhat arbitrary originating basis.

However, the notion of sovereignty as functionally absolute authority vested in the monarch gave way, in practical terms, to increasing notions of power sharing under a system of rules or laws. Indeed, the notion of absolute authority had always been contested, with varying degrees of success, and was at many times and places not the preferred model of government, with councils of various types existing, for example the Indian *sahba*, Islamic caliphates (*shura*), England's pre-Norman *witenagamot*, and previous associated Nordic councils, as well as the English, French and Scottish parliaments and so on.

The importance of such councils or parliaments is that they required a system of laws demarcating areas of responsibility, available powers and rules of political, social and economic behaviour. In this respect, notions of sovereignty are dispersed through the defined agencies of the state, in particular the executive, the legislature and the judiciary (*trias politica*), on behalf of the citizens. Sovereignty is thus commonly understood in post-monarchical environments as being vested in the state's citizens. Citizens of a state can reasonably claim the protection of the state both from abuses by state institutions but also from harm from external actors, such as other states, including being attacked or captured by another state. It is at this point that territorial integrity makes sense, in that it provides a basic guarantee of the security of citizens.

However, when a state or the citizens of a state act in ways that infringe on the safety and security of other citizens, including citizens of another state, as with the purposes of conventional law as 'protection from', the state has a right to defend itself on behalf of its citizens. Moreover, should the state be unable to defend itself or should the state be the perpetrator of an attack against its own citizens, then a duty of care falls upon citizens elsewhere, as represented by their states, to act in concert with or on behalf of those under attack. Krasner (1999) makes a distinction between types of sovereignty in which, in the first instance, states have never had the type of sovereignty they sometimes attempt to claim, that notions of sovereignty have been substantially modified by the process of globalisation, that Westphalian sovereignty excluding others from the internal affairs of states is (or should be and has often been) provisional, and that international recognition of states should be accorded only to those that are functionally juridically independent. Juridical independence implies not just the reach of state laws to the extent of state territory but also the sometimes contested legitimacy of such laws and the method of their implementation. As a result, claims to absolute sovereignty can be contested by its internal definitions, in particular when states operate on the basis of political discord and suppression. In this, Krasner details the sometimes arbitrary process of state creation and the consequences of the colonial legacy by way of challenging sovereign claims (Krasner 1999: ch. 7), as noted.

Colonialism itself stands as a major obstacle to R2P, with criticisms that the direct intervention it implies is just colonialism, or imperialism, with a new face. As Orford notes, for R2P to be effective, its practitioners, particularly from the formerly colonial West, need to 'forget' this 'aberration' and renew it by focusing on its humanitarian, global and liberating qualities (Orford 2003: 45–7), as indeed external and internal intervention once more commonly had. Yet both this intervention and what might also be called 'internal colonisation' have continued as a blight upon peoples and a continuing source of discord, conflict and war. This was noted by the pro-independence movement in Ireland, among many others:

> We declare the right of the people of Ireland to the ownership of Ireland, and to the unfettered control of Irish destines, to be sovereign and indefensible . . . In every generation the Irish people have asserted their right to national freedom and sovereignty . . . Standing on that fundamental right . . . we hereby proclaim the Irish Republic as a sovereign independent state.
>
> (Sinn Fein 1916)

Importantly, then, states that claim sovereignty on the basis of colonial unity in one sense cause permanent colonial iniquity, in which sometimes quite divergent peoples are unilaterally united under the umbrella of a sovereign state (e.g. see MacQueen 2006: 182 regarding the sub-Saharan African model).

Following the splits between NATO and Russia, China and the Non-Aligned Movement and the re-ordering of the global political and strategic environment, the first signs of a doctrine of humanitarian intervention occurred in 1991 following operations by the United States and France to protect Kurds and Shi'ites in Iraq. The UN Security Council endorsement of pushing Iraq from Kuwait was an important step in R2P (under the guise of protection of sovereignty), but offered no provision for protection of Kurds or Shi'ites who had been encouraged to rebel against their Sunni Iraqi masters. In response, France pushed for Security Council Resolution 688, calling for Iraq to end the repression of its civilian population and to allow access by humanitarian organisations, although not the use of force.

As a result of the debate over this and similar issues, at the time of his leaving the office of the UN Secretary-General, Javier Perez De Cuellar said:

> I believe that the protection of human rights has now become one of the keystones in the arch of peace, I am convinced that it now involves more a concerted exertion of international influence and pressure through timely appeal, admonition, remonstrance or condemnation and, in the last resort, an appropriate United Nations presence, than what was regarded as permissible under international law . . . With the heightened international interest in

> universalizing a regime of human rights, there is a marked and most welcome shift in public attitudes. To try to resist it would be politically unwise as it is morally indefensible. It should be perceived as not so much a new departure as a more focused awareness of one of the requirements of peace.
>
> (Perez De Cuellar 1992: 7)

This was followed soon after by the succeeding UN Secretary-General Boutros Boutros-Ghali who also advocated an even stronger role for the UN in conflict resolution based on his commitment to human rights (Boutros-Ghali 1992), in effect permanently expanding the rules of peacekeeping. Yet this shift towards a greater global responsibility, and in particular conflict resolution by authorised local groupings, proved to be of mixed success: 'The optimism of the Secretary-General in the *Agenda for Peace* has proved to overestimate the role to be played by regional organisations and to underestimate the difficulties' (Gray 2004: 325).

Of the numerous humanitarian interventions of R2P that stand out, the those of Kosovo and Timor-Leste in 1999 are critical (e.g. see Orford 2003: 2). The two cases are different in that the former did not enjoy UN Security Council approval nor the agreement of the state in question (Serbia, or former Yugoslavia), while the latter, Timor-Leste, did enjoy the endorsement of the UN Security Council and was undertaken with the agreement of the nominal state then in question, Indonesia, if under a significant degree of compulsion. The critical element that brings them together, however, is their timing, both being in 1999 at a time when the notion of 'humanitarian intervention' was high, even while R2P was still in its infancy.

More importantly, however, was that the UN Security Council failed to reach agreement on the Kosovo issue, not because of debate about the severity of the situation but, very clearly, because of strategic infighting within the organisation. Given the breach of promise by Serbia, its failure to comply with UN Security Council resolutions and the unfolding humanitarian catastrophe, it was a *prima facie* case of where external intervention was warranted and available under international law, if without the formal endorsement of a Security Council, not over law but over narrow self-interest. In effect, as noted by Orford, the Kosovo intervention was less about pro-active but more about reactive international law; the challenge for the Security Council was not to endorse the intervention but rather, once it had taken place, to adopt a resolution terminating such action. In this, the 'burden of veto' was reversed (Orford 2003: 45).

As a result of these debates and the failure of the Security Council to follow its own criteria, '[t]he central rule on the use of force, the prohibition of the threat or use of force contained in Article 2(4) of the UN Charter, is currently the subject of fundamental disagreement' (Gray 2004: 29). This has particularly become the case following the rationale for and intervention in Kosovo (Gray 2004: 29). As with any complex document trying to address the full range of issues in a particular field, the UN Charter contains ambiguities and even contradictions. However, there is little doubt that, despite the underlying respect for territorial sovereignty and the general prohibition on the use of force, there are circumstances that seriously breach the higher order or peremptory commitment (*jus cogens*) to the protection of human rights (see Article 28 of the UN Charter, UN 1945) and international stability from which derogation is not permitted and which may require just force in order to suppress unjust force (*jus ad bellum*). As with all such matters, the preference for interpretation for or against the right to intervention depends on the perspective of the party concerned. If it is the party likely to be intervened in then there is a greater chance of opposition to an interpretation that allows intervention. Conversely, if the party is likely to be one that intervenes or agrees with intervention, then their interpretation will tend to be more inclusive of a range of options.

It can be argued that the meaning of the provisions of the Charter is fixed, which it may be claimed to be in legislation, if in somewhat internally contradictory terms. But not only does argument also run the other way – that its meaning is contingent – when there is sufficient agreement around its meaning then that will tend to prevail, regardless of the precision that might – or might not – have been intended. Notably, given the changes to other aspects on international law since the drafting of the Charter, it may be that the Charter increasingly needs to be read within context and not as a document that exists outside the further legal elaborations of what constitutes right and wrong in an international context. This would be a fairly conventional perspective if one assumed that the Charter had the same type of status as, say, a state constitution. Of course, one problem is that many do not accept that it does have such status and, indeed, some also argue that their own constitutions should be minimally interpreted (e.g. by 'Tea Party' republicans in the United States).

Illustrating that NATO's intervention in Bosnia was not an exclusive case, in discussing the issue of mass killings in Darfur, former US Secretary of State Madeleine Albright argued in favour of intervention:

> there would've been time to do something if the international community had seen itself as feeling that it could, in fact, do something about it. I do think we need to . . . Ultimately, it is political will. All of it is political will.
>
> (Albright 2010)

In making this observation, Albright was appealing to two qualities in international law, the first being that political will combined with capacity militates in favour of employing international law, in this case supported by a normative argument in favour of human rights and in opposition to crimes against humanity, including genocide or in support of international peace and security (UN 1945: VII). In particular, Article 41 clearly notes that the UN Security Council may 'decide what measures not involving the use of armed force are to be employed to give effect to its decisions', including the interruption of the economy of an offending state. Articles 42 and 43 go further, noting that, if the provisions of Article 41 prove inadequate, the Security Council may employ armed forces 'for the purpose of maintaining international peace and stability'. Further articles outline how such employment of armed force should be coordinated.

Pre-dating the formal introduction of R2P, a nuanced version was that of international intervention in Timor-Leste in 1999. The situation in Timor-Leste was that, after 24 years of invasion and occupation by Indonesia, never recognised by the UN, and in which about a quarter of the population was killed or died as a direct consequence, the people of Timor-Leste were offered the opportunity to vote on whether they wished to remain as a part of Indonesia or to opt for independence. As a part of the agreement, Indonesia was to provide security for the ballot. Set against a backdrop of increasingly brutal violence and intimidation by the Indonesian army and their proxy militias, the people of Timor-Leste voted overwhelmingly for independence, in return for which the already high level of violence exploded. Within a few weeks, a third of the population had been forced at gunpoint across the border to West Timor and more into the mountains, around three-quarters of all infrastructure was destroyed and at least 1,500 people were murdered. In this case, outrage internationally, but in particular within Australia, meant that, despite it being contrary to strongly held Australian government policy towards Indonesia, a 'humanitarian intervention' was all but inevitable (see McDougal and Edney 2010: 214–16). In the end, the UN Security Council agreed to sponsor the intervention and the Indonesian government, under threat of losing international financial support from the International Monetary Fund at a time of desperate economic need, acceded to the intervention. The UN's Resolution 1264, which authorised the deployment of the Australian-led International Force in East Timor (Interfet) ahead of the deployment of a similarly constructed UN peacekeeping force, was later authorised under the provisions of Chapter VII.

Formally, the Timor-Leste case met all the legal conditions of R2P whereas, without UN Security Council endorsement or Serbian government agreement, the Kosovo case did not. However, both situations were clearly based on humanitarian principles and notions of global responsibility. It also seems clear that, had the Security Council not agreed to sponsor the Timor-Leste intervention, or if Indonesia had not reluctantly accepted the international intervention, it is quite possible and arguably probable that, parallel to the intervention in Kosovo, with US backing, Australia would have led a smaller coalition of forces into Timor-Leste in any case, again reversing the 'burden of veto'.

There was a widespread acceptance of what morality required in the case of Timor-Leste, with all members of the Security Council agreeing to endorse action. However, NATO's intervention in Serbia over Kosovo at around the same time was much more contested, principally because of its strategic significance and historical alliances, in particular with Russia. It could be reasonably argued that if morality required intervention in Timor-Leste then it equally required intervention over Kosovo. However, the distinction between the two rested on Security Council approval or lack of it and, hence, the formal status of the intervention under international law. 'There seems to be a widening consensus', according to Buchanan (2003: 131), 'that there is an unacceptable gap between what international law allows and what morality requires'. That is, variably applied international law as the sole source of authority for external intervention in turn raises the question of its legitimacy. However, both interventions, along with others, increased:

> the perception of international law has changed. In the twenty-first century, it has become professionally respectable for practitioners of both domestic and international law, when asked if a proposed course of action is lawful, to reply that, well, sometimes it is, sometimes it isn't, and sometimes it both is and isn't. A lot depends on the specific context in which the act occurs.
>
> (Franck 2003: 204)

That is, the law is what enough (strong) states say it is, in general compliance with the intentions of if not the source of authority for such law.

If R2P requires broad international support, if not explicit UN Security Council endorsement, to legitimise its actions, then the Bosnia-Herzegovina situation arguably stands as a case in point of Albright's dictum about political will. In this situation, the United States, Russia, the United Kingdom, France, Germany and Italy combined, under the name the 'Contact Group,'[3] to apply pressure to Serbia, Bosnia and Croatia to find a resolution to the Bosnian war. A NATO-led Implementation Force guaranteed the 1995 Dayton agreement to end the war in Bosnia, following which various groups of other states combined to assist with its implementation (Orford 2003: 129–34). Although this grouping of states can be said to constitute most of the UN Security Council and was otherwise, as Orford noted, a re-representation of the earlier 'Great Powers',[4] it did show that legitimacy, which has the same etymological root as 'law', could be derived from sufficient international agreement outside the formal confines of the UN. In a blending of realpolitik and idealism, international law was effectively written by an agreement for action. Even though the Security Council might have retained the 'burden of veto', with most of its permanent members represented in the Contact Group, such a veto would, somewhat absurdly, itself have faced a veto.

Although this situation could be considered as constituting part of the growing canon of international law, it did so by establishing a precedent, in much the same way that NATO's attacks on Serbia four years later extended that precedent. It is possible to argue that these interventions did not constitute, or make, international law. But if law is the codification of norms accepted by a community, in this case the international community, then it could be argued that these two interventions went a considerable way towards establishing new parameters and indeed precedent for international law (as well as increasingly basing its function on common law principles).

Notably, the UN Charter's Article 53 notes that regional forces can be employed against another state if they have the approval of the Security Council to do so. Examples of this include the deployment of Commonwealth of Independent States (CIS) forces in Abkhazia and Georgia, the Organisation for African Unity in Sierra Leone and NATO in Kosovo. Article 53 states that: 'The Security Council shall, where appropriate, utilize such regional arrangements or agencies for enforcement action under its authority.' This reference to 'enforcement action', then, allows fairly wide scope for interpretation and has been increasingly argued to imply decisions by the Security Council to re-establish 'international peace and stability'. What constitutes 'international peace and stability' may be argued to be not just the absence of international war but also the securing and maintenance of law and order within a state, on the grounds that its internal problems have the potential to spill across borders, or that they are a constituent part of the international community. It could even be argued, assuming that the most stable state is that which has the most accountable government, that the (re)-establishment of an accountable and representative, that is, democratic, political framework could be grounds for 'enforcement action' under Article 53. Its involvement in the direct internal politics of states can be seen, for example, in Libya in 2005, Côte d'Ivoire in 2006, the Central African Republic in 2007 with a military component in 2009 and the Côte d'Ivoire again in 2010–11.

It can be argued that the sovereignty that is claimed by states as absolute has never, historically, been that. The purity of the principle put by some, very often for narrow defined self-serving reasons, has rarely, if ever, existed in fact. Some states have had greater capacity to protect (or extend) their borders or to impose their will. But the nominal claim of states to entirely be a law unto themselves without regard for international norms or conventions, such as that by Sri Lanka, reflects a blinkered reading of the UN Charter and a complete ignorance of global political history. As noted by Glennon (2001: 149): 'International law as it has evolved thus deals with the incidents or attributes of *theoretical* sovereignty – not sovereignty as it has actually existed in the reality of day-to-day state practice'. At best, there is a very significant gap between theory and practice, but more accurately it can be read that there has sometimes been a wilful misreading of the theory in support of particular self-interested claims, much less a misreading of international law. Abiew suggests that Articles 52 and 53 demonstrate a legitimate basis for humanitarian intervention (Abiew 1999: 208), notably through the evolution of the theory and practice of the doctrine and in particular in the post-Cold War era (Abiew 1999: 228–58). He further argues that sovereignty is not incompatible with humanitarian intervention (Abiew 1999: 264) and that where human rights violations occur on a massive scale, either because of government action or internal conflict, then intervention is justified to protect those rights on the grounds that sovereignty as such has ceased to properly exist on a functional or humanitarian basis.

As Bellamy (2010) has noted, NATO's involvement in Kosovo was the watershed moment for both humanitarian intervention and the notion of sovereignty. It marked the advent of the idea that sovereignty had meaning only if it was on behalf of the interests and in fulfilment of the state's responsibility to protect its own citizens. Bellamy quoted former UN Secretary-General Kofi Annan as saying: '[S]tate sovereignty, in its most basic sense, is being redefined . . . States are now widely understood to be instruments at the service of their peoples, and not vice versa' (Bellamy 2010: 39). Annan went on to note that sovereignty also applied to individuals – the sovereign (physical) integrity of the person – and that it was the aim of the UN Charter to protect them rather than those who abuse them. As Bellamy further discusses, this then implies that states have responsibilities as well as rights, and that asserting one without due regard for the other is no longer tenable (Bellamy 2010: 39–40). The intervention in Kosovo reflected the fact that 'Western leaders decided that the protection of human rights outweighed the traditional importance attached to notions of sovereignty' (Ker-Lindsay 2010: 168). Extrapolating from that, he said that: 'in essence their positions can be reduced to an apparent contradiction in international law between the fundamental rights to self-determination and the principle of the territorial integrity of states' (Ker-Lindsay 2010: 169). Self-determination may be the driver for separatist conflict, which may in turn produce serious human rights abuses, or it may follow the perpetration of such abuses. But the default position of most states, other than those with a specific strategic or economic interest, is to endorse the status quo that reflects their territorial integrity. This is generally seen as the lowest risk strategy, endorses the principle of state sovereignty that all states claim, and conforms to the time-honored if increasingly tested realpolitik principles that the internal affairs of states are not the subject of external concern.

Insofar as this shift in the meaning of sovereignty applied to Serbia and Kosovo, it meant that Serbia was not entitled to abuse people (the Kosovars) it claimed as citizens. Despite strong opposition, in particular from Russia, NATO attacked Serbia, directly contravening Article 2(4) of the UN Charter but establishing a first-order regard for the UN's various human rights instruments. In that there has been argued to be a tension, or contradiction, between sovereignty and a minimum regard for human rights, Bellamy has proposed that these are in fact two sides of the same coin; that a failure of the state to protect its citizens constitutes a diminution of its sovereignty (Bellamy 2010: 51–7). *Ipso facto*, if sovereignty is diminished or disappears, then the illegality of intervention in the affairs of such a state is, in line with the status of its sovereignty, similarly diminished or disappears.

Indicating the shift away from claims of absolute sovereignty generally and their compromise by human rights considerations in particular, the Polish foreign minister, Bronislaw Geremek, said, in relation to NATO's intervention in Serbia over Kosovo, that: 'In the 21st century human rights will be the fundamental basis for defining international relations. Relations between nations can no longer be founded on respect for sovereignty – they must be founded on respect for human rights' (Gellman 1999). Despite some tensions between NATO partners and misgivings about the ultimate success of the Kosovo campaign, the Canadian prime minister, Jean Chretien, identified its purpose when he said: 'Right now in the heart of Europe, NATO is fighting for the cause of humanity' (Gellman 1999). Among the other leaders in favour of the intervention, Iceland's foreign minister, Halldor Asgrimsson, said: 'Indifference in the face of the atrocities would make us accessories to [Yugoslav president Slobodan] Milosevic's crimes of attempted genocide'. Identifying the critical central issue, he asked rhetorically: 'Haven't we yet learned the lessons of Auschwitz and Buchenwald?' (Gellman 1999). The moral compulsion of the issue, along with a capacity to prosecute it, and the will to do so, ultimately decided NATO in favour of intervention and led to the outcomes it was intended to achieve, in the first instance a cessation of Serbian slaughter in Kosovo and, eventually, the establishment of Kosovo as an independent state. However, a number of the states involved in the campaign remained uncomfortable about a ground presence in Kosovo and similarly would have liked the endorsement of the UN Security Council, even if retrospectively, to give formal legitimacy to their actions.

Especially in light of the Kosovo campaign, the increasing willingness of the international community to employ varying degrees of force or compulsion has meant that 'The events of the present decade have revealed international law to be an ambiguous force with respect to the distribution of security in global governance' (Sandvik 2010: 110). This 'ambiguity' that has arisen in the application of international law has reflected 'the move towards humanization [which] represents an important thematic reorientation', and '[t]his development also constitutes a significant shift in *how* and *through which sites* security is to be allocated' (Sandvik 2010: 113, emphasis in original).

Sri Lanka has long responded to any query, much less criticism, of its policies towards its ethnic Tamils by falling back on the 'absolute sovereignty' argument. In doing this, it has ignored the increasing international view that sovereignty is 'an insufficient excuse for maintaining an impenetrable barrier between victims and an effective humanitarian response' (Rice and Loomis 2007: 92). Not only have 'the tools that national governments had to address these concerns matured . . . they grew accustomed to using all the tools in their tool boxes' (Rice and Loomis 2007: 92). Sovereignty is thus not a sacrosanct privilege but an accountable responsibility. If it fails, then the burden of responsibility does not disappear but moves elsewhere.

As the first, and most inoffensive, 'tool' to come out of the 'international toolbox' following calls from the UN High Commissioner for Human Rights for an investigation into war crimes in Sri Lanka, the UN Secretary-General appointed a panel of experts to advise him on what had happened and was happening in Sri Lanka. Russia and China failed in their attempts to keep the subject of Sri Lanka off the agenda of the Security Council, but demanded a private briefing from the UN Secretary-General ahead of his visit to Sri Lanka in mid-2009.

In the case of the UN and Sri Lanka, it was determined that it was necessary to conduct an investigation into events during, especially towards the end of, and following the war by the Sri Lankan government against the Tamil Tigers. Despite trenchant criticism from Sri Lanka that the establishment of such a panel infringed on its sovereignty (e.g. see Botejue 2010), UN Secretary-General Ban Ki-moon said: 'I am convinced that it is well within my power as Secretary-General of the United Nations to ask such a body to furnish me with their advice of this nature. This does not in any way infringe on the sovereignty of Sri Lanka' (Reddy 2010). Mr Ban told journalists that the establishment of the panel was in line with a joint statement he issued with Sri Lankan president Mahinda Rajapaksa during his visit to the country the previous May after government forces defeated the LTTE (UN 2010).

Interestingly, although the Sri Lankan government portrayed the UN Secretary-General as intervening in its sovereign affairs, the head of his panel of inquiry, Ban's chief of staff, Vijay Nambiar, an Indian national, was also the principle diplomat who argued against Indian intervention in Sri Lanka during the final phase of the assault on the Tamil Tigers. Nambiar's opposition to India's intervention prevailed, directly leading to the perpetration of war crimes and the mass civilian deaths towards the end of the war. That is, if the UN was intent on being seen to take responsibility for investigating gross human rights violations in Sri Lanka without actually doing anything about it, then the appointment of Nambiar would seem to be entirely appropriate. Despite this, in response to government-led disruptions of UN activities in Sri Lanka, in mid-2010 the UN Secretary-General Ban Ki-moon recalled the UN Resident Coordinator and closed down its UN Development Program centre in Colombo (UNSG 2010). There was clearly some tension at work here, with perhaps the appointment of Nambiar wanting to be seen as a conciliatory gesture.

Having established a precedent, if in the opposite direction to that which prevailed in Sri Lanka, NATO's intervention in Kosovo continues to stand as the preeminent example of the contradiction, in international law, between what is legal and what is right. On one hand this intervention diminished the Security Council's authority to determine the circumstances that could allow international intervention. It also failed to comply with the other criteria for military intervention: the right of an individual or a collective to respond to armed attack. On the other hand, the Security Council's failure to act in its own right was self-diminishing, showing that the competing interests of the Security Council's permanent members was its greatest shortcoming and that which compromised its legitimacy in the eyes of the world, in particular among those people of states requiring intervention or among those states feeling compelled to provide such intervention. It was out of this dilemma that then UN Secretary-General, Kofi Annan, announced that it was the:

> core challenge to the Security Council and to the United Nations as a whole in the next century [is] . . . to forge unity behind the principle that massive and systematic violations of human rights – wherever they take place – should not be allowed to stand.
>
> (Annan 1999)

It was a grand statement that, like all words that lack action to back them (if admittedly after his time), rang hollow, if not cheap. Fine rhetoric from powerful people matters only if they back it with action.

Although not constituting law, Annan's words highlighted the ways in which understandings of what is acceptable, what is legal and what ultimately constitutes law change. 'As we seek new ways to combat the ancient enemies of war and poverty, we will succeed only if we adapt our Organisation to a world with new actors, *new responsibilities*, and new possibilities for peace and progress' (Annan 1999, emphasis added). Again, these were fine sentiments, no doubt sincerely intended. But as the occupant of an office, and not as an individual, the implied institutional responsibility was not fulfilled.

The issue that Annan raised in light of the Security Council's failure and NATO's intervention in Kosovo was that the global community increasingly accepted that it did have 'new responsibilities' and that, implicitly, it had failed to act on those responsibilities, thus opening the way for a regional community to effectively supplant the UN at times of crisis. It was Annan's intention, as a consequence, that the UN rise to, and address, this challenge.

In large part, Annan's recognition of this challenge highlights both the limitations and the dynamism of law, in particular international law, and the debates that occur in relation to legal interpretation (see Carvin 2008). There are, broadly, two schools of thought regarding law: one that law is made by law makers and should be applied in a literal and narrowly defined sense, and on the other that law is open to interpretation and should be applied according to context and changing values. The more formalistic argument in international law tends to arise among supporters of a 'realist' school of international relations theory, in that they believe that law has little place in international affairs, which is essentially a contest of self-interest, and should be limited to such in its application. From an ideological perspective, this view is also linked to opposing notions of 'world government' and various conspiracies, which argue that such a move is intended to limit individual freedom.

An 'idealist' perspective, on the other hand, suggests that not only should there be laws for the governing of the actions of the international community but also the extent of this law should be increased and more flexibly adapted to particular circumstances. Notably, this view has it that the lack of law between states allows for the continuation of abuses that actually limit personal freedom. Conversely, the introduction, extension and more open interpretation of such laws implies not global domination by a single entity (much less a conspiracy to this end), but an agreed system of mutual guarantees of protection.

In large part, the debate is not about law as such, but about a confusion of categories. The argument against greater international law, and presumably the intervention that it could imply, derives from a concern with government interference in and limitations upon the affairs of individuals, the inefficiency and self-serving nature of bureaucratisation, and the unnecessary cost of, ultimately, a job poorly done. There is some legitimacy in this argument, especially around the inefficient, inflexible and self-serving nature of bureaucracies in general and the UN in particular. However, law does not necessarily imply bureaucracy, apart from its immediate administration, much less the types of problems believed to arise with greater global governance.

More importantly, though, law – including international law – is not just intended to standardise practices between states, such as over the resolution of boundary disputes or contractual matters. It is to limit or contain harm to oneself or to others by parties that act in ways that take unfair advantage of their strength, circumstances or some other material advantage. In this respect, the purpose of law is to prevent injustice and to enhance freedom. This common interpretation of the purpose of law has special meaning if the custodian of the legal process, be it the sovereign state or some other body, operates on the basis that people are not subservient to it but that it is subservient to and an expression of their will. Just as state law provides 'rules for' and 'protection from', so too international law normatively functions in the same manner. Because international law may fail to formally provide 'rules for' and 'protection from', there is then a claim under natural law that the community (of states) has an obligation to adjudicate. Because the highest international body, the UN, and in particular its Security Council, sometimes fails to act through lack of internal agreement and especially when that disagreement is predicated not upon interpretations of law or other matters of principle but on issues of strategic interest then, assuming appropriate deliberation, there are grounds for regional groupings of states to act in concert to assume this abrogated responsibility and to intervene in the affairs of another regional state. This has led to the view that:

> Many are uneasy about the recognition of a new norm allowing for unilateral humanitarian intervention because of its potential for abuse, yet want to allow for situations in which collective action without Security Council authorisation is permissible, particularly in the light of the Kosovo precedent. Thus they adopt a natural law argument, suggesting there are situations in which the international community must act outside *positive* law, in ways that are nevertheless legitimate because of the demands of morality and justice.
>
> (Orford 2003: 44, emphasis in original)

Apart from the obvious example of NATO's attack on Serbia, the 2003 war in Iraq is perhaps the most notable example of a coalition of states going to war without Security Council endorsement. The 'Coalition of the Willing', led by the United States and including 48 other states,[5] invaded Iraq in March 2003. The 'Coalition of the Willing' was constructed under the rationale of ridding Iraq of weapons of mass destruction, following what was argued to be the failure of Iraq to comply with Security Council Resolution 1441. Resolution 1441 gave Iraq a 'final opportunity to comply with its disarmament obligations' as set out in a series of previous resolutions and was predicated on the position that Iraq was allegedly and probably in breach of the terms of its ceasefire concerning the acquisition of particular types of weapons and its failure to compensate Kuwait following its invasion in 1991.

The situation of Iraq's status was compounded by its limited willingness to comply with weapons inspections and later its cancellation of those inspections, and by it providing inaccurate information about its weapons status. To add to this, the United States further outlined Iraq's breaches of international law, including allegedly harbouring a terrorist organisation, 'extremely grave' human rights violations, and the use of funds from oil sales to purchase weapons rather than food. Despite Iraq saying that it would comply with Security Council requirements, the Security Council did not accept its sincerity, with Resolution 1441 being passed unanimously.

There was then debate about whether Resolution 1441 created the legal conditions – a 'hidden trigger' – for going to war with Iraq. Although some political leaders argued that this was the case, the Security Council, including US and UK representatives, did not accept that this was so. The Security Council was adamant that any use of force in relation to Iraq would have to be referred back to the Security Council for further agreement. Fuel was added to this debate with reports from UN weapons inspectors Hans Blix and Mohamad Al Baradei stating that Iraq could not adequately explain how it had 'misplaced' 1,000 tonnes of a deadly nerve gas or whether it had destroyed the potentially deadly bacterial agent anthrax.

The United States then used this finding, along with its own 'intelligence' reports, to launch the invasion of Iraq. Most importantly, it did so not just without the support of the Security Council but against Iraq's opposition to the invasion, thus invalidating one aspect of an 'ideal' R2P context. Had the United States been able to demonstrate that its grounds for the invasion were founded, it might then at least have had the opportunity to present a case justifying the invasion under the terms of Resolution 1441. Had this been established, despite the invasion being in breach of formal international law, a defence could have been mounted on the grounds of self-defence, global stability and natural justice. However, this was not to be the case, with the UN Secretary-General, Kofi Anan, stating bluntly that the invasion was 'not in conformity with the UN Charter from our point of view, from the charter point of view, it was illegal' (BBC 2004). In short, the US-led invasion of Iraq pretended to have an R2P fig leaf of modesty, but in fact even this did not exist.

The US Iraq Survey Group (ISG), established to determine whether weapons of mass destruction had existed at the time of the invasion, stated that they believed that Iraq would resume production of weapons of mass destruction if the opportunity arose. This was supposing inferred intent, which is not usually accorded legal status. It is, though, accorded strategic status. However, and more importantly, the group stated that:

> While a small number of old, abandoned chemical munitions have been discovered, ISG judges that Iraq unilaterally destroyed its undeclared chemical weapons stockpile in 1991. There are no credible indications that Baghdad resumed production of chemical munitions thereafter, a policy ISG attributes to Baghdad's desire to see sanctions lifted, or rendered ineffectual, or its fear of force against it should WMD (Weapons of Mass Destruction) be discovered.
>
> (ISG 2004)

The importance of the Iraq invasion was that it constituted a clear breach of international law as such law is commonly agreed. Although the ICC was unlikely to pursue this line, there have been allegations that the invasion of Iraq and its consequences, including the deaths and serious maiming of untold numbers of people,[6] constituted war crimes and crimes against humanity. Regardless of the success or otherwise of any such ICC investigation or prosecution, there is no doubt that the invasion of Iraq significantly strengthened the argument against international intervention.

The subsequent arguments rationalising the Iraq invasion, that Saddam Hussein abused human rights, that he was a dictator, that he brutalised his own people and attacked neighbours, can all be held to be true of many other countries. Yet these have not been subjected to such invasion. A number of possible options have been put forward as the reasons behind the invasion of Iraq, not least being to control a significant proportion of the world's oil supplies, as an assertion of the 'Bush doctrine', interpreted as US global hegemony, and as 'unfinished business' for US president George W. Bush following the US-led war against Iraq prosecuted by his father, President George H. W. Bush, in 1991. But the result has been, because non-Security Council-sanctioned invasion on legal grounds could have been established, the Iraq invasion all but demolished the proposition that it was a legal, internationally sanctioned use of force.

This is not to say that there are not legal grounds for regional or unilateral action against states beyond those authorised by the Security Council. The Vietnamese invasion of Cambodia in 1978, although strongly criticised at the time, has increasingly looked more palatable with the benefit of hindsight. But it is to say, post Iraq, that the international opprobrium resulting from further invasion would be significant and may in turn lead to Security Council sanctions against the actor, assuming it was not a Security Council member with the power of boycott over such a retaliatory action.

Any unilateral intervention, then, would have to be undertaken either by a permanent Security Council member (e.g. Russia's intervention in trans-Caucasian conflicts) or, more palatably, by a regional grouping with some international credibility (e.g. NATO in Serbia). What this means for Sri Lanka is that, short of the Security Council endorsing intervention, which seems unlikely given Sri Lanka's increasingly close relationship with permanent Security Council member China, there would need to be a coalition of regional states in agreement about the status of their collective regional security and/or grievous human rights concerns. No such coalition is likely to be formed, given that neighbouring states are themselves often in disagreement and separately strategically aligned. Nor is India, as the regional power, likely to act independently, given its previous experience in Sri Lanka and its geo-strategic interest in maintaining reasonable relations with the government of Sri Lanka.

Moreover, on the scale of humanitarian concern, as serious as Sri Lanka's human rights abuses have been and in many respects continue to be, they do not represent a threat to regional order and stability. Unless Sri Lanka were to turn 'feral' and become a direct threat to its neighbours, for example as a base to a hostile power, its strategic significance at the crossroads of the Indian Ocean, along with its physical isolation, count, on one hand, for not creating a potentially more unstable environment and, on the other hand, for not caring much what actually happens within Sri Lanka while it remains contained.

6 Opposition to R2P

There are compelling moral and practical arguments in favour of R2P, which is why the idea was endorsed by the UN General Assembly in 2005 and the Security Council in 2006, and by actors as varied as the Non-Aligned Movement and UN US Ambassador John Bolton (Weiss 2006: 745). Of 192 possible UN member states, 191 endorsed the proposal. However, despite this near absolute endorsement, in a somewhat contradictory manner, many states have since not accepted it as a principle, much less a practice, and in particular do not accept its premise that state sovereignty is not absolute and sacrosanct. 'One doesn't have to spend too much time in the UN corridors, or in some Asian capitals in particular', according to Gareth Evans, 'before hearing expressions of regret, or even denial, that so far-reaching a doctrine could possibly have been agreed by national leaders' (Evans 2007a: 2).

There have broadly been four categories of reasons why R2P has been objected to. They include that it violates national sovereignty, that it may cause more harm than it resolves, that it relies on a self-interested UN Security Council and that it imposes neo-imperialist agendas. Sri Lanka strenuously rejected the idea of R2P, along with its related rejection of other international instruments, and has similarly strenuously endorsed the notion of the absolute inviolability of state sovereignty. It has also claimed that calls for R2P and other forms of intervention reflect neo-imperialist agendas.

Although global realpolitik rarely turns on moral considerations, and noting that views change in response to changing values and circumstances, the reluctance of the global community to embrace external intervention is long-standing and predicated on the intersection between practical sovereign considerations and the methods employed by some states in attempting to resolve internal political issues. This position was articulated as early as the 1965 Declaration on the Inadmissibility of Intervention and Interference in the Internal Affairs of State (reaffirmed in 1981). According to a statement by the UN General Assembly: '(n) o State or group of States has the right to intervene, in any form or for any reason whatsoever, directly or indirectly, in the internal or external affairs of any state' (UNGA 1965; see also UNGA 1981). Continuing this consistent theme within the UN was the 1993 review of the Declaration on the Strengthening of International Security, in which the UN General Assembly again reinforced the necessity to 'refrain from the use or threat of use of force, aggression, intervention, interference' (UNGA 1993).

According to Glennon:

> The Assembly has thus construed the Charter as imposing a rule of *per se* invalidity with respect to intervention. The rule admits of no exception: Intervention is always unlawful, regardless of the identity of the state undertaking the intervention, and regardless of the motive or effects. The Charter's prohibition applies to individual states as well as to states acting in coalitions, including military alliances such as NATO and even the Security Council and General Assembly.
>
> (Glennon 2001: 21)

Glennon also noted that NATO's intervention over Kosovo was in violation of NATO's own charter (Glennon 2001: 21).

Opposition to R2P began almost immediately following its establishment, both in discussion about its principles and in rather more agitated discussion about its potential actions. No sooner had the UN Secretary-General appointed Edward Luck as Special Adviser on the responsibility to protect than a number of states, principally from Latin America, Africa and the Middle East, claimed during the UN Budget Committee session in 2008 that 'the concept of responsibility to protect has not been adopted by the General Assembly' (UNGA 2008). Rather than fight an unproductive and possibly unwinnable battle, which would have seen R2P diminished or removed, the Secretary-General instead added to the title of Francis Deng that of 'Special Adviser on the Prevention of Genocide and Mass Atrocities', by way of circumventing specific concern over the terminology of R2P. From this time it became clear that many states intended to undermine or obstruct the establishment of R2P. In some cases these states objected to R2P on grounds of neo-colonialism or neo-imperialism, although this was all too often a blind for their real concern that they could become subject to R2P's provisions. Even humanitarian Noam Chomsky (2008), among others, has criticised R2P on the grounds of it constituting 'humanitarian imperialism'. However, during a talk a year later, he also said that the West was interested only in protecting people when it gave a strategic or economic advantage, and that the failure to intervene in Sri Lanka reflected this lack of advantage. 'There was plenty of early warning. This [conflict] has been going on for years and decades', Chomsky said, answering a question on Sri Lanka following a talk on R2P at the UN. 'Plenty of things could have been done [to prevent it]. But there was not enough interest' (Chomsky 2009a). Chomsky said, 'there is no protection for any people who it doesn't do any good [to the West] to protect, and basically Sri Lankans are in that unfortunate position' (Chomsky 2009b).

A key criticism of R2P, employed in varying guises, is that overall it allows the legitimisation of some forms of international violence, such as Western counter-insurgency or anti-terrorism, in some states while criminalising genocide – widely interpreted – in other states. The argument here is that the legal distinction of stated or implied intent is a blind for acts that have a substantively similar outcome, this being the deaths of non-combatants, and that the notion of legitimate external intervention employs the same logic that rationalised colonialism (Mamdani 2010).

In decrying the global imbalance of power and R2P's requirement that it not produce more harm than it resolves, objections were also raised on the grounds that it is a tool to be used only against weak or vulnerable states, and not against larger and powerful states. Although this criticism fails on the criterion of the core principle of R2P, it does have some validity when considered in light of the 'Blair Doctrine' (Blair 1999). In this, there was required to be a high likelihood of success for an intervention to be undertaken (see also ICISS 2001: 4.41, 4.42). As Evans noted, despite its universal applicability, 'there will be some countries for whom such measures will never be a practical option – [this is a] a fact of life' (Evans 2008: 64). By way of illustration, some states may engage in practices that could qualify them as subjects of R2P, but either the states are relatively powerful and able to resist such intervention or they enjoy the support of more powerful states that could assist their resistance to such intervention.

Concern over R2P also followed memories of other interventions, which did not always or even often occur with altruistic motives. Such interventions include the more covert operations of the CIA in Iran in 1953 and Guatemala in 1954, that of the United States in Vietnam from the late 1950s (notably from 1965) and those of the United Kingdom and France in Egypt in 1956. In some cases, 'invitations' by unpopular or puppet governments have paved the way for invasion, such as by the Soviet Union in Hungary in 1956 and Czechoslovakia in 1968, by Indonesia in Timor-Leste in 1975[1] and by the Soviet Union in Afghanistan in 1978. 'The potential for facilitating hegemonic interventions by regional powers, particularly for maintaining docile, collaborative governments, is one cause for concern about a view of Chapter VIII [of the UN Charter] that allows for military coercion without prior Security Council authorization' (Farer 203: 73). This is not to mention the activities of client states of great powers, notably the United States, the USSR and China, in intervening in the affairs of neighbouring or other states. The United States has rationalised unauthorised interventions in Grenada, Panama and the states of Central America as justified by humanitarian concerns, along with Security Council-authorised interventions in Kuwait/Iraq, Somalia and Haiti. In short, external intervention has very often had a negative connotation, regardless of the rationale presented for it at the time.

Criticism of the R2P principle was, as noted, again given a boost with the 2003 invasion of Iraq. Although R2P was not cited as a reason for the invasion, following the failure of the United States and its allies to find evidence to support claims of Iraq's possession of 'weapons of mass destruction' or links to the terrorist organisation Al Qaeda, the R2P principle was later rolled out by UK prime minister Tony Blair as its justification. Disturbingly for advocates of R2P, Blair even linked the rationale for intervention in Kosovo to the invasion of Iraq (Blair 2010: 374, 399), where the case for the former was compelling in terms of evidence of war crimes and arguably genocide being committed but the case of the latter was predicated upon unsubstantiated claims of 'weapons of mass destruction'. Blair later attempted to justify his support for the Iraq invasion, saying that the issue of weapons of mass destruction was only one of many – precisely 22 according to Blair, referencing Stan Rosenthal – reasons for going to war (Blair 2007). However, despite Iraqi leader Saddam Hussein at different times qualifying his state for R2P intervention, such as the massacres of Kurds and Shia Muslims, R2P or something like it was not invoked at that time.

In all, the Iraq invasion and the inaccuracy of its rationale seriously damaged the idea that countries could intervene in the affairs of others for necessary altruistic reasons. Critics of R2P from the right argued against R2P's multilateralism and its assumption that there is a sense of international responsibility while critics from the left argued that it was but another form of neo-imperialism or a blind for other agendas (in the case of Iraq, securing oil supplies).

As discussed, Iraq had previously met the criteria for R2P under the leadership of Saddam Hussein, but this was not the rationale employed for its invasion in 2003. Had it been, it could equally have applied to a number of other regimes that have to date escaped such imposition. Similarly, the 1994 US invasion of Haiti, nominally in 'defence of democracy', was a normative but highly selective rationale for intervention that has not been, moreover, applied elsewhere. The promotion of democracy has since been cited as a key factor in what has become known as the 'Bush Doctrine' (e.g. see Monten 2005), although this reference more properly applies to the 2002 US National Security Strategy (Bush 2002: 21–3). Yet such democratic outcomes that did eventuate could, at best, be claimed to be no more than procedural, in the cases of both Iraq and Afghanistan simply providing a veneer of electoral legitimacy to pre-existing warlords and power brokers.

The Bush Doctrine, as it has been applied to the Iraq intervention, and some others, has been characterised as implying the legitimacy of unilateral pre-emptive war. This unilateralism was celebrated by President Bush, who said that 'The United States welcomes our responsibility to lead in this great mission', although without identifying the source of legitimacy of such 'leadership' (Bush 2002). This was intended to apply in cases in which there was a likely or potential attack against the United States, although the invasion of Iraq could not be justified on such grounds. In practice, this doctrine of unilateral pre-emption is conceded by the United States as being allowed for some states, such as Israel and India, but not others, such as Iran. In this, there is no equity in the application of the principle, nor upon closer examination is there a principle at all. Rather, there is simply a practice that is applied if and when it suits a hegemonic power or one of its strategic allies. Moreover, unilateral pre-emption precludes recourse to institutions such as the UN and the plurality of views and concerns that implies.

Specifically in relation to Sri Lanka, opposition to R2P being applied in Sri Lanka also came from legal academic Mary Ellen O'Connell, who at the height of the Sri Lankan army attacks on the remnants of the LTTE and the civilians with them proposed instead a ceasefire, which the government had already rejected. O'Connell cited calls for R2P in Burma following Cyclone Nargis in 2008, saying 'cooler heads prevailed and the junta was persuaded to allow aid to flow – presumably following firm assurances that there would be no military intervention. With the cooperation of the Burmese government, the humanitarian response is considered a major success' (O'Connell 2009). In fact, however, R2P was not an option in Burma because of Chinese opposition, while foreign assistance was rejected (CNN 2008). Much aid was turned back and such aid that did eventually get in was poorly distributed and the overall relief effort was widely considered a disaster, with the government hampering relief efforts and not distributing aid properly, with the military stealing aid and other aid ending up on the black market. The situation was so bad that one group even said it amounted to genocide (Ogden 2008). O'Connell went on to say that 'Classic mediation is exactly what is needed now in Sri Lanka. Reaching an effective cease-fire and then sending in UN peacekeepers, following classic peacekeeping doctrine, has a history of success. Reaching a true and effective ceasefire will not be easy' (O'Connell 2009). Yet Sri Lanka had explicitly rejected 'classic mediation', claiming that it was unwanted interference in sovereign affairs; the 'effective ceasefire' that had existed had been abandoned by the government and there was no scope for peacekeepers to be sent in with the agreement of the Sri Lankan government. O'Connell was correct, however, in her understated observation that 'Reaching a true and effective ceasefire will not be easy'. This view, as with so many opposed to R2P that did not reflect a direct interest, tended to reflect a broader ideological opposition to multilateralism, whatever its circumstances, reconstructing facts to diminish the issue at hand. In short, O'Connell got it wrong.

A further aspect of opposition to R2P rests on the assertion that it does, or can do, more harm than good. This is particularly so of the humanitarian intervention, or military engagement, aspect of R2P. In citing the 'Doctrine of Double Effect', Quinn (1989) argues that the ends of R2P do not justify the means, especially if a humanitarian outcome means targeting innocent civilians in the process. This essentially means that unintended bad consequences are acceptable but intended bad consequences are not. Quinn argues that 'bad consequences' are acceptable if they are unintended or 'merely foreseen' and only 'less acceptable' if they are intentional (Quinn 1989: 335). For anyone concerned with notions of humanitarian intervention, this proposition at best casts into doubt the overall good of such intervention, weighing as it does the benefits to some over the costs to others. The unanswerable question in this, though, is what ratio of human cost is acceptable if the intention is to intervene on humanitarian grounds. There may be a point at which such an argument can be sustained, where the ratio is of vastly inverse proportions, although even this retains serious moral dilemmas. But if R2P is taken as the rationale for the intervention, the issue of 'protection' becomes an even more serious problem for such a utilitarian proposition. There is, then, a strong moral argument against R2P when it involves intervention that can harm unintended and innocent victims.

There is no doubt that any broad action against a state will ultimately affect some unintended victims and this has to be a significant concern, given that a basic tenet of R2P is not to do more harm than good, or to create more problems than it solves. Yet Aoi, de Coning and Thakur's (2007) concerns over the 'unintended consequences of peacekeeping', which might be argued to parallel those of R2P, are, frankly, relatively insubstantial. Without intending to diminish the importance of protecting women from exploitation or other negative consequences of their own opportunism, Aoi *et al.* focus their first concerns on the spread of sexually transmitted diseases (STD) and, to a lesser extent, unwanted pregnancies, and the potential for increased prostitution. These are indeed problems that can arise when there is an increased number of men who have disposable income and who are new to a particular social context. It was Cambodia's strong-man prime minister Hun Sen who, answering a question following the UN's intervention in Cambodia as to what was its greatest legacy, replied: 'AIDS' (Downie 1998). This, however, was widely seen more as an effort to discredit the United Nations Transitional Authority in Cambodia (UNTAC) and, a year after a coup against the coalition government, to belittle the democratic process that it established rather than being a genuine expression of concern for the victims of such STDs (see also Hun 2008).

Other negative consequences of such military operations include the unintended impact upon the economy of the host country, in particular the potential impact on inflation and undermining local food production, orienting the provision of goods and services towards the foreign force, and the manner in which military actions can collide with or take priority over humanitarian relief operations (Ammitzboell 2007; Lee 2007; Gordon 2008). Although there are no doubt problems associated with an influx of troops, the 'unintended consequences' on troop donor countries outlined in Aoi *et al.* (2007) are perhaps worth even less serious attention set against the compelling necessity of an established case of R2P intervention.

More substantively, establishing a humanitarian right to intervention undermines the claim to absolute sovereignty and threatens to 'unravel the entire fabric of international relations' (Zakheim, quoted in Traub 2001). Sri Lanka was also quick to raise the issue of sovereignty as a defence against external investigation: 'The Ministry [of External Affairs] points out that Sri Lanka is a sovereign state with a robustly independent judiciary and a tried and tested system for the administration of justice' (Colombo Page 2010a). The Ministry of External Affairs went on to say that Sri Lanka:

> has consistently promoted and protected human rights. Indeed, this has been explicitly acknowledged by legitimate organs of the United Nations system. The Human Rights Council of the United Nations has formally adopted, after the cessation of the conflict situation, a resolution commending, inter alia, the commitment of Sri Lanka to the promotion and protection of human rights.
>
> (Colombo Page 2010a)

What the Ministry of External Affairs did not say, however, was that, despite the claim that the Human Rights Council was a 'legitimate' organ of the UN, it was also a highly controversial body that was roundly criticised by human rights groups and even by the Secretary-General of the UN himself (UNDPI 2008; Evans 2008). The Council was dominated by a number of Islamic and African states backed by Cuba, China and Russia, each of whom protect each other from criticism. China and Russia in particular were close allies of the Sri Lankan government and were instrumental in protecting and supporting it in the final phases of the war, and so the Ministry's claim as to the value of the Council's support had to be taken, at best, in a circumspect manner.

Beyond this, claims in general and Sri Lanka's claim in particular to absolute sovereignty are (and perhaps should be) challenged, while a world order built upon such hardcore 'realism' in which the only constant of international affairs is its anarchy increasingly appear as dated, if not to some degree incorrect.

Sri Lanka's opposition to R2P

The government of Sri Lanka strenuously rejected the idea of R2P, along with its related rejection of other international instruments, and has similarly strenuously endorsed the notion of the absolute inviolability of state sovereignty. It has also claimed that calls for R2P and other forms of intervention reflect neo-imperialist agendas. This opposition to both the idea and the practice of R2P, since its inception, would have made any on-ground R2P intervention difficult if not impossible, assuming the criterion of permission of the affected state. Its opposition to external intervention includes India's disastrous intervention, which it accepted only very reluctantly, and the subsequent opposition to and ultimate failure of the Norwegian-led ceasefire monitoring mission. Importantly, Sri Lanka's external relations have since changed, in particular under the Rajapaksa government, and the types of countries that the government of Sri Lanka now feels most able to freely deal with, including China and Iran, reflect Sri Lanka's international outcast status. Similarly, Sri Lanka has shifted its position more negatively towards other more conciliatory countries, including Norway, overall marking a distinct shift in its international orientation.

As a sign of stronger international concern over events in Sri Lanka, some sanctions, primarily in the area of aid, were brought to bear on it. However, the efficacy and the extent of these sanctions were limited, in part due to their moderate nature and in large part due to Sri Lanka turning away from its traditional allies and supporters. 'They don't like me!', President Rajapaksa said by way of explaining international sanctions on Sri Lanka. 'They don't like my independent views! My preference is for my country. Why should I be loyal to any other country? I'm not a Green Card holder, am I?' [with reference to Green Card holder and rival presidential candidate, former army general Sarath Fonseka]. 'We reject foreign intervention, in whatever form, in the internal affairs of our country and fiercely defend our right to determine our own economic, social, political and cultural system, and our sovereign right to control our natural wealth and resources for the benefit of our own people' (Kunanayakam 2010).

In rejecting offers of assistance from Western governments, Rajapaksa argued that such offers implied interference in Sri Lanka's internal affairs and were subterfuge for other agendas:

> Referring to offers for international assistance to resettle the over 300,000 displaced persons who had been held hostage by the LTTE and to the

> reconstruction of the North and East, my Government made clear that we were looking for partners not Trojan horses! As at 4th February 2010, i.e., within a period of some 8 months, my Government had resettled more than 72% of the internally displaced persons, while others have been cleared to leave the temporary villages at any time. In combating terrorism, we make a distinction between solutions to terrorism and solutions to the national question. However, Western countries have – not innocently – sought to create confusion between the two so as to legitimize the actions of the LTTE and to impose the terrorist organisation as the sole representative of the Tamil people.
>
> (Kunanayakam 2010)

Rajapaksa also argued that Sri Lankan soldiers had not committed any human rights abuses during the war. 'Our troops carried a gun in one hand and the human-rights charter in the other', he said rhetorically, claiming that the military did not 'fire at a single civilian' (Deen 2010). Such dissembling was not uncommon in states rejecting international expressions of concern about human rights abuses.

The use of economic and diplomatic sanctions as a mechanism to achieve change have been applied elsewhere, with differing degrees of success; sanctions made a significant contribution to ending apartheid in South Africa, but have done little to modify the character of the military regime in Burma.[2] That is, sanctions have a mixed record in bringing about compliance with international humanitarian law. In a bid to bring about some degree of change, in mid-2010, the European Commission set 15 conditions on continuing preferential trade relations with Sri Lanka until it complied with the a range of conditions consistent with the International Covenant on Civil and Political Rights (ICCPR). The conditions included the appointment of independent figures to key public institutions, repealing the 2006 Emergency Regulations including detention without trial and immunity from prosecution, repealing sections of the Prevention of Terrorism Act inconsistent with the ICCPR, the right of suspects to immediately see a lawyer, implementation of outstanding UN Human Rights Committee opinions, extension of an invitation to UN Special Procedures to conduct an investigation on war crimes in Sri Lanka, identifying LTTE prisoners held and granting access to all places of detention by the Red Cross (EU 2010).

Somewhat predictably, if not entirely logically or consistently, President Rajapaksa characterised the European Commission's conditions as requiring a betrayal of 'the freedom of the land and people' (Colombo Page 2010b). Sri Lanka's External Affairs minister Professor Gamini Peiris similarly said in relation to the EC's conditions that:

> The government's view is that the conditions imposed by the EC under the guise of what is essentially a trade agreement, amounts to an intervention, the range and depth of which inevitably erodes in every significant respect, the authority of the government to decide upon and to deal with a series of domestic issues.
>
> (Gunesekera 2010)

It was notable that the internationally respected and politically moderate Professor Peiris was appointed as External Affairs minister a year after the defeat of the LTTE, it was widely assumed to be able to deflect international criticism of the government of Sri Lanka for its handling of the war. States with poor human rights records had often appointed similar types of people to such positions as a way of deflecting international criticism. They were most often understood, though, for what they were, which is essentially a public relations 'flack'.

In part, the lack of impact of such sanctions has been as a consequence of their limitations, which in turn have been predicated on how external governments have attempted to calibrate such sanctions based on their understanding of events in Sri Lanka. The government of Sri Lanka has contradicted or has impeded knowledge of or investigation into war crimes as a means of avoiding such forms of external intervention. It has also criticised such claims as reflecting how the LTTE similarly engaged in a propaganda war.

When photographs and videos came to light in 2010 showing what appeared to be the massacre of unarmed, bound and blindfolded Tamil prisoners in the final stages of the war, the Sri Lanka government continued to refuse to allow an external investigation into what were, on face value, war crimes. However, when the first of the videos of the execution of an unarmed Tamil by a Sri Lanka soldier was released in May 2010, President Rajapaksa said that his government would not punish the army for 'defeating terrorism'. Rejecting calls to allow an international investigation into war crimes, Sri Lanka instead established its own 'Lessons Learnt and Reconciliation Commission'. The Sri Lankan Minister for External Affairs claimed that, among other things, the commission was engaged in a process of 'restorative justice', which in usual parlance implies focusing on the needs of the victims and offenders. It was difficult, however, to see any 'restorative justice' in Sri Lanka, with tens of thousands of Tamils still displaced and tens of thousands of others unable to engage in earning a meaningful livelihood, while 'offenders' were summarily executed, disappeared or, if they were lucky, were prosecuted. Critics, including Human Rights Watch and Amnesty International, had described the commission as a 'whitewash' and refused to be associated with it. The ICG noted that

> the Commission's members, many of them retired senior government employees, have made no attempt to question the government's version of events and have instead offered current officials a platform for continued misrepresentations of the facts . . . These failings are reinforced by the absence of any provisions for the protection of witnesses to alleged crimes – a particularly crippling factor given that government officials have labeled as 'traitors' Sri Lankans who have made claims or provided evidence of violations of international humanitarian law by government forces.
>
> (ICG 2010b)

In addition, the ICG, Human Rights Watch and Amnesty International said:

> Should a genuine and credible process eventually be established – featuring truly independent commission members, effective powers of witness protection, and a mandate to explore the full range of alleged violations of national and international law; and backed up by government action to end impunity and ensure that police and courts launch effective and impartial prosecutions – we all would be pleased to appear.
>
> (ICG 2010b)

The UN's former special rapporteur on Sri Lanka, Philip Alston, said that he believed a video of a Sri Lankan soldier executing an unarmed and bound Tamil prisoner was genuine (Al Jazeera 2010). The credibility gap between what the government of Sri Lanka claimed and what the evidence showed grew increasingly wide.

Similarly, Sri Lanka claimed support for its war in cases in which that support did not exist. In April 2009, in the final weeks of the government offensive against the LTTE, the Sri Lankan government claimed that Mexico, which had requested UN Security Council briefings on the issue, had reverted to requesting that the matter be kept off the UN Security Council agenda. The Sri Lankan government's foreign secretary Palitha Kohona claimed that he was told by Mexican vice-minister Gomez-Robledo that Mexico did 'not have any intention of permitting the Sri Lankan situation to be placed on the Security Council agenda'. Kohona also claimed that Gomez-Robledo said that 'the Mexican authorities saw the parallels between their own experience in Chiapas and the negative impact of a cleverly manipulated propaganda machine'. This claim was strenuously denied by the Mexican ambassador, Claude Heller: 'It is not an accurate statement . . . We were very clear that in the case of Sri Lanka there is a concern of the responsibility to protect the population' (Lee 2009). This was consistent with Sri Lanka's 'cognitive dissonance' in misquoting US Secretary of State Hillary Clinton and UN Secretary-General Ban Ki-Moon, saying that they had not raised any humanitarian issues concerning Sri Lanka's handling of the war when it was later revealed that they had (Lee 2009).

Some critics of R2P, in particular in Sri Lanka, have opposed it on grounds related to the imperialist imposition of civil and political rights, and likened it to the twenty-first-century version of the 'white man's burden' (Wijeyawickrema 2007). According to pro-government commentator C. Wijeyawickrema, the question of whether or not to consider employing R2P is 'Just like in the past when Columbus in 1492 and Vasco da Gama in 1498 came with the Bible and the sword, the likes of Gareth Evans now come in 2007 with R2P' (Wijeyawickrema 2007).

Similarly, 'the so-called responsibility to protect is nothing but a licence given by the white man to himself [to] intervene in the affairs of dark sovereign countries, whenever the white man thinks it fit to do so' (de Silva 2007). This type of argument, in which the logic is both internally referential and externally exceptionalist, has been extensively used in arguments against the application of civil and political rights and even against environmental protection by a number of authoritarian and dictatorial states. The underlying assumption of this argument is that there is a universal divide between 'white' and 'dark' peoples and that the states that represent them do so with the blessing of all of their citizens. Further, the accusation that humanitarian concern is a 'white' only position is supported each time a person of European descent raises R2P (or other ethical concerns), the logic being that 'white' people are or should be disenfranchised from being able to legitimately comment on such matters (see also Wijesinha 2008b). As Teson argues, if the view that people have rights is agreed on then it is, by definition, universally so. The origin of those rights, despite their often cross-cultural recognition, is irrelevant to the status of their fact. As Teson notes, this is to confuse categories: the problem of the origin of an idea with the problem of its justification (Teson 2003: 100).

Moreover, the retreat to racial distinction invariably derives from self-serving political elites who may or may not be representative of a majority or who might be so, such as in the case of Sri Lanka, but at the exclusion or diminution of the minority. That is, the majoritarian principle of 'dictatorship of the majority' – the assertion of majority requirements at the unreasonable expense of the minority – abrogates the state's sovereign responsibility to its citizens and in doing so confirms the legitimacy of external intervention.

When several Western governments called for investigations into war crimes committed by the Sri Lankan government, the Sri Lankan ambassador to the United Nations in Geneva rejected claims that war crimes could have been committed as 'outrageous'. He likened such critical commentary to asking the triumphant Allies of World War II to be tried for war crimes over the atomic bombing of Hiroshima. Sri Lanka's Minister of Disaster Management and Human Rights, Mahinda Samarasinghe, stated that his government was 'sick and tired' of what he called 'foreign meddling' (Reuters 2009). This was an inadequate response when an explanation was called for.

Consistent with the view of the Sri Lankan government, Walzer defended the idea of national borders on the basis that there is generally a 'fit' between governments and people that makes injustice an internal, not external, matter, and that only the citizens of that state may overthrow a tyrant. It is only when this lack of fit is radically apparent, according to Walzer, that intervention is acceptable. Examples of such a radically apparent lack of 'fit' include cases of genocide, enslavement or mass deportation. Walzer's position is based upon the idea that the histories and loyalties of nations that define their political processes should be protected on the grounds of 'communal integrity' (Walzer 1980). This, of course, assumes historical continuity of 'nations', that there is a 'fit' between nations and the states into which they are sometimes arbitrarily incorporated and that the citizens of states agree with the 'integrity of their community', or the privileging of the communal and hence organicist over the minority or individual. Similarly aligned with the Sri Lankan government's claims that its war against the LTTE was legitimate, Heine said: 'The last thing South Asia needs is a finger-pointing exercise aimed at questioning the Sri Lankan state's legitimate right of self-defence and of using military force to respond to a separatist uprising to protect its territorial integrity' (Heine 2009). Consistent with wider Sri Lankan government claims, this claim to territorial integrity focused on the claimed legitimacy of Sri Lanka's sovereignty and the fact that the LTTE was a recognised terrorist organisation. It did not, however, go into the question of government responsibility for the deaths of tens of thousands of Tamil civilians in the last months of the war, nor address the issue of war crimes, crimes against humanity or genocide.

Much of the ire of Sri Lanka's government against the international community arose following comments by the then head of the ICG, Gareth Evans, in his 2007 Neelan Thiruchelvam lecture advocating R2P. Evans said:

> In recent Sri Lanka history offers all-too-many examples of large scale atrocities, mass graves, war crimes and ethnic cleansing. It was Louise Arbour's reports that prompted US State Department official to assert that 'we remain concerned about the deteriorating humanitarian situation in Sri Lanka as confirmed in the recent assessment of the UN High Commissioner for Human Rights [Louise Arbour], an international human rights presence in Sri Lanka would be an important step in improving human rights, accountability and the rule of law and ultimately resolving the conflict in Sri Lanka'.
>
> (Evans 2007b)

This speech brought a hail of official and unofficial criticism from numerous quarters in Sri Lanka, paralleling attacks against other less prominent people who dared to question Sri Lanka's human rights record and its failure to find a political solution to the Tamil problem. In attacking the ICG and in particular its then head Gareth Evans, on behalf of the Sri Lankan Ministry of Defence, Dayasri alleged that funding for the ICG from philanthropist George Soros 'reveals funding sources of the ICG are of a suspicious nature and dubious character; at times its funding sources appear to be tilted in favour of terrorist objectives' (Dayasri 2010). That is, the internationally respected ICG was claimed to be linked to or to support 'terrorist objectives', which could not be rationally understood as other than absurd.

According to the Sri Lankan Ministry of Defence, the purpose of an international inquiry into war crimes, as proposed by the ICG, 'is to bring Sri Lanka into disrepute in the eyes of the international community . . . They are the front-runners on whose doctored reports the Western Powers and NGOs can activate their objectives of attempting to shame Sri Lanka (Dayasri 2010). The stridency of this and related views and the ethnic chauvinism they reflect set alarm bells ringing for anyone who had read the history of genocide; either in advance of or parallel with genocide are strident accusations against specific groups and anyone associated with them, as a means of detaching existing or future actions from accountability.

Similarly, pro-government commentators were blunt in their rejection of external concerns. Writing in the *Sri Lanka Guardian* on the appointment of a UK envoy to Sri Lanka by the then UK prime minister Gordon Brown, Mahindapala Don said that 'His brash action is as welcome as dog's vomit at the breakfast table'

(Mahindapala 2009). Mahindapala was a sometime commentator and propagandist for the Sri Lankan government, formerly heading the radical Sinhalese organisation in Australia, the Society for the Protection of Human Rights (SPUHR). As well as attacking public figures, Mahindapala and other members of SPUHR also harassed (see Wije 2009[3]) and threatened non-Sri Lankans who did not share their extremist views or who simply promoted alternative views.

His views on observations that did not agree with his own were outlined in the seemingly non-ironically entitled article 'The Brave New World is Leaving the Tamil Separatists Behind':

> Rejecting patronizing neo-colonialism Sri Lanka has reacted assertively with the clear intention of teaching its former colonial master some telling lessons in diplomacy. First President Ranasinghe Premadasa unceremoniously sent home David Gladstone, the then British High Commissioner to Sri Lanka, for trying to poke his unwanted nose in the domestic affairs of Sri Lanka. Gotabaya Rajapakse did one better: he sent two Foreign Ministers of big powers in the West – Bernard Kouchner (France) and David Milliband (Britain) – back to the hole from which they came when they tried to interfere in the internal affairs of the nation. The importance of dismissing two Foreign Ministers, asking them to put their own house in order first, cannot be underestimated, coming especially from a tiny island with no comparable clout of the combined power of two Big Brothers. Snubbing both England and France in one stroke is, perhaps, one of the biggest political statements Sri Lanka ever made on the world stage. Ever since then Sri Lanka has grown in confidence telling the West to jump in the Atlantic Ocean with their hypocritical morality.
>
> (Mahindapala 2010)

Similarly, the former Norwegian foreign minister who brokered the 2002 Sri Lanka ceasefire, Erik Solheim, was also criticised by Mahindapala, despite having been invited by the then Sri Lankan government to assist: 'The main man who was acting as the agent of the Tamil Tigers, Erik Solheim, is now sitting at the bottom of one of Norway's political fjords trying to figure out what hit him' (Mahindapala 2010).

The standing position of the government of Sri Lanka has been that it set up its own internal 'Lessons Learnt and Internal Reconciliation' panel on the events of 2008–9 and that it 'strongly opposed' the UN Panel of Experts established to enquire into those events as 'unwarranted and unnecessary interference with a sovereign nation' (MEA 2010). In mid-2010, UN Secretary-General Ban Ki-Moon appointed 'a panel of experts that would advise him on the issue of accountability with regards to any alleged violations of international human rights and humanitarian law during the final stages of the conflict in Sri Lanka' (Xinhua 2010). The three-person panel was chaired by former Indonesian Attorney-General and human rights investigator Marzuki Darusman, who also served on the UN independent commission to investigate the 2007 assassination of former Pakistani prime minister Benazir Bhuto. The other two members of the panel were former South African Truth and Reconciliation Commissioner, Yasmin Sooka, and US legal academic, who advised on bringing former Khmer Rouge to trial, Steven Ratner. The panel was to advise the Secretary-General on the implementation of the commitment on human rights accountability made in a joint statement issued by Sri Lankan president Mahinda Rajapaksa and Ban during Ban's visit to Sri Lanka in May 2009. The panel was to 'look into the modalities, applicable international standards and comparative experience with regard to accountability processes, taking into account the nature and scope of any alleged violations in Sri Lanka' (Xinhua 2010). Darusman had previously served on a panel of international monitors observing a Sri Lankan commission investigating a number of major human rights violations. The observers subsequently resigned, citing the commission's failure to meet international standards, political interference and its failure to produce substantive results (Reuters 2010). As the panel was about to begin its work, Sri Lanka announced that its members would not be allowed to enter Sri Lanka to undertake investigations. External Affairs minister Professor Peiris said that Sri Lanka would not accept the panel and that its three members would 'not be welcome' in Sri Lanka (Gunesekera 2010).

The findings of the panel were, not entirely surprisingly given the evidence that had been mounting, damning of the government of Sri Lanka in its conduct of the war, especially in the final phases. It was also damning of the LTTE for using civilians as human shields and for shooting civilians who tried to flee the LTTE's encampment in the final days of the war. The panel found credible the allegations that, between September 2008 and 19 May 2009, the Sri Lankan army advanced its military campaign into the Vanni using large-scale and widespread shelling causing large numbers of civilian deaths. This campaign was deemed to have constituted the persecution of the area's Tamil population. More than 300,000 civilians were found to have been trapped into a decreasing area, fleeing the shelling but kept hostage by the LTTE. When the media attempted to report on the unfolding humanitarian catastrophe, the panel's report found that the government attempted to intimidate and silence the media and other critics of the war through a variety of threats and actions, including the use of white vans to abduct people and make them 'disappear'. The report also found that the army shelled on a large scale in three consecutive 'no-fire zones', where it had encouraged the civilian population to concentrate, even after saying that it would cease the use of heavy weapons. Among its targets was the United Nations hub, food distribution lines and near Red Cross ships arriving to pick up the wounded and their relatives from the beaches. Despite intelligence reports detailing the impact of the shelling, the government continued its attacks. The report found that most civilian casualties in the final phases of the war were caused by this government shelling:

> The Panel's determination of credible allegations reveals a very different version of the final stages of the war than that maintained to this day by the Government of Sri Lanka. The Government says it pursued a 'humanitarian rescue operation' with a policy of 'zero civilian casualties'. In stark contrast,

> the Panel found credible allegations, which if proven, indicate that a wide range of serious violations of international humanitarian law and international human rights law were committed both by the Government of Sri Lanka and the LTTE, some of which would amount to war crimes and crimes against humanity. Indeed, the conduct of the war represented a grave assault on the entire regime of international law designed to protect individual dignity during both war and peace.
>
> (Panel of Experts 2011: ii)

The panel's report found credible allegations that comprised five core categories of serious violations committed by the government of Sri Lanka. These included the killing of civilians through widespread shelling, shelling of hospitals and humanitarian objects, the denial of humanitarian assistance, human rights violations of victims and survivors of the conflict including both internally displaced people and suspected LTTE cadres, and human rights violations outside the conflict zone including against the media and other critics of the government. The panel's report also found credible allegations against the LTTE associated with the final stages of the war, covering six core categories of serious violations. These included using civilians as a human buffer, killing civilians attempting to flee LTTE control, using military equipment in the proximity of civilians, the forced recruitment of children, forced labour, and the killing of civilians through suicide attacks (Panel of Experts 2011). Despite these findings and a call by the report for the establishment of an independent international inquiry into the possibility that both Sri Lankan forces and the LTTE committed crimes against humanity, the UN Secretary-General only requested further investigations into the findings, without calling for specific investigations into war crimes or crimes against humanity. He said that such specific investigations would proceed only if the government of Sri Lanka requested them, which, given its objections, seemed highly unlikely, or if UN member states called for such an inquiry, also unlikely given China and Russia's objections (Buncombe 2011).

Despite the even-handedness of the report – and no doubt to protect itself should charges relating to war crimes or crimes against humanity eventually be raised – Sri Lanka adopted the full range of objections to the panel, its investigation, its findings and, of course, R2P, including that it compromised state sovereignty and territorial integrity, that its grounds were not justified, that it implied the imposition of a neo-imperialist agenda and that it functionally supported terrorist activities. The claim to national sovereignty was perhaps the strongest put by the Sri Lanka government, arguing that its affairs were its own and that moreover it had a legitimate right to defeat terrorism using whatever means it believed were appropriate. In that there was any recognition of the impact that this had on Tamil civilians, the government of Sri Lanka denied that civilians were harmed or targeted, blamed the LTTE for civilian casualties or, in rare and slightly more candid moments, admitted that there were always a few casualties in any war. When video footage showed two men being executed by Sri Lankan soldiers and a further seven bodies of bound and blindfolded victims, the Sri Lankan High Commission to the UK said:

> The High Commission of Sri Lanka categorically denies that the Channel 4 News TV video is authentic. Last year when Channel 4 News telecast a similar video the Government of Sri Lanka clearly established, by reference to technical considerations, that it was not genuine but fake. The present video is nothing more than an elongated version of the same video.
>
> (Channel 4 2010)

However, based on its public expressions, there was little doubt that the government of Sri Lanka believed that almost any tactic – other than a genuine political solution – was justified if it rid the country of the LTTE. Between the vehemence of the anti-LTTE rhetoric and the assertion of Sri Lanka as the home of the Buddhist Sinhalese, it seemed as though the existence of Sri Lanka's Tamils were only barely tolerated. Within this context, any attempt to subvert or override the authority of the government and of this disposition would always be seen within the context of a battle not just of wills but of peoples, more or less to the death. With such an outlook, regardless of moral persuasion, diplomatic and economic pressure, or the possibility of intervention, the government of Sri Lanka would object to R2P or any element of it until the last.

7 Geo-strategic factors, R2P and Sri Lanka

Sri Lanka occupies a geographic position that is highly strategically relevant while at the same time, in some respects, quite irrelevant. This chapter therefore considers these strategic implications and their influence on decision making concerning possible R2P in relation to Sri Lanka. It then illustrates the types of complexities that face external actors when contemplating R2P, beyond the simple evidence that the grounds for R2P are established.

The island has been a stopping-off point for traders for many centuries and was colonised by three different European states. Just a short distance across the easily navigable Palk Straights sits the world's second most populous state, India, with which Sri Lanka has historical links, in particular for its Tamil-speaking population but also with many cultural commonalities shared by the Sinhalese majority.

Sri Lanka is located at the crossroads of major shipping routes, with more than two-thirds of the world's oil and half its container shipping passing nearby in the Indian Ocean. It enjoys one of the best deep-water harbours in the world at Trincomalee and, with a high level of Chinese assistance, is rapidly developing another major port at Hambantota. Sri Lanka's strategic location at the centre of the Indian Ocean is, therefore, the primary reason for its strategic relevance. However, Sri Lanka does not share land borders with any country, lives in India's geographic and strategic shadow and is otherwise a relatively insignificant global player. Sri Lanka also tends to be of little if any strategic concern to most other countries – with the exception of part of India, with which its shares a Tamil heritage. What happens within Sri Lanka, therefore, has little bearing on the rest of the world.

In a world still dominated by 'realism' in international relations, Sri Lanka is not big enough to be an aggressor, has little ability and no identifiable purpose in trying to destabilise near countries and is not a significant economic power. In particular, other than India's interest by dint of proximity and China's interest as a counter to India, the rest of the world is little troubled by the affairs of a small and more or less inconsequential island state. Even when humanitarian concerns arise, as in the case of its Tamil population, there is little to be gained from external involvement and potentially much to be lost in terms of antagonising two relatively powerful, nuclear-armed states.

However, Sri Lanka does have some potential for strategic significance if other powers seek to employ it as a base to project their interests into the Indian Ocean. The internationally significant deep-water naval base at Trincomalee can host and supply a major fleet in the Indian Ocean and, alongside the world's second most populous country, India, can play an unfriendly game by choosing as allies states that are antithetically positioned towards India, such as China and Pakistan and perhaps even Burma. Sri Lanka's relationship with India has been mixed and its more recent closeness to China as a principle arms supplier, more general trading partner and diplomatic supporter was precisely calculated to neutralise potential Indian manipulation or interference.

As an island in the Indian Ocean, however, Sri Lanka does not present a threat to neighbouring states nor, with the exception of the attack on Rajiv Gandhi and some (long since ended) training of LTTE cadres[1] in southern India, do its internal issues spill over into other states. Sri Lanka is formally non-aligned and balances its increasing closeness with China with its proximity to India through its 'dialogue' status in the Shanghai Cooperation Organisation (SCO), which includes India and China as well as Russia (and other states effectively irrelevant for its purposes). China and India vie for Sri Lanka's attention, with China being the more dominant of the two, and India checking any return to its own earlier self-regard as the sole arbiter of regional affairs.

The war for Tamil liberation began when the Cold War was still a major factor in geo-strategic considerations and continued throughout the post-Cold War period. At that time, Sri Lanka was not considered to be in either the Western or the Soviet Bloc camps. As a member of the non-aligned movement and as a nominally socialist state, at no time was Sri Lanka regarded as a likely ally for the then Soviet Union or, later, Russia, despite their otherwise supportive relations. Sri Lanka began to be considered more closely by other states as a consequence of the post-Cold War US-led 'war on terror' rebounding on the LTTE, given its broad international status as a terrorist organisation. This status was enhanced by the government of Sri Lanka as it assiduously courted numerous governments[2] and international organisations (e.g. the UN) to proscribe the LTTE as a terrorist organisation.[3] These countries in turn agreed to limit the international activities of the LTTE, particularly around fund-raising, which made a significant contribution to supporting the LTTE's separatist campaign.

From the perspective of the government of Sri Lanka, it believed that its geo-strategic significance was central to what it perceived to be efforts to undermine its sovereign authority by claims of support for the LTTE. This was notably the case with some sections of the Tamil Indian community in the neighbouring Indian state of Tamil Nadu. Towards the end of the war, Sri Lanka became increasingly concerned that attempts to influence the conduct of the war were actually intended to weaken the sovereign authority of the state by creating a breathing space for the increasingly retreating LTTE. In this, questions over the conduct of the war against the LTTE and expressions of concern over human rights issues, particularly towards and following the end of the conflict, were conflated with neo-imperialist ambitions. According to the ambassador of Sri Lanka in Cuba, Tamara Kunanayakam (2010):

> For imperialism, our part of the Indian Ocean is not merely a market to be conquered or a source of raw materials to be pillaged. It is the gateway to the control of resources and markets in the Near East, Middle East, Africa and Asia.

Despite the extent of this claim as overstating Sri Lanka's significance, Ms Kunanayakam went further, proposing that the United States and NATO had conducted naval exercises in the Indian Ocean with a view to gaining a toehold in Sri Lanka. But, Kunanayakam said, in particular in relation to the role of the UN Security Council:

> There is no longer any doubt that Russia, China and Iran will be successful in frustrating US attempts to conquer this geo-strategic position. Its maritime decline in the Indian Ocean will continue and many observers consider as realistic the emergence in the next decade of China as a superior naval force.
> (Kunanayakam 2010)[4]

Visits by Sri Lankan politicians and military officers to Iran, Russia and China in 2007 and 2008 to access arms and financial support helped set the stage for the military defeat of the LTTE (Nazemroaya 2009). The government of Sri Lanka understood that these states were equally opposed to separatist tendencies and had little practical regard for notions of human rights. In a community of ethically challenged states, Sri Lanka found new friends.

In particular, this move towards a closer strategic relationship with China meant two things. Sri Lanka both was protected from arms and trade embargoes, such as they existed, and moved the country out of the overwhelming sphere of Indian influence and into a position where it was able to balance itself as more or less between, and perhaps to some extent astride, these competing strategic interests. Sri Lanka further neutralised India's capacity to act against it, in particular regarding investigations into war crimes, by holding Indian intelligence reports that assisted the Sri Lankan army in its final assault on the LTTE at the beach at Mullivaykkal:

> A Delhi stunned by an angry Gothabhaya Rajapakse took his 'loop' signals [intelligence reports] as lethal enough to implicate Delhi's South Block [intelligence base] in the war crimes should SL [Sri Lanka] ever be forced to face such charges. A harried and alarmed Delhi reacted speedily to appease Colombo launching a swift diplomatic offensive to save the murderous SL regime by killing off the international community's war crimes initiatives in the UN specifically supporting the infamous May 2009 UNHRC resolution.
> (Vssubramaniam 2010)

In part, Sri Lanka's more recent confidence in Russia and China stemmed from, as noted, its signing up as a 'dialogue partner' to the Shanghai Cooperation Organisation, originally established in 1996, which is a group of mainland Asian countries with the primary purpose of ensuring the military security of land borders between them. The SCO, comprising China, Russia, Kazakhstan, Kyrgyzstan, Uzbekistan and Tajikistan, has since expanded its remit to include economic and cultural cooperation. India, Iran, Mongolia and Pakistan have observer status to the SCO, with Belarus and Sri Lanka having 'dialogue' status. Sri Lanka signed its 'dialogue' status agreement in Colombo in May 2010, just one year after the end of the war against the LTTE. From a different perspective:

> The strange lineup of the member countries of the United Nations Human Rights Council (UNHRC) for or against Sri Lanka at the special session of the body scheduled to take place in Geneva on Tuesday underscores the maritime Great Game unfolding in the Indian Ocean.
>
> (Bhadrakumar 2009)

Perhaps, though, this was less a 'maritime Great Game' unfolding, and more an alignment of countries having a vested interest in attempting to resist complying with the global human rights paradigm and thus seeking support in each other's company. The UN Human Rights Council, including China, India, Egypt and Cuba, was ultimately challenged:

> Sri Lanka claimed a propaganda victory last night after the United Nations Human Rights Council passed a resolution praising its defeat of the Tamil Tigers and condemning the rebels for using civilians as human shields . . . China, India, Egypt and Cuba were among the 29 developing countries that backed a Sri Lankan-proposed resolution describing the conflict as a 'domestic matter that doesn't warrant outside interference'. Western diplomats and human rights officials were shocked by the outcome at the end of an acrimonious two-day special session to examine the humanitarian and human rights situation in Sri Lanka after the blitzkrieg of the final military offensive that wiped out the Tiger force . . . 'The vote is extremely disappointing and is a low point for the Human Rights Council. It abandons hundreds of thousands of people in Sri Lanka to cynical political considerations,' Amnesty International said . . . In Colombo, by contrast, there was a mood of jubilation for a government that has cast itself as a plucky minnow fighting the hypocrisy of large Western powers. Sri Lanka's resolution passed with the support of powerful new allies such as China, which provided much of the weaponry used in its decisive defeat of the rebels.
>
> (Philp 2009)

In significant part, the 'war on terror' also allowed the government of Sri Lanka to more freely launch a conventional ground war against the LTTE, which gave rise to expressions of serious concern over such human rights issues by sections of the international community. However, despite criticism by sections of the international community, Sri Lanka found that between employing the rhetoric of the 'war on terror' on the one hand and its new-found friends on the other it was less restricted in its actions than it had previously been. The LTTE was increasingly isolated, while the hard-line actions of the government of Sri Lanka were increasingly supported.

In that these factors presented a case for or against R2P, they meant that, although factors in favour of intervention were present, there were no compelling strategic reasons to intervene militarily in any coordinated way in Sri Lanka's internal affairs, there was significant domestic and international opposition to such intervention, and the countries most likely to mount a case for intervention were themselves either ambiguous about the overarching and human rights security situation in Sri Lanka or, although concerned about human rights issue, actively opposed to the LTTE. There were, then, strong strategic reasons to consider carefully any such intervention, not least the reaction from China on one hand and India on the other. Similarly, even though less effective, there were and remain strong reasons for economic and diplomatic sanctions against the government of Sri Lanka, although, again, also potential costs around such action.

This suggests that any action that might be taken in relation to Sri Lanka would be weighed against a possible backlash from either China or India, both of which are nuclear-armed giant states or, barring full-scale military intervention, would risk pushing the government of Sri Lanka into an even closer strategic, economic and diplomatic alliance with China or, less likely, India. The only factor playing against China become a fully-fledged ally of Sri Lanka was that such a move would be viewed in a very negative light by India and would likely result in some type of strategic posturing unhelpful to Sri Lanka's future stability. Sri Lanka's ability to balance Indian and China, then, was critical to its own survival and the non-intervention of other parties.

Because Sri Lanka has traditionally followed a policy of non-alignment, it was able to employ this to also seek friendly nations further abroad (e.g. Cuba). Sri Lanka's membership of the Non-Aligned Movement dated back to Indian prime minister Jawaharlal Nehru announcing the five principles of non-alignment in Colombo in 1954, with Sri Lanka formally becoming a founding member of the Non-Aligned Movement in 1961. Despite having non-aligned status, like many other states, Sri Lanka has been closer to or more distant from various states at different times and for different reasons. Each of these variations in its external relations has reflected its internal politics at the time and how the state has ordered itself to help ensure its preferred outcomes. Until the early 1980s, Sri Lanka maintained a relatively even balance of relations with the United States and the Soviet Union, and more or less cordial relations with it immediate neighbour, India. Although other relations remained much as they were, relations with India began to develop in ways that the Sri Lankan government was not always comfortable with, notably complicated by the close relations felt by Sri Lanka's Tamil community with many Indians, in particular in the nearest state of Tamil Nadu.

Indian intervention

As the conflict in Sri Lanka escalated and in particular after the 1983 riots, India chose to become involved, based on what has been called its 'Doctrine of Regional

Security' (Hagerty 1991). The basis for this doctrine was that India opposed external intervention in regional conflicts and that if external intervention was required this should fall to India to undertake it. There has been some debate about the existence of such a 'doctrine', with some analysts suggesting that India's regional relations were marked more by ambivalence than by any doctrine that could be equated with those such as the US's Monroe Doctrine or those of subsequent US leaders (e.g. Eisenhower, Nixon) (see, for example, Thomas 1986: 14). However, India's intervention in the separatist war between Pakistan and what was to become Bangladesh did indicate that India regarded itself as a regional hegemonic power. In 1983, India's doctrine of regional assertion was more fully expressed in relation to Sri Lanka, resulting in the first direct international intervention and a string of processes that would, unintentionally at the time, mark a change in the direction of, if not an equitable political solution to, the war in Sri Lanka.

What was notable about India's interventions in Sri Lanka was that they were initially motivated by a degree of support for the Tamil separatist cause, or were at least in response to such sympathy within India. However, the overriding factor in India's considerations was its own strategic position, both in terms of excluding other states from being involved in the region and hence challenging India's self-perceived (or desired) regional hegemony and in terms of demonstrating that it was the dominant regional power. There were instances of humanitarian intervention in India's involvement and indeed India's airdrop of supplies to a desperate Tamil population in Jaffna could be seen as an instance of R2P at work. But as with most matters in international affairs, it was a confluence of factors that made India feel compelled to become involved in Sri Lanka and humanitarian considerations were only one among a number of factors, and generally not the dominant one.

Based on the claim that excluding India from regional security matters could allow intervention by other states, such exclusion would hence be construed by India as an 'anti-India' move (Hardgrave 1984: 167). Following close interest in and concern for the conflict in the Indian state of Tamil Nadu, which had been covertly supporting the LTTE (Swamy 2006: 72–8, 97, 106, 111–13), in addition to the even more covert support from the Indian intelligence Research and Analysis Wing (Swamy 2006: 106–11, 113–14), Indian prime minister Indira Gandhi announced that Sri Lanka's president Jayewardene had accepted India's offer to hold talks with Sri Lankan Tamil leaders to find a resolution to the conflict. From this came an Indian proposal to establish functionally autonomous elected regional councils in the north and east of Sri Lanka. Despite talks between the Tamil United Liberation Front and a number of Sinhalese organisations, the proposal failed to find agreement between the parties.

In 1985, following a further escalation in the war and Sri Lankan government moves to resettle 3,000 Sinhalese families in Tamil areas of the north of Sri Lanka, India's new prime minister, Rajiv Ghandi,[5] organised further talks to be held in Thimpu, Bhutan. These talks also failed, leading to heavy fighting in the north and east of Sri Lanka. It was from around this time that the LTTE came to assert its dominance among the Tamil separatist groups.

Under further Indian pressure, in 1986 Sri Lanka's president Jayewardene met with Rajiv Gandhi, Tamil Nadu chief minister Maruthur Ramachandran and LTTE leader Velupillai Prabhakaran in Bangalore, India. Jayewardene's proposal to break up the eastern province into three units representing Tamil, Muslim and Sinhalese areas contravened the LTTE's claim to a traditional homeland, which it thus rejected. Fighting subsequently resumed, including a food and fuel embargo on the Jaffna Peninsula. The humanitarian crisis that unfolded there as a result led to a backlash in the neighbouring Indian state of Tamil Nadu. Relief ships from India were blocked by the Sri Lankan navy, leading to Indian air force food drops in Jaffna. In the face of escalating tensions between Sri Lanka and India, President Jayewardene ended the blockade of Jaffna, released a number of political prisoners and agreed to seek a political solution. This event led to the signing of the Indo-Sri Lankan Accord in 1987.

There were six conditions under the terms of the Indo-Sri Lankan Accord. First, the territorial integrity of Sri Lanka was reaffirmed, ending Tamil hopes for an independent homeland. Second, the state was recognised as multi-ethnic comprising Sinhalese, Tamils, Moors (Tamil-speaking Muslims), Malays and Burghers. Third, the northern and eastern districts were recognised as the historic habitation of Tamil-speaking people while allowing others the right to live in those areas. Fourth, there was to be a temporary merger of the northern and eastern provinces following provincial council elections with a referendum to determine the permanency of the merger. Fifth, Tamil insurgents were to surrender their weapons and the Sri Lankan military was to return to barracks, and, sixth, there was to be a repeal of emergency and anti-terrorist laws and the release of political prisoners.

To counter Sri Lanka's growing use of Pakistani and Israeli advisers, India was to be guarantor of the accord, providing military assistance to implement aspects of the accord if requested to do so by the government in Colombo. India also secured its own regional security dominance and effectively ended the influence of other states by having Sri Lanka agree that neither country would enter into external military or security relations in ways that could be prejudicial to the other, that the port of Trincomalee would not be made available to any foreign military power prejudicial to the security interests of the two countries (along with some infrastructure redevelopment work), and that foreign broadcasting from Sri Lanka would not be used for military or intelligence purposes.

Tamil separatists were not a part of the signing of the accord and were disappointed with its conditions following the intervention of what they considered to be a friendly power. Similarly, more nationalist Sinhalese were also disappointed with the accord or opposed it, seeing it as compromising the state's territorial integrity and debasing more chauvinist Sinhalese claims. Yet the day after it was signed, under the ambiguous terms it outlined, India sent 8,000 peacekeepers to Sri Lanka to ensure that the accord was implemented. Because the Indian Peace Keeping Force was supposed to be peacekeeping in orientation, it did not bring heavy weapons with it. At the same time, the Sri Lankan government continued with its policy of resettlement of Sinhalese in previously Tamil areas, which led to fighting between the Sri Lankan army and the LTTE, increasing tension around the accord. Then the LTTE refused to surrender its weapons to the IPKF under the terms of the accord, which immediately escalated tensions and quickly led to fighting between the IPKF and the LTTE.

The IPKF was criticised by both the Sri Lankan government and the LTTE for failing to protect civilians and restrain the other party. Indian prime minister Rajiv Gandhi responded by ordering a crackdown on anyone breaking the rules of the ceasefire. Fighting broke out between the LTTE and the IPKF in November 1987. Given its lack of preparedness for such an eventuality and the relatively high level of organisation of the LTTE, the IPKF fared poorly in battle. Further, the IPKF had alienated both the Tamil and the Sinhalese communities, meaning that it could rely on almost no local support. Added to sensitivity in India about fighting Tamils, the IPKF could not adequately prosecute this aspect of the conflict. At one point, the Sri Lankan government, which resented what it also regarded as the imposition of the IPKF in a violation of Sri Lankan sovereignty, even supported the LTTE by supplying it with weapons in its fight. Meanwhile, the ultra-nationalist Janatha Vimukthi Peramuna (JVP, or People's Revolutionary Front) unleashed a wave of terror against Tamils, ethnic Indians and Sinhalese 'traitors', which further destabilised the situation. As a result of criticism from its own government and within Sri Lanka, falling morale and a high number of casualties, the decision was taken to end IPKF engagement in December 1989 followed by a complete withdrawal in March 1990. The mutual distrust of Indian motives for intervening in the Sri Lankan war led the Sri Lankan government and the LTTE into talks, but as they talked both sides prepared for a return to war.

Despite signing a free trade agreement in 1998 and India's subsequent economic favouritism towards Sri Lanka, meaning a fourfold increase in trade to almost US$3 billion, Sri Lanka became more distant from India and began to develop closer relations with India's sometimes combative neighbour, Pakistan, particularly in areas of military training (SLG 2007), notably at the suggestion of China. Pakistan has since come to develop an even closer relationship with Sri Lanka, although this has to some extent been countered by India also improving its own relationship with Sri Lanka, not least through intelligence assistance given to the Sri Lankan army during the final phases of the war with the LTTE. The efforts of both of these countries to develop closer relations with Sri Lanka have been purely strategic, not least as a counter to each other and in India's case to counter China's use of Pakistan as its proxy.

Since the election of Mahinda Rajapaksa as president in 2005, India has maintained a formally cordial relationship with Sri Lanka. Notably, in the last year of the war against the LTTE, India supplied Sri Lanka with intelligence, although not weapons, to assist it in its final battles. As noted by one observer: 'both sides appear to have worked out a flexible model of collaboration, co-ordination and at times mutual condescension' (Hariharan 2010). Despite this, and a desire for it to go away, the Sri Lanka Tamil issue is still important in India, as a human rights issue, because of the greater involvement of China, through continuing sensitivities in Tamil Nadu towards the Sri Lankan Tamil cause and as a result of closer and rapidly growing economic relations – Sri Lanka has grown to become India's second largest trading partner (Hariharan 2010). Despite, or because of, these factors, President Rajapaksa remained lukewarm towards India, with his visit in June 2010 reflecting more diplomatic courtesy than substantive improvement.

While India's star in Sri Lanka has at best remained steady, it has declined relative to that of China. In the twenty-first century, China has developed very much closer relations with Sri Lanka and has become a major trading partner, a major source of foreign investment and, since the 1990s, its largest arms supplier, notably as a result of India refusing to sell weapons to Sri Lanka for use in the war. China's pre-eminence in supplying arms to Sri Lanka increased following a US embargo on the supply of weapons in 2007 as a result of concerns over human rights abuses. Notably, China not only sold arms to Sri Lanka, but also gave six Chengdu F7 interceptor aircraft as a gift to counter the LTTE's then developing but modest air wing. An LTTE air attack in 2007 on Katunayake air field destroyed a number of Sri Lankan air force Israeli-supplied Kfir C2 and C7 and Russian-supplied MiG 27 military aircraft, which had been used to attack LTTE positions. China's US$36 million ammunition and ordnance sales to Sri Lanka were credited with having tipped the war against the LTTE in Sri Lanka's favour (Macartney 2009). Notably, both China and Russia have been engaged in suppressing their own separatist movements, in the former case in Tibet and Xinjiang and in the latter in Chechnya and to a lesser extent in other constituent republics (e.g. others of the North Caucasus, Tyva, Karelia in the north-west and more eastern republics such as Yakutia). Both have also been widely accused of perpetrating human rights abuses in doing so and have chosen not to be accountable on such charges. Both China and Russia warmly congratulated the government of Sri Lanka when it finally defeated the LTTE in May 2010.

As elsewhere, China's relationship with Sri Lanka served its commercial and strategic interests, with one view being that China's construction of a US$1 billion port at Hambantota in Sri Lanka's south was part of a plan to establish port facilities throughout the Indian Ocean (joining with bases already established at Laem Chabang and Sittwe in Burma, Chittagong in Bangladesh and Gwadar in Pakistan). These ports had not yet been deployed as naval bases, but had the potential to become so. Hambantota could therefore have been viewed as another 'pearl' in China's 'String of Pearls' strategy (BAH 2005). As with other Chinese international projects (the above and those in Timor-Leste and Fiji among the more regional ones), several thousand Chinese labourers were sent to Sri Lanka and China had a newly visible presence on the island.

The strategic importance of this port was made explicit by the Sri Lankan ambassador to Cuba, Tamara Kunanayakam (2010), when she said: 'For China, Sri Lanka represents a major attraction. Not only will it [Hambantota] facilitate the supply of its fleet, but will strengthen links with its southern province of Yunnan'. If Sri Lanka's distinct move away from Western countries was not already clear, Kunanayakam ensured that it now was when commenting on the significance of the results of the 2010 elections: 'The vote in favour of Mahinda Rajapaksa has a dual significance: First, it was a popular vote – or an anti-elite vote! Second, it was an anti-Western vote!' (Kunanayakam 2010).

China was also a useful ally to Sri Lanka by managing to deflect criticism and opposing extensive investigations into its conduct of the war and its consequences by the UN Security Council. 'Beijing had managed to prevent the Security Council from even discussing the situation. When a debate was conceded, Chinese objections ensured there was no resolution and the Council took the minimalist option of releasing a statement of concern' (Blair 2009). 'China's quiet assertion in India's backyard has put Sri Lanka's government in a position not only to play China off against India, but also to ignore complaints from outside Asia about human rights violations in the war' (Sengupta 2008). Both China and Russia opposed UN investigations into alleged war crimes by the Sri Lankan army, particularly in the closing months of the war.

As head of the Non-Aligned Movement of which Sri Lanka remained a strong member, Egypt also strongly opposed any investigation into allegations of war crimes.

Among Sri Lanka's emerging allies was Iran, which provided a $US1.9 billion low-interest loan to buy military equipment, develop a hydro-electric scheme and buy Iranian oil and develop an oil-refining capacity (BBC 2008). In return, Sri Lanka supported the development of Iran's independent nuclear energy capability. As Sri Lanka's foreign secretary Palitha said: 'Asians don't hector each other from public pulpits. They're more ready with assistance and less ready with gratuitous advice' (BBC 2008). Again, and as with China, Iran's interest in Sri Lanka was very much less humanitarian and more about securing a new ally in its continued international diplomatic difficulties.

The United States has also played a small but important role in the outcome of the war in Sri Lanka. Apart from supporting the government against the LTTE over the issue of state unity, when the possibility of reconstruction following the 2002 ceasefire was mooted the United States effectively scuttled it. In April 2003, talks were to be held in Washington concerning reconstruction. However, the United States barred LTTE representatives from attending the talks on the grounds that it had declared the LTTE a terrorist organisation, in effect excluding the LTTE from participating in the allocation of resources and all that implied for the economic marginalisation of the LTTE in areas it controlled under the terms of the 2002 ceasefire. A week after being excluded from the talks regarding the allocation of reconstruction resources, the LTTE withdrew from further peace talks (Smith 2009: 98).

The LTTE being declared a terrorist organisation, by the UN and a number of individual states, was a critical blow against it in the Sri Lankan government's prosecution of the war. The intention of the government was not just to win a moral argument, of which it was already convinced. The intention was to cut off the LTTE from its external sources of income and supplies from the Tamil diaspora, which were critical in helping the LTTE wage its own part of the war. The government began to prosecute its case for having the LTTE declared a terrorist organisation in the 1990s, with the United States complying in 1997, along with 31 other countries, including the United Kingdom, India and Canada, as well as the European Union.

The status of the LTTE as a terrorist organisation was made much more real in its international dealings following the events of 11 September 2001, in which all listed terrorist organisations (not just those associated with Islamist causes) became a target of US foreign policy and were increasingly viewed with disdain by other states. The LTTE found itself isolated, not least as the government of Sri Lanka stepped up its campaign to have foreign governments prosecute alleged LTTE members and procurers for actively supporting the LTTE. The international network that had helped sustain the LTTE increasingly began to crack and by 2007 had begun to crumble. By the time the government of Sri Lanka launched its final offensive against the LTTE, its international support base had effectively stopped working.[6]

Strategic implications

The strategic implications of Sri Lanka, as noted at the outset, are both important and unimportant. They are important because Sri Lanka occupies a strategically vital position at the crossroads of one of the world's major trading routes, because it has one deep-water harbour of international standing and because it is developing other such facilities. It has also demonstrated that it is prepared to forge strong relations with countries that have internationally controversial policies. In particular, Sri Lanka's closeness to China is of major interest (and concern) to India, while its closeness to Iran is viewed as disturbing by the United States and other Western powers. A large arms shipment seized in Bangkok at the end of 2009 from a Russian plane on route from North Korea was also believed to be destined for Colombo (*Bangkok Post* 2009), indicating a link between Colombo and Pyongyang, probably at the behest of China. In a sense, these strategic partnerships reflect what might be referred to as an 'unpleasant countries club', in which members 'join' to mutually support each other and in spite of or to effectively block prevailing world opinion.

However, Sri Lanka's closeness to China has to be weighed against its proximity to India and national security. Despite much earlier conflict between China and India and China's closeness to Pakistan, China has not intervened when Indian and Pakistani forces have exchanged fire over the Siachen Glacier on the border between India's province of Jammu-Kashmir and Pakistan. The government of Sri Lanka would be aware that its friendship with China has extended to the provision of weapons and substantial aid but is very much less likely to include going to war with India. Having said that, India would be aware that China could lend Sri Lanka tactical support, particularly in keeping open its shipping lanes, and that this might open up some potential for more limited forms of military engagement, which India would prefer to avoid in order to forestall possible escalation.

According to a leading Sri Lankan government propagandist, Sri Lanka was only too aware of its ability to play off China against India and in doing so snub the rest of the world:

> In the new era Sri Lanka can afford to ignore the West primarily because no meddlesome son of a witch can touch the president who is now sitting comfortably between China and India. The growing importance of Sri Lanka to India and China makes the West almost irrelevant to Sri Lanka.
>
> (Mahindapala 2010)

For the rest of the world, despite Sri Lanka's geographic position, it does not have a major trading port and is not a necessary stop on trans-Indian Ocean routes as it was before the advent of more modern shipping. Other powers have little concern that Sri Lanka would intentionally interrupt international shipping or allow itself to be used for such purposes, given that this would invite an almost immediate and probably military response. Thus, Sri Lanka's geographic position is on one hand neutralised and on the other hand irrelevant. Other than in exceptional circumstances and in particular those that involve threats to national security, intervening in Sri Lanka for any state has the potential to create a great deal of strategic, not to mention diplomatic, difficulty. Without a strategically compelling reason, then, the only state with the capacity and possible potential interest in intervening militarily in Sri Lanka – India – is unlikely to do so in any circumstances that can reasonably be envisaged.

States further afield do not regard Sri Lanka as sufficiently important and, on a scale of global humanitarian problems, those of Sri Lanka are widely seen as worthy of investigation and perhaps grinding over the slow wheels of international justice. But they are not at the forefront of international concerns: the war that gave rise to them is now ended and the LTTE's widespread status as a terrorist organisation does little to encourage sympathy for advocates of the remnants of its cause. Moreover, taking such matters through the UN Security Council would almost certainly continue to be blocked by permanent members China and Russia. Doing nothing, then, has become the lesser of two undesirable possible outcomes.

8 Conclusion

In the months between January and May 2009, the Sri Lankan army unleashed a full military offensive against the separatist Liberation Tigers of Tamil Eelam (or Tamil Tigers) in Sri Lanka's northern districts. This was to be the final phase of a war for a separate Tamil state that killed more than 100,000 people, damaged the country's economy and fundamentally changed and arguably diminished the Sri Lankan polity. According to a former UN spokesman, up to 40,000 people were killed in the final weeks of the war (Stein 2009[1]).

Following the war, more than 250,000 Tamils were held in internment camps in which they did not have access to adequate food, clean water or health care, with a death rate averaging 200 per day (AI 2009). Also deeply disturbing, between 10,000 and 15,000 individuals 'disappeared' from the internment camps (UNOCHA 2009), consistent with previous practice and presumably murdered by soldiers or police without recourse to trial or any other form of justice. These actions continued as a profound reminder of the nature of the state that had evolved to assume authority of its sometimes reluctant peoples. Most internees were eventually released, if to an uncertain future, and in many cases not being able to return to the homes or to the land they once owned. In some cases their homes were destroyed, but in many cases they had also become the site of or were in close proximity to army camps in what remained occupied areas or were occupied by internal migrants shifted from the Sinhalese south. Unsurprisingly, the government used the terms 'returns' and 'resettlement' interchangeably, with many displaced people being unable to return to their homes (Fonseka 2010: 10–12). Even more tellingly, the government's budgetary allocation in 2010 was Rs215 billion compared with Rs1.7 billion for resettlement appropriation. This followed the 2009 allocations of Rs201 billion compared with Rs3 billion respectively. This high level of expenditure on new weapons and Sri Lanka's 500,000 strong police and military followed the defeat of the LTTE. By way of illustration of the government's disinclination to engage in 'reconciliation', when the International Committee of the Red Cross gave 400 two-wheeled tractors to local farmers in the Mullaitivu and Vavuniya districts, a minister present at the ceremony overturned the ICRC's list of recipients and instead gave them to people of his own choice (*Sunday Times* 2010). This followed the transfer of the government 'NGO Secretariat' from the civilian Ministry of Social Services to the

Ministry of Defence, consequently denying many NGOs access to areas in most humanitarian need (IRIN 2010b). The directive from the director of the National Secretariat for Non-Governmental Organizations, Douglas Nanayakkara, issued a statement including the following:

> 1 Heads of all the NGOs/INGOs operating projects in Northern Province should register all the officials of such organizations in the Presidential Task Force (PTF) with immediate effect.
> 2 PTF will forward with its recommendation, all such lists of names as referred to in (1) above to the Director General of the National Secretariat for Non Governmental Organizations (NGO Secretariat). DG of the NGO Secretariat will forward with his recommendation all such lists as received from the PTF to the Military Liaison Office (MLO) for further clearances and final approval.
> 3 Further, all human and material movements of NGOs/INGOs to Northern Province referred to above need to be channeled through PTF with a copy to DG of the NGO Secretariat, to the MLO for further approval.
> 4 Heads of all NGOs and INGOs are strictly advised to adhere to the procedure above before any further action is taken in respect of projects in Northern Province.
>
> (Nanayakkara 2010)

In the period after the war, Tamils continued to flee Sri Lanka, in reasonable fear of persecution or for their lives. Despite the clear grounds they were able to present for seeking refugee status, receiving countries such as Australia and Canada treated them not with compassion but as, in effect, criminals or as potential criminals (Maley 2009a). The government of Sri Lanka, meanwhile, called for Tamil asylum seekers to be returned to Sri Lanka, employing the logic that they would only flee if they were members or sympathisers of the LTTE (Maley 2009b). In spite of the fact that many LTTE sympathisers simply sought equity, that many LTTE soldiers had been forced to join the organisation and that Tamils felt persecuted on the basis of their ethnicity rather than their political activity, the assumption was that they were all 'terrorists'. Being returned to Sri Lanka, then, meant at least a brutal interrogation and a period of detention without trial, and at worst joining the legion of 'disappeared'. The grounds for international concern were overwhelming in practice, if consistently underwhelming in terms of responses.

Over the 12 months or more since the end of the fighting, increasing evidence has emerged of a military operation that systematically and deliberately ignored the lives of civilians in its pursuit of LTTE rebels or which targeted civilians as LTTE sympathisers. There was also growing evidence of war crimes having been committed by SLA troops and some have argued that intentional disregard for or attack upon Tamil lives constituted an attempted genocide.[2] This all followed the formal and informal marginalisation of, and increasingly attacks against, the Tamil people dating back to the period just after Sri Lanka's independence in

1948. The question, then, appears to be not whether there were grounds for invoking the principles of a responsibility to protect but, if they have meaning beyond words on paper, why such principles were not invoked.

Notably, assuming that the Rome Statute constitutes the basis for determining and prosecuting war crimes, crimes against humanity and possibly genocide, it appeared that there was evidence to support charges for such crimes. However, the Rome Statute applies only to those states that are signatories to it and Sri Lanka has never accepted its jurisdiction, not least because it has been involved in two wars in which its criteria for war crimes and crimes against humanity could, as noted below, be claimed to have been breached. However, although Sri Lanka is not a signatory to the Rome Statute, these key provisions are a part of international customary law and, as such, could be reasonably argued to constitute a basis for invoking R2P.

A responsibility to protect?

As noted at the outset, the idea of R2P is relatively new in formal terms, bringing a sense of an international duty of care to the conduct of world affairs. From inauspicious beginnings surrounding various mass killings, the principle of R2P was endorsed by the General Assembly in 2005 under the explicit title of 'Responsibility to Protect Populations from Genocide, War Crimes, Ethnic Cleansing and Crimes against Humanity' and unanimously reaffirmed by the Security Council in 2006. Despite being adopted by the UN General Assembly, R2P was, however, not universally endorsed in principle and is less committed to in practice. This continues to reflect the tension between notions of international law or international responsibility concerning globally acceptable behaviour on one hand and the self-interest of states and disregard for others' internal affairs on the other.

The limits to international law were nowhere more keenly felt than in 1999 when the UN Security Council failed to reach agreement on the Kosovo issue, not because of debate about the severity of the situation but because of strategic infighting within the organisation. The Security Council failure to act in its own right was self-diminishing, showing that the competing interests of the Security Council's permanent members was its greatest shortcoming and that which compromised its legitimacy in the eyes of the world, in particular among those people of states requiring intervention or, on the other hand, among those states feeling compelled to provide such intervention. It was out of this dilemma that Annan announced that it was the:

> core challenge to the Security Council and to the United Nations as a whole in the next century [is] . . . to forge unity behind the principle that massive and systematic violations of human rights – wherever they take place – should not be allowed to stand.
>
> (Annan 1999)

In opposing R2P, the government of Sri Lanka has fallen very firmly into the literalist, realist camp of self-interest, and has been opposed to the idea and the practice of R2P in all its nuanced forms since its inception. This meant that attempts at limiting Sri Lanka's internal behaviour were, and would likely have remained, unsuccessful and would have made any last resort on-ground R2P intervention very difficult, given that it would be likely to be militarily resisted. Not least, this would have been resisted on the grounds that R2P was just another form of neo-colonialism and that states pushing an R2P agenda or even accountability for war crimes had secret strategic interests at stake, rather than being genuinely concerned about humanitarian issues.

The Tamil Eelam war

The Tamil Eelam separatist war, which led to the conditions that might otherwise have implied R2P and in which 'whites' have mostly shown limited interest, was a result of a series of injustices that built up to the point where they were regarded, by many Tamils, as no longer tolerable. The Sinhalese majority increasingly saw the island of Sri Lanka as their sole home and continued to marginalise the Tamil minority. Conflict was all but inevitable.

Having established its authority over other Tamil separatist groups, the LTTE grew to become one of the largest and most dangerous separatist organisations in the world. It also managed to have itself put on global terrorist lists, principally for its murder of Indian former prime minister Rajiv Ghandi and its attacks against civilians. There is no serious argument against the fact that the LTTE employed methods that fall under the conventional heading of 'terrorism', including assassinations, generalised bombings and attacking uninvolved civilians in a number of highly publicised cases. The Sri Lankan state could similarly be accused of employing terrorism, notably in relation to mass killings of civilians, presiding over the 'disappearances' of suspected activists and in relation to indiscriminate attacks against civilian-populated areas. The problem was, however, at a time of 'war on terrorism', states were more easily able to claim legitimacy for their actions and non-state actors were increasingly regarded as not just illegitimate but, almost by default, as terrorist organisations. By having the LTTE so listed, the government of Sri Lanka was able to bring international pressure to bear on the LTTE's international operations, which eventually isolated the organisation from its international support base.

Despite early sympathy for the Tamil cause in India, especially in the state of Tamil Nadu, and support from India's external intelligence agency, the Research and Analysis Wing, India's support was always informed by its own strategic interests, which was largely to counter Sri Lanka's support for (and from) Pakistan and later China. India had never supported a separate state in Sri Lanka and its deployment of the IPKF was intended to stabilise the situation in Sri Lanka, appease Indian popular concerns and, no doubt, assert India's strategic hegemony in the region. However, it ended badly, with the IPKF at war with the LTTE, departing two years later in ignominy. This misadventure has continued to remind external actors of the potential futility and likely cost of directly and especially unilaterally intervening in Sri Lanka's affairs.

On the back of military successes, the Sri Lankan state eventually agreed to a Norwegian-brokered ceasefire agreement (CFA) in 2002, which allowed the creation of the unarmed Norwegian-led Sri Lanka Monitoring Mission (SLMM) as a muted version of R2P. However, the ceasefire did little more than allow the LTTE to consolidate its control over the Vanni area of the north of the island and both sides to re-arm and re-equip ahead of what was seen by both sides as an almost inevitable return to war. Following the signing of the CFA in 2002, in 2003 in Tokyo, the EU, Norway, the United States and Japan pledged money for the economic development of Sri Lanka and declared themselves to be the 'co-chairs of the Tokyo Conference', which then took joint responsibility for monitoring the peace process within the context of the CFA. After the Sri Lankan government withdrew from the CFA in 2008, the 'co-chairs' issued a statement expressing their support for a negotiated settlement and their belief that there was no military solution to the conflict in Sri Lanka.

Both the LTTE and the government had been using the period since the ceasefire agreement to build up stockpiles of weapons[3] and by the end of 2004 it appeared that the two parties were ready to resume fighting. This perception was reinforced on 12 August 2005 when the LTTE was widely held responsible for the assassination of the stridently anti-LTTE Sri Lankan foreign minister (and ethnic Tamil) Lakshman Kadirgamar, resulting in the renewal of a state of emergency. Similarly, the government and its front groups engaged in extra-judicial killings of public Tamil figures and political activists. The government in particular used remaining Karuna group defectors with assistance from India's by now anti-LTTE Research and Analysis Wing to conduct what amounted to an insurgency campaign against the LTTE.[4] As the government hardened its position in 2004, President Kumaratunga declared a state of emergency, suspended parliament, took control of the mass media and Ministries of the Interior and Defence and called new elections for April 2004. The People's Freedom Alliance in coalition with the JVP won the elections, with Mahinda Rajapaksa becoming prime minister. Despite formally acknowledging the 2002 ceasefire agreement, from the outset Rajapaksa intended to seek a military victory over the LTTE.

The 2004 Boxing Day Tusnami which killed 30,000 people only hardened divisions that arose over the allocation and distribution of relief funds. The LTTE claimed that under the provisions of the 2002 ceasefire agreement it should be responsible for the allocation of aid in areas under its control. However, the government believed that the aid would be used to support more pro-LTTE areas and would not be used to benefit those that did not support the LTTE. Moreover, given what appeared to increasingly be the government's longer-term intention of returning to war, whoever controlled the flow of aid also controlled economic resources, which in turn equalled military resources. The problem was not the tsunami so much as it was the lack of good faith on the part of both the government and the LTTE to find further political compromise without first returning to war.

The return to war

In November 2005, Rajapaksa was elected to the presidency on a clear policy of militarily defeating the LTTE but with a slim margin of just 1.8 per cent, which many attributed to the LTTE stopping or 'discouraging' people under its control from voting, in this case for the opposing candidate. Following Rajapaksa's election and the appointment of his brother Gotabhaya Rajapaksa as defence minister, the Sri Lankan government became significantly more aggressive towards the LTTE, escalating its attacks via proxy militias, and engaging in direct kidnappings, murders and assaults, and eventually full-scale military confrontation. The government's policy of having the LTTE listed as a terrorist organisation by other state governments became increasingly successful and its effect was to limit fund-raising for the LTTE, which denied it an important source of income. The ceasefire agreement was more or less respected until early 2006 but from then it began to fall apart, with both sides escalating attacks against the other (BBC 2007). By mid-year, following full-scale government attacks in both the north and the east, what was referred to by Tamils as Eelam War IV had begun. This return to war demonstrated that there was little scope for a negotiated settlement and that both sides were belligerent. Only significant external intervention at this time could have halted the continued slide into full-scale war and the atrocities that accompanied it.

Despite many – perhaps most – Tamils not wanting a return to war, there also remained profound impediments to sustaining or returning to peace. But both the LTTE and the Sri Lankan government had acted in less than good faith throughout the ceasefire and both had always appeared to have as their intention to settle their differences on the battlefield. This lack of support for a negotiated outcome was confirmed at the beginning of January 2007, giving public acknowledgement to what already existed: that the government intended to seek a military solution to the LTTE issue (Balachandran 2007). This should have set the alarm bells ringing for the international community, especially among its R2P advocates. But it did not. Beyond this return to a military solution, Sri Lanka was also moving away from open democratic processes and towards a type of bureaucratic authoritarianism[5] in which Tamils were increasingly a persecuted minority. Sri Lanka had been shifting from a parliamentary to a presidential-led system in 1978 and, since then, executive authority had been more and more located in the hands of the president, who appoints ministers as well as the Supreme Court judges who decide on constitutional issues. The role of the prime minister, in contrast, had become increasingly ceremonial. The president appoints, among others, the defence minister, who was from late 2005 an army brigadier-general and brother of the president. This was accompanied by increasing impunity for extra-judicial killings and other grave human rights violations. Parliamentary politics continued, if in a more limited fashion, although the use of army-linked death squads and torture and the denial of habeas corpus contributed to an increasingly constrained political climate and real concerns about the orientation of the state towards its Tamil minority.

Any genuine democratisation and political devolution could have theoretically worked but was hamstrung by the organisation of Sri Lanka's political parties and the voting patterns of its citizens, which ensured that ethnic Sinhalese parties dominated the parliament. Any encouragement for such a political settlement became less and less likely as Sri Lanka drifted further from its pro-democracy states and closer to single-party authoritarian states that were not squeamish about war crimes, much less human rights issues. As noted by one scholar, the:

> Systematic weakening of public institutions and the consolidation of power through a largely unchecked security apparatus and a centralisation of power in the Presidency have created a culture of abysmal lawlessness in Sri Lanka. I share the deep concerns expressed by Louise Arbour, President of the International Crisis Group, and The Elders about the potential 'multiplier' effect of the GoSL's exploitation of security rhetoric to justify its methods and policies.
>
> (Scott and Yap 2010)

As noted by another close observer:

> Death squads remain active as enforcers of the government's writ. Dissent is punished, newspapers and public opinion tamed by an even more rigid ideology of Sinhalese supremacy. The yearning for freedom of expression is an equation of diminishing returns for those who wish to make a living – or indeed to live at all – in Sri Lanka. The central issue of political and social equality for Sri Lankan Tamils remains unsatisfied, with the triumphant state less inclined than ever to make meaningful political concessions.
>
> (Weiss 2011)

The small, unarmed and, in terms of human rights violation monitoring, poorly trained and inadequately resourced Sri Lanka Monitoring Mission, established to oversee the 2002 CFA, was unable to prevent Sri Lanka's slide back into conflict. Indeed, the SLMM became a subject for antipathy from the Sri Lankan government for what it perceived to be its unwanted interference and the implicit assumption that, if it was at all even-handed towards the LTTE, then it was diametrically opposed to the government's increasingly strident claims and interests. All ceasefire agreements require the active support of all combatant parties otherwise, almost by definition, they break down. However, the intention of R2P is that it brings an element of external compulsion to such arrangements and it was clear from the outset that the SLMM lacked the resources, political will and especially the mandate to impose its will on the combatant parties. The SLMM represented a type of R2P but it was a weak and ultimately futile interpretation of the intention of the paradigm and was consequently unable to prevent subsequent mass atrocities. These included more than 4,000 people being killed between late 2005 and early 2007 and more than a quarter of a million made homeless over that time. Another 2,000 or more either were killed or 'disappeared' between then and August 2007. The resumption and escalation of the war were further clear signals that a 'circuit breaker' – external intervention – was required.

In large part, the LTTE's aspirations to the trappings of statehood were its undoing. The LTTE had evolved from a highly mobile if heavily armed and highly skilled guerrilla organisation to become a conventional army fighting a largely conventional rather than asymmetric guerrilla war. In the final analysis, if the government put into the war as much determination as the LTTE had demonstrated, its overwhelming size and access to funds and military hardware meant that it would ultimately succeed. The LTTE had become a captive to its own dream and, along with its increasing international isolation, in particular from India, entered into the final phase of a conventional war that it could not possibly win.

The unfolding of a humanitarian disaster

The renewal of fighting in 2006 marked the beginning of the end of the Eelam wars. Despite initial signs of LTTE strength, the Sri Lankan army conducted a series of successful campaigns. The first was to push the LTTE out of the eastern provinces including an LTTE artillery sight near Trincomaleee, followed by the capture or destruction of LTTE-owned ships carrying weapons and supplies. The LTTE resumed its bombing campaign, with one suicide attack at Habaraba killing around 100 sailors in the single deadliest attack of the war. In 2007, the army assaulted the LTTE's northern bases, initially targeting the LTTE's leadership with air strikes. In November 2007, the LTTE's political leader, Thamilchevan, and five other senior leaders were killed in what was described by the LTTE as a precision air strike.[6] Despite these setbacks, LTTE forces on the ground put up a stiff defence against continuing army assaults. In a somewhat odd statement two years after the fact, the government formally withdrew from the 2002 ceasefire agreement in January 2008. After a number of setbacks, from August 2008 the SLA eventually advanced, taking Mannar in the west and then assaulting the LTTE's 'capital' of Kilinochche from three sides in November 2008, capturing it in January 2009. With the loss of their 'capital', the LTTE, civilians under its protection and others retreated to Mullataivu where they underwent a sustained air attack, including against civilians sheltering with or being held by the LTTE. Again overwhelmed, by the end of January 2009 the remaining LTTE forces and civilians retreated further. It was clear from this time that a humanitarian catastrophe was unfolding but, due to the veto powers of two of its permanent members, China and Russia, the UN Security Council remained helpless to act.

It is possible to mount a case that R2P could have been applicable at several stages throughout the war in Sri Lanka, but towards the end of 2008 and into the first months of 2009, despite government efforts to restrict media coverage and to mislead about the facts on the ground, it was becoming increasingly clear to the outside world that war crimes and crimes against humanity were being committed under the 'complete operational freedom' granted to Sri Lanka army commanders to ensure the war's success (see Smith 2010: 40; Shashikumar 2009). It was this explicit 'operational freedom' as part of government policy that led to mass deaths which contravened the Rome Statute's Article 7 concerning 'crimes against humanity'. Thus, the grounds for R2P were established, if not in terms so absolute that the UN Security Council could not help but take concrete steps (although recognising China and Russia's role in limiting such steps). In that there had been arguments that genocide or ethnic cleansing was under way this was, as discussed, more difficult to sustain. But genocide and ethnic cleansing were not required to be proven for war crimes and crimes against humanity to be committed.

Despite LTTE overtures that it was in the last weeks willing to discuss a negotiated settlement, the government pressed the SLA's attack while foreign governments refused to intervene. The last months of the war were marked by unremitting brutality against civilians with consequently rapidly mounting civilian casualties. Human Rights Watch accused the SLA of 'slaughtering' civilians through indiscriminate air and artillery attacks against positions where large numbers of civilians were known to be sheltering. This not only made President Rajapaksa's 'zero civilian casualties' policy and the army's claim that the area being shelled was a 'no-fire zone' look decidedly empty but again should have spurred the international community to action. Indeed, at this point there could have been a case made for unilateral or regional action. The international community, however, procrastinated, despite some hand wringing and ineffectual calls for the LTTE to release civilians being held on the narrow, 14-kilometre strip of beach near Mullaitvu. With some 20,000 civilians killed in the 'no-fire zone' in the last weeks of the war, at the almost inconceivable rate of about 1,000 a day, the world stood by and watched this humanitarian disaster unfold. Meanwhile, the dissembling continued and the Sri Lankan High Commissioner in London rejected claims that any civilians had been killed, later qualifying this by saying that if civilians had been killed it had been by the LTTE. There was no doubt that the LTTE was indeed trying to shoot fleeing civilians, but there was similarly no doubt that the Sri Lankan army continued to bomb and shell civilian areas, which the government continued to reject as LTTE propaganda.

The blocking by the United States of Sri Lanka's application for a $1.9 billion emergency loan from the International Monetary Fund, backed by the United Kingdom, over its conduct of the war had no effect. Notably, China's support for Sri Lanka's war against the LTTE and its lack of concern over its methods stopped dead any moves by the Security Council towards sanctions or intervention. R2P was not even beginning to be on the international agenda. In particular, China's blocking of Security Council resolutions regarding Sri Lanka meant that the requirements for implementing R2P could not be established and it was clear that it would not allow the imposition of R2P. Russia's further support was simply another nail in the coffin of the LTTE and for tens of thousands of Tamil civilians, whose lives were sacrificed on the altar of narrow strategic interest. The Security Council's expression of 'deep concern' was remarkable only for its complete irrelevance to anything that was then happening.

The failure of R2P in Sri Lanka

A major reason why the international community was not able to exercise more authority in relation to Sri Lanka, particularly in the final stages of the anti-LTTE war, was because it was both blocked in the UN Security Council by China and Russia and blocked on the ground by China and India both actively supporting the government of Sri Lanka – India with intelligence and China with weapons and funds. There was also considerable reluctance by Western states to do anything more than apply economic pressure to Sri Lanka, which might have been influential had it not been countered by China's economic support for the country's government. It was particularly China's economic and military support for the government of Sri Lanka that effectively stopped international intervention and which limited the efficacy of economic sanctions. 'The most remarkable aspect of Sri Lanka's recent victory over the Tamil Tigers is [that] . . . [w]ithout that Chinese backing, Rajapaksa's government would have had neither the wherewithal nor the will to ignore world opinion in its offensive against the Tigers' (Wen 2009). China's involvement had compelled India to support the government of Sri Lanka, to ensure that its influence was not neutralised in favour of its regional competitor:

> Sri Lanka was able to vanquish the Tigers also due to India's tacit support, which included providing training and logistical support such as naval surveillance to cut off Tigers' weapons supply. There were two motives: India wanted to be rid of the LTTE and, second, India could not sit back and see its regional influence overwhelmed by its main strategic competitor. Against the combined military might of Sri Lanka, India and China, the LTTE was hopelessly outclassed.
>
> (Pratap 2009)

Setting aside India's mixed motives and disastrously handled implementation in 1987, Norway's efforts to achieve the 2002 ceasefire agreement supported by the European Union, the United States and Japan were as close as Sri Lanka came to R2P intervention. However, without a geo-political stake in its outcome, the international parties to the CFA were not able or – more importantly – sufficiently motivated and hence willing to extend their involvement when the ceasefire began to break down from 2006 (Goodhand 2001: 27). Having initially backed peace efforts in Sri Lanka as a mechanism for resolving terrorism, the United States moved its position towards one of overall declining interest and increasing disenchantment with what it perceived to be the LTTE's problematic demands (Lunstead 2007: 33, 36–7). This corresponded with its 'war on terror', a more global trend towards banning the LTTE as a terrorist organisation, and US positioning as a balance between India and China (Kaplan 2009: 16–32).

Considering the above details and *prima facie* case for intervention and how it did not come about, it appears that there were four key reasons why R2P was not applied in Sri Lanka. The first reason was that the international community was (and remains) divided over whether or not R2P is a legitimate form of international activity. In particular, a number of states with questionable human rights records, which include areas challenged by separatist movements or that have strategic alliances with such states, have been reluctant to endorse or have been actively opposed to the implementation of R2P principles. These include Sri Lanka and, as its main sponsor, China.

The second reason for the failure to invoke R2P principles in the case of Sri Lanka was that, as a result of Sri Lankan appeals, the LTTE was widely classified as a proscribed terrorist organisation, notably at a time when the US-led 'war on terror' helped define much of the way in which otherwise more liberal states responded to 'terrorist' threats. There was little international sympathy for the LTTE and considerable international support for the continued unity of the state of Sri Lanka. This should not have impacted upon international concern for the welfare of civilians, but the government of Sri Lanka was clever in the way that it obscured the plight of the Tamil civilians and the circumstances under which they were with the LTTE.

The third reason for the failure to invoke R2P principles in the case of Sri Lanka was that the economic sanctions that were applied were too little, too uncoordinated, too late and ultimately countered by China's economic support. Beyond economic or other sanctions, should members of the international community have contemplated on-ground R2P intervention, under its generally accepted (if not specifically endorsed) terms, it must have had a reasonable chance of success and must not have caused more harm than it resolved. Following India's unsuccessful intervention in 1987, neither of these criteria could be guaranteed. Indeed, given increasing Sri Lankan belligerence, there was a high likelihood of official military resistance, backed by China and possibly India. Finally, the fourth reason for the failure to invoke R2P principles was that such an attempt would ordinarily require the endorsement if not active participation of the UN Security Council, which was blocked by China and actively opposed by Russia.

These four factors – international disagreement over R2P, reservations about or being antithetical towards the LTTE, the likely human cost of intervention and the lack of support from the UN Security Council – all contributed to making an R2P intervention either ineffective as sanctions or all but impossible in an on-ground capacity. In the end, no country cared enough about Sri Lanka's Tamils to want to go to the trouble of invoking R2P. The UN Security Council was stymied by China and Russia, late and relatively minor sanctions by Western countries had little effect given that China had stepped into the military and economic breech, India vied with China to support the government, and the R2P principle of benefits exceeding cost could not reasonably be established.

A resolution to the Sri Lankan conflict had not been likely, or possible, without significant international pressure to adopt measures that reflected a fundamental compromise on the part of both parties, and support for such measures once adopted. It may be that the earlier employment of R2P could have produced this effect, especially if it had been around the time of or as part of the SLMM (noting that this pre-dated the establishment of R2P). Such an intervention would have implied, among other measures, a more substantial version of the SLMM, the promise of extra aid and the threat of serious sanctions on either party should they break the agreement. Having said that, the LTTE came to a point of genuine preparedness to compromise only in 2008–9, well after the government of Sri Lanka had embarked on an opposite course.[7] From the election of Rajapaksa as president in 2005, the die was effectively cast, yet it was only at that time that the international community had formally adopted the idea of R2P and had not yet moved to a position of enacting it. Had a sustainable solution been available at any time, Sri Lanka needed to return to being a more substantive democracy, working gradually back towards a notion of civic nationalism in which equity under rule of law rather than ethnicity was the effective basis for a sense of inclusion and participation, or at least the equitable management of different interest claims. This appeared an increasingly distant goal, following a change to the Sri Lanka constitution in September 2010 to end limits on presidential terms, end the presidential advisory council and implement the direct political appointment of judges.[8] Assuming that these changes did not imply 'the last nail in the coffin of democracy' (Cowan 2010) or 'absolute power'(The Australian 2010), after perhaps generations, a sense of normalcy and unity might have returned to Sri Lanka, although not without deep and far-reaching changes. Following the end of the war, such an outcome appeared to be further away than ever and such a potential path appeared littered with significant obstacles that the international community showed little interest in trying to surmount.

The world had a clear opportunity and, in terms of civilian deaths, a moral obligation to bring R2P principles to bear in the Sri Lanka war. Instead, tens of thousands of people were killed in a relentless and barbaric act of warfare that finds parallel only with the mass killings of Bosnia and Kosovo, Rwanda and Darfur. Indeed, it is probably inappropriate to try to compare acts of barbarity and inhumanity, as though there was some sliding scale by which some could be deemed more or less cruel and inhuman than others. All such acts of barbarism and inhumanity have the same intent and malignant lack of regard for human life; it has been only the efficacy of application that differentiated them. Sri Lanka was no different. Perhaps the timely application of R2P could have averted the humanitarian disaster that was the Sri Lanka Eelam war, but by the time R2P existed it was probably already too late, not least because of the structural impediments placed in its way by China, Russia, India and the government of Sri Lanka and probably the LTTE itself.

It may be that, had R2P been properly implemented in a timely manner, Sri Lanka could now be rebuilding as a prospering, liberal democratic state with respect for civil and political rights and in which there was devolved authority for ethnically specific areas. At different times different relevant parties have aimed for such an outcome. The problem was that none of them aimed for such an outcome at corresponding times, the international community paid too little attention for too long and such opportunity, as it ever existed, was lost.

Notes

Introduction

1 The United States had said that the International Monetary Fund would withhold a tranche of funds required to assist the Indonesian economy recover from its previous economic collapse.
2 Farer (2003: 58) referred to this situation as a 'very close cousin' of humanitarian intervention.
3 The precipitous nature of the withdrawal was reflected in Australian and New Zealand military forces having to return to Timor-Leste in 2006 to quell social and state breakdown that was arguably allowed to develop by the international community leaving before state institutions could be properly established.
4 Estimates of the number killed, including Hutu moderates, begin with 'at least 500,000' (Human Rights Watch 1999), or about 75 per cent of the Tutsi population in Rwanda, and commonly refer to around 800,000 deaths.
5 Conflict preceded this date, but it is often used as the formal entry point of the Liberation Tigers of Tamil Eelam (LTTE).

1 The meaning, theory and application of R2P

1 Co-founder of Médecins Sans Frontiers, among other achievements.
2 I have also had Muslim, notably Acehnese, friends discuss with me at length the importance of reason as a gift of God, and the ability to make rational decisions about good and evil as the purpose of that gift.
3 Second-generation rights include economic, social and cultural rights, with third-generation rights including peace and a sustainable environment.
4 Weber first enunciated this idea in the modern era, although the legitimacy of state violence was a given of prior state rule, and has since become commonplace in political theory.
5 The word 'felt' is used intentionally here, as this is a sub-rational response to conflict, which in reality can strike almost anywhere, especially in an age of long-range aircraft and missiles.

2 The politics of ethnicity

1 There is believed to have been a settlement on this site since around the ninth century BCE.
2 This is the historic equivalent of claiming the national illegitimacy of English people derived of a Norman heritage, for example with French-derived surnames.
3 This was intended to limit the proportion of Tamils in universities and in effect set a higher and hence inequitable university entrance requirement for Tamils. It had the effect of cutting Tamil university enrolments by about three-quarters.

4 The island had been historically known by the Sinhalese as Lankaa and by the Tamils as Ilanki/Ilankai. The addition of 'Sri' to 'Lanka' followed its use in the 1940 song, 'Ananda Samarakoon', which subsequently became the national anthem; it had been in increasingly common use in Sinhalese, from 1948 on postage stamps and from 1956 on currency notes.
5 This ministry pre-dated the Ministry of Religious Affairs and again replaced this ministry under President Mahinda Rajapaksa in 2006. 'Sasana' is Buddhist doctrine or teaching.
6 From a talk given by this activist to an expatriate Tamil community meeting, Melbourne, 10 April 2010.

3 The war in Sri Lanka

1 Interview, head of the LTTE Peace Secretariat, Seevarasiah Puledevan, Kilinochche, 11 May 2006.
2 Personal communication, unnamed LTTE negotiator, May 2010.
3 Observed by the author, northern Vanni technical control line, 9 May 2006.
4 This number was hinted at by an LTTE cadre travelling with the author, but not confirmed. Other estimates have put the LTTE's numbers around 10,000, while Sri Lankan sources have quoted figures as low as 800 regular fighters and 2,000 militia (Balachandran 2007).
5 This observation is based on the Sri Lankan military's mixed record in battling the LTTE, leading to the establishment of the 'liberated zone' in the Vanni.
6 This observation is based on discussions by the author with senior members of the LTTE international branch, in particular in 2006, a time when there was also a marked breakdown in the 2002 CFA. These views are supported in particular by interviews with the head of the LTTE Peace Secretariat, Pulidevan (single name attrib.), on 10 and 12 May 2006, the head of the LTTE International Secretariat, Castro (*nom de guerre*), on 11 May 2006, and the political head of the LTTE, Suppiah Paramu Tamilchelvan, on 13 May 2006.
7 Observed by the author, 9–14 May 2006.
8 This view was explicitly stated by the head of the Aceh Monitoring Mission Pieter Feith in discussions with Gerakan Aceh Merdeka (Free Aceh Movement or GAM), at which the author was present, during negotiations that ultimately ended the Aceh conflict.
9 Based on personal conversations with the LTTE leadership in the Vanni in 2006.
10 The second factor was the LTTE's assassination in 1991 of former Indian prime minister Rajiv Gandhi, which effectively ended any possible future Indian support for the LTTE as well as ensuring its increasing international status as a terrorist organisation and consequent international isolation. The third factor was the LTTE stopping ethnic Tamils voting in the 2005 elections, which gave a slim victory to the nationalist Mahinda Rajapaksa, whose policy was to wipe out the LTTE rather than negotiate with it. This is what ultimately transpired.
11 This view was unofficially supported by a number of LTTE cadres (date and place of discussions not noted for ethical reasons).
12 These claims were made by leading Tamil figures within Sri Lanka who cannot be identified because of the continuing climate of fear and retribution that remains.

4 Cultural dominance, genocide and crimes against humanity

1 In which Nazi propagandist Julius Streicher was sentenced to death for directly inciting the extermination of Jews.

5 Sri Lanka and international law

1 Socrates' acceptance of his sentence of death as a social obligation.
2 The United States failed to ratify the Covenant of the League of Nations because of the US Senate's refusal to pass the requisite legislation.
3 Representatives of the European Union Council and Presidency, the European Commission and NATO also attended most Contact Group meetings.
4 That is, states that had an ability to assert their authority on the global stage, usually characterised by the United Kingdom, France, Italy, Japan and the United States following the Great War, and by the UN Security Council permanent members following World War II.
5 Many of the countries involved offered only a token presence or in some cases even only verbal support, with Costa Rica withdrawing because of limitations imposed by its constitution and most other states subsequently withdrawing according to a range of timelines. At the time of writing, it appeared that 2014 might constitute a final timeline for all external involvement, although even this could be shifted by interpretation.
6 The number of people killed in Iraq to the end of 2010 has been estimated to range from around 100,000 (IBC 2010) to more than one million (JFP 2010), including those who have died as indirect results of the war.

6 Opposition to R2P

1 The 'Balibo Declaration' signed by representatives of four pro-Indonesia parties on 30 November 1975 was used as a justification for Indonesia's invasion of Timor-Leste on 8 December that year. Despite its name, the Balibo Declaration was actually signed in Bali, Indonesia, after being drafted by Indonesian military intelligence the previous September.
2 The sham 2010 elections not withstanding.
3 The author was among those subject to a barrage of harassing and occasionally threatening e-mails as well as defamatory e-mails to his school between 2007 and 2009.

7 Geo-strategic factors, R2P and Sri Lanka

1 The word 'cadre' was developed by Lenin to denote professional revolutionaries. It was adopted by the LTTE to denote full-time military members of the LTTE.
2 The government of Sri Lanka provided a number of other governments with information and occasionally evidence with which to prosecute cases against suspected LTTE members or supporters, in particular Australia, the United Kingdom, the United States and Canada.
3 Australia has recognised the LTTE as a terrorist organisation only under the UN's listing of the LTTE as a terrorist organisation. The LTTE was not proscribed as a terrorist organisation as such by the Australian government.
4 Claims of neo-colonial aspirations were also common among Sri Lanka's media opinion writers.
5 Rajiv Gandhi was elected as India's prime minister following the assassination of his mother, Indira Gandhi, in October 1984.
6 Based on discussions with alleged LTTE supporters at that time.

8 Conclusion

1 Also Gordon Weiss, personal communication, July 5, 2010.
2 There was considerable debate about whether genocide was being committed, although the unremitting brutality and ethnic character of the war did tend to push it towards a conventional definition (see Fein 2009; Surendiram 2009; Shaw 2010).

3 Acknowledged by senior LTTE officers to the author (see also Bedi 2007).

4 The general belief that this was the case was supported when RAW sent officers on a reconnaissance mission to Kilinochche after its recapture by the Sri Lankan army in late 2008 (see Malik 2009).

5 In September 2010, a two-thirds majority of the parliament changed Sri Lanka's constitution to allow successive presidential terms beyond the prescribed two, handed control of the judiciary to the president and effectively severed legal accountability.

6 The claim of a precision air strike may have been an accurate account of events, although requiring close observation of this group in safe LTTE territory. An alternative account was that growing divisions in the senior leadership of the LTTE over whether to fight or talk led the hard-line leadership to permanently remove soft-liners. Neither account was able to be substantiated.

7 Based on discussions by the author with senior LTTE members in Sri Lanka in 2006 and outside Sri Lanka from that time until the defeat of the organisation.

8 The constitutional changes were approved by the Sri Lanka Supreme Court, which was also politically beholden.

References

Abiew, F. (1999). *The Evolution of the Doctrine and Practice of Humanitarian Intervention*, The Hague: Kluwer Law International.

Acharya, A. (2004). 'How ideas spread: Whose norms matter? Norm localization and institutional change in Asian regionalism'. *International Organisation* 58(2): 239–75.

Acharya, A. (2009). *Whose Ideas Matter?: Agency and Power in Asian Regionalism*. Ithaca, NY: Cornell University Press.

AFP (2009). 'Over 20,000 Tamils killed in Sri Lankan onslaught'. Agence France Presse, 29 May 2009.

AI (2009). 'Amnesty International Report – Sri Lanka', 28 May 2009. London: Amnesty International.

AI (2010). 'Sri Lanka's New Parliament Must Drop Emergency Laws'. London: Amnesty International, 20 April 2010.

Albright, M. (2010). 'Madeleine Albright on redefining NATO', National Public Radio, 20 May 2010.

Al Jazeera (2010). 'Photos allege Sri Lanka massacre', 10 November 2010.

Aluwihare, A. (2000). 'Patterns of displacement: Responsibilities and consequences: Can Sri Lanka provide any lessons/ideas for the AsiaPacific region', *Refugee Survey Quarterly* 19(2): 216–23.

Ammitzboell, K. (2007). 'Unintended consequences of peace operations on the host economy from a people's perspective', in C. Aoi, C. de Coning and R. Thakur (eds) *Unintended Consequences of Peacekeeping*, Tokyo: United Nations University Press.

Anderson, B. (1991). *Imagined Communities*, New York: Verso.

Anderson, B. (ed.) (2001). *Violence and the State in Suharto's Indonesia*, Ithaca, NY: Cornell University Press.

Angiolillo, P. (1979). *A Criminal as Hero*, Lawrence: Regent Press of Kansas.

Annan, K (1999). 'Secretary-General Presents his Annual Report to the General Assembly', New York: United Nations, 20 September 1999.

Anon (1991). 'Tamil Eelam National Flag' (trans. from Tamil), *Viduthalai Puligal*, March 1991.

Aoi, C., de Coning, C., and Thakur, R. (eds) (2007). *Unintended Consequences of Peacekeeping*, Tokyo: United Nations University Press.

Asian Tribune (2010a). 'Sri Lanka is South Asia's most liberal economy: President Rajapaksa', Asiantribune.com, 2 July 2010. Available at http://www.asiantribune.com/news/2010/07/02/sri-lanka-south-asias-most-liberal-economy-president-rajapaksa (accessed 21 July 2010).

Ayton-Shenker, D. (1995). 'The Challenge of Human Rights and Cultural Diversity', United Nations Background Note, UN Department of Public Information, DPI/1627/HR, March 1995.

BAH (2005). 'Energy. Futures in Asia', Washington DC: Booz Allen Hamilton.

Baines, E. (1818). History of the Wars of the French Revolution, Vol. II, London: Longman, Hurst, Rees, Orme and Brown.

Balachandran, B. (2007). 'Lankan army hopes to clear East by March', *Hindustan Times* (New Delhi), 3 January 2007.

Balasingham, A. (2003). *The Will to Freedom: An Inside View of the Tamil Resistance*, 2nd edn, Mitcham, UK: Fairmax.

Ban, K. (2008). 'Statement Attributable to the Spokesperson for the Secretary-General on the Situation in Kenya', New York: United Nations, 2 January 2008.

Bangkok Post (2009). 'Huge N Korea arms cache seized', 13 December 2009.

Barns, G. (2010). 'Arbiter of asylum claims casts doubt on Rudd's application freeze'. Crikey.com, 13 April 2010. Available at http://www.crikey.com.au/2010/04/13/arbiter-of-asylum-claims-casts-doubt-on-rudds-application-freeze/ (accessed 11 September 2011).

Barro, R. (1996). *Getting It Right: Markets and Choices in a Free Society*, Cambridge, MA: MIT Press.

Bass, G. (2008). *Freedom's Battle: The Origins of Humanitarian Intervention*, New York: Alfred A. Knopf.

BBC (2004). 'Iraq war illegal, says Anan', British Broadcasting Corporation News, 16 September 2004.

BBC (2007). 'War victory party in Sri Lanka', British Broadcasting Corporation News, 12 July 2007.

BBC (2008). 'Iran president in Sri Lanka visit', British Broadcasting Corporation World News, 28 April 2008.

BBC (2009). 'Tamil war zone hospital hit again', British Broadcasting Corporation News, 13 May 2009.

Bedi, R. (2007). 'Sri Lanka turns to China, Pakistan, for military needs', Indo Asian News Service, 6 February 2007.

Bellamy, A. (2009). *Responsibility to Protect: The Global Effort to End Mass Atrocities*, Cambridge: Polity Press.

Bellamy, A. (2010). 'Kosovo and the advent of sovereignty as responsibility', in A. Hehir (ed.) *Kosovo, Intervention and Statebuilding*, London: Routledge.

Bentham, J. (1781). 'The principles of morals and legislation'. Available at http://www.constitution.org/jb/pml.htm (accessed 8 August 2006).

Bentham, J. (1843). *The Principles of International Law, Vol. II*, in *The Works of Jeremy Bentham*, ed. J. Bowring, Edinburgh: Tait.

Berlin, I. (1958). *Two Concepts of Liberty*, Oxford: Oxford University Press.

Bettati, M. (1987). *Le Droit d'indigence: mutation de l'ordre international*. Paris: Odil Jacob.

Bettati, M. and Kouchner, B. (eds) (1987). *Le Devoir d'ingérence: peut-on les laisser mourir?* Paris: Editions Denoel.

Bettati, M. (2004). 'The use of force by the United Nations', *Pouvoirs: Revue Française d'Etudes Constitutionnelles et Politiques* 109: 111–24.

Bhadrakumar, M. (2009). 'Sri Lanka wards off Western bullying', Asia Times Online, 27 May 2009. Available at http://www.atimes.com/atimes/South_Asia/KE27Df01.html (accessed 7 June 2010).

Blair, D. (2009). 'Sri Lanka analysis: China emerges as key player in victory over Tamil Tigers', *The Telegraph*, 18 May 2009.

Blair, T. (1999). 'Doctrine of the International Community', address to Chicago Economic Club, 22 April 1999.

Blair, T. (2007). 'Iraq – 22 reasons why it was right to invade', 1 August 2007. Available at http://keeptonyblairforpm.wordpress.com/iraq-pm-announces-military-action-20-march-2003-transcript/iraq-why-it-was-right-to-invade/ (accessed 25 November 2011).

Blair, T. (2010). *A Journey: My Political Life*, New York: Alfred A. Knopf.

Bodin, J. (1992). *On Sovereignty*, ed. J. Franklin, Cambridge: Cambridge University Press.

Bond, G. (1992). *The Buddhist Revival in Sri Lanka: Religious Tradition, Reinterpretation and Response*, Delhi: Shri Jainendra Press.

Boot, M. (2001). *Nullum Crimen Sine Lege and the Subject Matter Jurisdiction of the International Criminal Court*, Mortsel, Belgium: Intersentia.

Botejue, V. (2010). 'Hats off to president', *Ceylon Daily News*, 17 March 2010.

Boutros-Ghali, B. (1992). 'An Agenda for Peace: Preventive Diplomacy, Peacemaking and Peace-keeping', report of the Secretary-General pursuant to the statement adopted by the Summit Meeting of the Security Council on 31 January 1992, New York: United Nations, 17 June 1992.

Brown, C. (1999). 'War in the Balkans: Blair's vision of global police', *The Independent*, 23 April 1999.

Brundage, E., King, W., Vahali, R., Vladeck, S. and Yuan, X. (2004). 'Indonesian Human Rights Abuses in West Papua: Application of the Law of Genocide to the History of Indonesian Control', paper prepared for the Indonesia Human Rights Network by the Allard K. Lowenstein International Human Rights Clinic, Yale Law School, April 2004.

Buchanan, A. (2003). 'Reforming the international law of humanitarian intervention', in J. Holzgrefe and R. Keohane (eds) *Humanitarian Intervention: Ethical, Legal and Political Dilemmas*, Cambridge: Cambridge University Press.

Buncombe, A. (2011). 'Hopes fade for full UN investigation into Sri Lankan "war crimes" ', *The Guardian*, 27 April 2011.

Bush, G. (2002). 'The National Security Strategy of the United States of America', The White House, Washington DC, 17 September 2002.

Carvin, S. (2008). 'Threats, Challenges and Changes: International Law and the Evolution of "Threat" Since the End of the Cold War', unpublished paper presented to Bridging Multiple Divides, International Studies Association 49th Annual Convention, San Francisco.

CCC (1997). *Catechism of the Catholic Church*, 2nd edn, Pope John Paul II, The Vatican.

CDHRI (1990). 'Cairo Declaration of Human Rights in Islam', Cairo: Organisation of the Islamic Conference.

Channel 4 (2010). 'Sri Lanka execution video: new war crimes claims', Channel 4 News, 30 November 2010.

Chomsky, N. (2008). 'Humanitarian imperialism: the new doctrine of imperial right', *Monthly Review*, September 2008.

Chomsky (2009a). 'Thematic Dialogue on the Responsibility to Protect', panel discussion, United Nations, New York, 23 July 2009.

Chomsky, N. (2009b). 'Crises and the Unipolar Moment', talk to the School of Oriental and African Studies, University of London, 27 October 2009.

Cicero, M. (1998). *The Republic and the Laws*, trans. N. Rudd, Oxford: Oxford University Press.

Cleghorn, H. (1799). 'Cleghorn Minute', Colombo: UK government.

CNN (2008). 'US admiral: Myanmar junta unconcerned by cyclone', 13 May 2008.

CNN (2009). 'UN seeks full access to Sri Lankan refugee camps', 24 May 2009.

Colombo Page (2010a). 'Sri Lanka rejects UN panel of experts', 23 June 2010. Available at http://www.colombopage.com/archive_10A/Jun23_1277301393CH.php (accessed 23 November 2010).

Colombo Page (2010b). 'Conditions set by European Commission for GSP+ "unacceptably intrusive", Sri Lanka says', 24 June 2010. Available at http://www.colombopage.com/archive_10A/Jun24_1277402211CH.php (accessed 24 November 2010).

Connor, W. (1994). *Ethnonationalism: The Quest for Understanding*, Princeton, NJ: Princeton University Press.

Cowan, J. (2010). 'Sri Lankan president extends grip on power', ABC News, Australia, 9 September 2010.

Dayasri, G. (2010). 'ICG Report: The Lying Game', Ministry of Defence, Sri Lanka, 10 April 2010.

Deen, T. (2010). 'UN panel rankles Sri Lanka', Asia Times Online, 25 June 2010. Available at http://www.atimes.com/atimes/South_Asia/LF25Df03.html (accessed 29 November 2010).

Deng, F., Kimaro, S., Lyons, T., Rothchild, D. and Zartman, I. (1996). *Sovereignty as Responsibility: Conflict Management in Africa*, Washington DC: Brookings Institute.

De Silva, K. M. (1981). *A History of Sri Lanka*, London: C. Hurst.

De Silva, N. (2007). 'White man's burden in black and white or R2P the LTTE?', *The Island*, 8 August 2007.

De Votta, N. (2004a). 'Chauvinism and Ethnic Conflict in Sri Lanka', BASAS Annual Workshop, University of Bristol, 13 November 2004.

De Votta, N. (2004b). 'Ethnic domination, violence and illiberal democracy', in M. Alagappa (ed.) *Civil Society and Political Change in Asia*, Stanford, CA: Stanford University Press.

Dhanapala, J. (2010). 'Outline of submission made by Janatha Dhanapala to Commission on Lessons Learnt and Reconciliation', *Groundviews, 30 August 2010.*

Diokno, J. (1981). Untitled lecture, International Council of Amnesty International, Cambridge, 21 September 1978, mimeo in Alston, R. (ed.) *Development, Human Rights and the Rule of Law*, London: Pergamon Press.

Downie, S. (1998). 'Cambodia: Rebuilding society', *Background Briefing*, ABC Radio National, 23 August 1998.

Dr'eze, J. and Sen, A. (1987) *Hunger and Public Action*, Oxford: Clarendon Press.

DuBois, M. (2008). 'Protection: The new humanitarian fig-leaf', *Humanitarian Exchange* 46(6), April.

Emon, A. (2007). *The Origins and Evolution of Islamic Law*, Cambridge: Cambridge University Press.

EU (2010). 'Implementing Regulation (EU) No. 143/2010 of the Council of 15 February 2010 temporarily withdrawing the special incentive arrangement for sustainable development and good governance provided for under Regulation (EC) No. 732/2008 with respect to the Democratic Socialist Republic of Sri Lanka', *Official Journal of the European Union*, 15 February 2010.

Evans, G. (2007a). 'The Responsibility to Protect and the Use of Military Force', World Legal Forum, The Hague, 11 December 2007.

Evans, G. (2007b). 'Eighth Neelan Thiruchelvam Memorial Lecture', International Centre for Ethnic Studies, Colombo, 29 July 2007.

Evans, G. (2008). *The Responsibility to Protect: Ending Mass Atrocity Crimes Once and for All*, Washington DC: Brookings Institution Press.
Evans, P. (1994). *Embedded Autonomy: States and Industrial Transformations*, Princeton, NJ: Princeton University Press.
Evans. P. (1995). *Embedded Autonomy: States and Industrial Transformation*, Princeton, NJ: Princeton University Press.
Evans, R. (2008). 'UN chief tells rights body to drop rhetoric, blocs', Reuters, Geneva, 12 December 2008.
Fanon, F. (1970). *A Dying Colonialism*, Harmondsworth: Pelican Books.
Farer, T. (2003). 'Humanitarian intervention before and after 9/11', in J. Holzgrefe and R. Keohane (eds) *Humanitarian Intervention: Ethical, Legal and Political Dilemmas*, Cambridge: Cambridge University Press.
Fein, B. (2009). 'United States of America vs. Gotabaya Rajapaksa and Sarath Fonseka', Grand Jury Indictment, Department of Justice, United States District Court, Central District of California, by Bruce Fein and Associates, Washington DC, 5 February 2009.
Fenton, A. (2005). 'Legalized imperialism: "Responsibility to Protect" and the dubious case of Haiti', *Briarpatch Magazine*, 3 December 2005.
Fernandes, C. (2004). *Reluctant Saviour: Australia, Indonesia and the Independence of East Timor*, Melbourne: Scribe Publications.
Finnemore, M. and Sikkink, K. (1998). 'International norm dynamics and political change', *International Organization* 52(4): 887–917.
Fisher, H. (1984). *A History of Europe Vol II*, Glasgow: Fontana.
Fonseka, B. (2010). *Commentary of Returns, Resettlements and Land Issues in the North of Sri Lanka*, Colombo: Centre for Policy Alternatives.
Fonseka, B. and Raheem, M. (2010). *Land in the Eastern Province: Politics, Policy and Conflict*, Colombo: Centre for Policy Alternatives.
Fontgalland, G. de. (2009). 'State aided colonisation: The destruction of the Tamil homeland', in A. Pararajasigham (ed.) *Sri Lanka: 60 Years of 'Independence' and Beyond*, Emmenbrucke, Switzerland: Centre for Just Peace and Democracy.
Franck, T. (2003). 'Interpretation and change in the law of humanitarian intervention', in J. Holzgrefe and R. Keohane (eds) *Humanitarian Intervention: Ethical, Legal and Political Dilemas,* Cambridge: Cambridge University Press.
Geertz, C. (1989). *Works and Lives: The Anthropologist as Author*, Cambridge: Polity Press.
Geertz, C. (1993). *The Interpretation of Cultures*, London: Fontana Press.
Gellman, B. (1999). 'Question: Can alliance muster will to win?', *The Washington Post*, 25 April 1999.
Gellner, E. (1983). *Nations and Nationalism*, Ithaca, NY: Cornell University Press.
Glennon, M. (2001). *Limits of Law, Prerogatives of Power*, Palgrave: New York.
Goodhand, J. (2001). 'Aid, Conflict and Peace Building in Sri Lanka', Conflict Assessments, University of London: Centre for Defence Studies, King's College.
Gopalakrishnan, R. (2006). 'The struggle for Tamil Eelam: Very little of Sri Lanka in Kilinochche', Reuters, 2 February 2006.
Gordon, S. (2007). 'Unintended consequences of civil–military cooperation in peace operations', in C. Aoi, C. de Coning and R. Thakur (eds) *Unintended Consequences of Peacekeeping*, Tokyo: United Nations University Press.
GoSL/LTTE (2002). 'Oslo Declaration between the Government of Sri Lanka (GOSL) and the Liberation Tigers of Tamil Eelam (LTTE)', Norway, 2–5 December 2002.
Gray, C. (2004). *International Law and the Use of Force*, Oxford: Oxford University Press.

Gunasingham, M. (2005). *Primary Sources for History of the Sri Lanka Tamils*, Chullora, NSW: World-Wide Search MV Publications.
Gunesekera, L. (2010). 'UN snoopers will not be given visa to enter SL – Govt', *The Island*, 24 June 2010.
Hagerty, D. (1991). 'India's regional security doctrine', *Asian Survey*, April 1991.
Hardgrave, R. (1984). *India under Pressure: Prospects for Political Stability*, Boulder, CO: Westview Press.
Hariharan, R. (2010). 'India's concern in Sri Lanka', *Sri Lanka Guardian*, 7 June 2010.
Harris, S. (2010). *Humanitarianism in Sri Lanka: Lessons Learned?* Medford, MA: Feinstein International Center, Tufts University.
Heard, A. (1997). 'The challenge of utilitarianism and relativism'. Available at http://www.sfu.ca/~aheard/417/util.html (accessed 2 October 2007).
Heine, J. (2009). 'Misapplying R2P in Sri Lanka', *The Hindu*, 27 June 2009.
Hobbes, T. (1962). *Leviathan, or the Matter, Forme and Power of a Commonwealth Ecclesiasticall and Civil*, New York: Collier.
Holzgrefe, J. (2003). 'The humanitarian intervention debate', in J. Holzgrefe and R. Keohane (eds) *Humanitarian Intervention: Ethical, Legal and Political Dilemmas*, Cambridge: Cambridge University Press.
Horowitz, D. (2000). *Ethnic Groups in Conflict*, 3rd edn, Berkeley: University of California Press.
Hovenkamp, H. (1985). 'Evolutionary models in jurisprudence', *Texas Law Review* 54(4): 645.
Human Rights Watch (1992). 'Indivisible Human Rights: The Relationship between Political and Civil Rights to Survival, Subsistence and Poverty', New York: Human Rights Watch.
Human Rights Watch (1999). 'Leave None to Tell the Story: Genocide in Rwanda', New York: Human Rights Watch.
Human Rights Watch (2007). 'Complicit in Crime: State Collusion in Abductions and Child Recruitment by the Karuna Group', New York: Human Rights Watch, 24 January 2007.
Hun, S. (2008). 'Hun Sen: UNTAC brought AIDS to Cambodia', K I Media, 23 January 2008.
Huntington, S. (1957) *The Soldier and the State: The Theory and Politics of Civil–Military Relations*, Cambridge, MA: Harvard University Press.
Hutchcroft, P. (1991). 'Oligarchs and cronies in the Philippine state: The politics of patrimonial plunder', *World Politics* 43(3): 414–50.
IASC (2007). 'Conflict-Related Internal Displacement in Sri Lanka: A Study on Forced Displacement, Freedom of Movement, Return and Relocation', Inter-Agency Standing Committee, WorldWide Operations, 1 August 2007.
IBC (2010). 'Iraq body count'. Available at http://www.iraqbodycount.org/ (accessed 23 March 2010).
ICC (1999). 'Rome Statute of the International Criminal Court', 12 July 1999.
ICG (2007). 'Sri Lanka's Human Rights Crisis', Asia Report No. 135, 14 June 2007, Brussels: International Crisis Group.
ICG (2010a). 'War Crimes in Sri Lanka', Asia Report No. 191, 17 May 2010, Brussels: International Crisis Group.
ICG (2020b). 'Sri Lanka: Crisis Group Refuses to Appear before Flawed Commission', open letter, Brussels: International Crisis Group.

ICISS (2001). 'International Commission on Intervention and State Sovereignty: Report', International Commission on Intervention and State Sovereignty, Toronto.

ICTR (1998). 'Prosecutor vs. Kambanda', Case No. ICTR-97–23-S, Chapter 4, September 1998, International Criminal Tribunal for Rwanda.

Indrapala, K. (2007). *The Evolution of an Ethnic Identity: The Tamils in Sri Lanka c. 300 BCE to c. 1200 CE*, 2nd edn, Colombo: Vijitha Yapa Publications.

IRIN (2010a). 'The Dangers of Promising to Protect', Dakar: UN Office for the Coordination of Humanitarian Affairs, 25 May 2010.

IRIN (2010b). 'Analysis: NGOs Question Tighter Access to Sri Lanka's North', Bangkok: UN Office for the Coordination of Humanitarian Affairs, 11 August 2010.

ISG (2004). 'Saddam Wanted Chemical Weapons but Industry Was Destroyed', Iraq Survey Group Report, Washington DC: Department of Defense.

JDS (2011). 'Extra-judicial killings, abductions, burglaries haunt Sri Lanka's north', Journalists for Democracy in Sri Lanka, 7 January 2011. Available at http://www.jdslanka.org/search/label/News?updated-max=2011–01–12T09%3A27%3A00%2B01%3A00&max-results=350 (accessed 25 January 2011).

JFP (2010). 'Iraq deaths'. Available at http://www.justforeignpolicy.org/iraq (accessed 23 march 2010).

Kalyvas, S. (2006). *The Logic of Violence in Civil War*, Cambridge: Cambridge University Press.

Kant. I. (1997). *Critique of Practical Reason*, Cambridge: Cambridge University Press.

Kantha, S. (2005). *Pirabhakaran Phenomenon*, Gifu City, Japan: Lively Comet Imprint.

Kaplan, R. (2009). 'Center stage for the twenty-first century', *Foreign Affairs*, March/April 2009.

Kearney, R. (1967). *Communalism and Language in Ceylon*, Durham, NC: Duke University Press.

Ker-Lindsay, J. (2010). 'Kosovo, sovereignty and the subversion of UN authority', in A. Hehir (ed.) *Kosovo, Intervention and Statebuilding*, London: Routledge.

Klip, A. and Sluiter, G. (2001). *Annotated Leading Cases of International Criminal Tribunals, Vol. VII, The International Criminal Tribunal for the Former Yugoslavia*, Oxford: Hart Publishing.

Krasner, S. (1999). *Sovereignty: Organised Hypocrisy*, Princeton, NJ: Princeton University Press.

Kravtsov, V. (2006). 'Norm Diffusion in the Globalizing World: Building a Conceptual Framework', paper presented to International Studies Association, San Diego, 22 March, 2006. Available at http://www.allacademic.com/meta/p100866_index.html (accessed 9 March 2010).

Kunanayakam, T. (2010). 'Sri Lanka, Geostrategic Importance, Present Situation and Challenges Ahead', Havana: Centre for Studies on Asia and Oceania, 11 March 2010.

Kurland, P. and Lerner, R. (eds) (1987). *The Founders Constitution*, Chicago: University of Chicago Press.

Lang, A. (2010). 'Global constitutionalism and Kosovo' in A. Hehir (ed.) *Kosovo, Intervention and Statebuilding*, London: Routledge.

Lanka News Web (2010). '"Yes, we are Sinhala. The country is also Sinhala. So listen you Demala (Tamil)" president tells the Tamil people in Jaffna', Lankanewsweb.com, 3 April 2010. Available at http://www.lankanewsweb.com/news/EN_2010_04_03_003.html (accessed 13 April 2010).

Larmore, C. (1996). *The Morals of Modernity*, Cambridge: Cambridge University Press.

Lederer, E. (1999). 'Annan accepts blame in Bosnian massacre', *Milwaukee Journal Sentinel*, 16 November 1999.

Lee, S. (2007). 'Unintended consequences of peace operations on humanitarian action', in C. Aoi, C. de Coning and R. Thakur (eds) *Unintended Consequences of Peacekeeping*, Tokyo: United Nations University Press.

Lee, M. (2009). 'On Sri Lanka, Mexico invokes Responsibility to Protect, rebukes Colombo's "inaccuracies"', *Inner City Press*, 13 April 2009.

Locke. J (1960) *Two Treatises of Government*, Cambridge: Cambridge University Press.

LTTE (2004) *The Judicial System of Tamil Eelam: Structure Function and Duties of Officials in Charge*, Kilinochche, Sri Lanka: ANBU Printing Press.

Lukes, S. (1974). *Power: A Radical View*, London: MacMillan.

Lunstead, J. (2007). *The United States' Role in Sri Lanka's Peace Process 2002–2006*, Colombo: The Asia Foundation.

Lyon, A. and Malone, M. (2010). 'Kosovo's call for humanitarian intervention', in A. Hehir (ed.) *Kosovo, Intervention and Statebuilding*, London: Routledge.

Macartney, J. (2009). 'Analysis: China arms may have secured rout of Tigers', *The Times*, 15 May 2009.

McDougal, D. and Edney, K. (2010). 'Howard's way? Public opinion as an influence on Australia's engagement with Asia, 1996–2007', *Australian Journal of International Affairs* 64(2).

MacQueen, N. (2006). *Peacekeeping and the International System*, London: Routledge.

Mahindapala, D. (2009). 'Brown+browne=white imperialism', *Sri Lanka Guardian*, 13 February 2009.

Mahindapala, D. (2010). 'The brave new world is leaving the Tamil separatists behind', LankaWeb, 3 November 2010. Available at http://www.lankaweb.com/news/items/2010/11/03/the-brave-new-world-is-leaving-the-tamil-separatists-behind/ (accessed 17 November 2010).

Maley, P. (2009a). 'Philip Ruddock predicts flood of 10,000 boatpeople', *The Australian*, 13 October 2009.

Maley, P. (2009b). 'Boatpeople facing expulsion over security concerns on former Tamil fighters', *The Australian*, 6 October 2009.

Malik, A. (2009). 'RAW goes on recce mission', *Times of India*, 7 January 2009.

Mamdani, M. (2010). 'Responsibility to protect or right to punish', *Journal of Intervention and Statebuilding* 4(1): 53–67.

Massaro, T. (1999). 'Show (some) emotions', in S. Bandes (ed.) *The Passions of Law*, New York: New York University Press.

MEA (2010). 'UN Panel an unwarranted unnecessary interference in sovereignty – Sri Lanka', Ministry of External Affairs, Government of Sri Lanka, Colombo, 23 June 2010.

Mill, J. S. (1984 [1825]) *A Few Words on Non-Intervention*, in *The Collected Works of John Stuart Mill Vol XXI*, ed. J. Robson, London: Routledge and Kegan Paul.

Miller, J. (2010). 'Sri Lanka Tamil killings "ordered from the top"', *Channel 4 News*, 18 May 2010.

Milner, A. (1999). 'What's happened to Asian values?', in D. Goodman and G. Segal (eds) *Beyond the Asia Crisis*, London: Routledge.

Monten, J. (2005). 'The roots of the Bush Doctrine: Power, nationalism, and democracy promotion in U.S. strategy', *International Security* 29(4): 112–56.

Morris, C. (1998). *An Essay on the Modern State*, Cambridge: Cambridge University Press.

Nanayakkara, D. (2010). 'Issued New Circular for Head of all the NGOs/INGOs', Colombo: National Secretariat for Non-Governmental Organizations, 17 July 2010.

Nazemroaya, M. (2009). 'Great power confrontation in the Indian Ocean: The geopolitics of the Sri Lankan civil war'. Available at http://www.globalresearch.ca/index.php?context=va&aid=15667 (accessed 5 February 2010).

NDTV (2006). 'NDTV exclusive with LTTE chief negotiator Anton Balasingham', New Delhi Television, 27 June 2006.

Nelson, D. (2009). 'Tamil Tigers prepare for last stand in Sri Lanka – but military victory is not political peace', *The Daily Telegraph*, 6 January 2009.

Nuremburg Tribunal (1950). 'Principles of the Nuremburg Tribunal', adopted by the International Law Commission of the United Nations.

Ober, J. (2000). 'Quasi-rights: Political boundaries and social diversity in democratic Athens', *Social Philosophy and Policy* 17(1): 27–61.

O'Connell, E. (2009). 'Sri Lanka needs peace, not R2P', *International Relations*, 28 April 2009.

O'Donnell, G. and Schmitter, P. (1986). *Transitions from Authoritarian Rule: Tentative Conclusions about Uncertain Democracies*, Baltimore, MD: Johns Hopkins University Press.

Ogden, T. (2008). 'When do we start calling it genocide?', *Philanthropy Action*, 26 May 2008. Available at http://www.philanthropyaction.com/nc/when_do_we_start_calling_it_genocide (accessed 25 November 2010).

Orford, A. (2003). *Reading Humanitarian Intervention*, Cambridge: Cambridge University Press.

OUNHCHR (2010). 'Working Group on Enforced or Involuntary Disappearances', Office of the United Nations High Commissioner for Human Rights, United Nations, New York. Available at http://www2.ohchr.org/english/issues/disappear/index.htm (accessed 8 November 2010).

Page, J. (2009). 'Sri Lanka soldiers fight Tamil Tigers, trapping civilians on beach', *The Times*, 16 May 2009.

Panel of Experts (2011). Report of the Secretary-General's Panel of Experts on Accountability in Sri Lanka, 31 March 2011, New York: United Nations.

PBS (1998). 'Promoting peace', *NewsHour*, Public Broadcasting Service, 25 March 1998.

Pemberton, J. (1994). *On the Subject of 'Java'*, Ithaca, NY: Cornell University Press.

Pereira, R. (1983). 'Sri Lanka's pogrom, *New Internationalist* 128, October.

Perera, J. (2009). 'State failure to provide for multi ethnic society', in A. Pararajasigham (ed.) *Sri Lanka: 60 Years of 'Independence' and Beyond*, Emmenbrucke, Switzerland: Centre for Just Peace and Democracy.

Perera, K. (1983). 'Twenty-eight years gone and still with "Sinhala Nittaewo', *The Sunday Leader*, 28 July 1983.

Perez De Cuellar, J. (1992). 'Report of the Secretary-General on the Work of the Organisation: 1991', in 'Yearbook of the United Nations 1991', New York: United Nations.

Philp, K. (2009). 'Is the U.N. complicit in Sri Lankan war crimes?', *The Australian*, 26 May 2010.

Pirapaharan, V. (2006). 'Sinhala Leaders' Duplicity of War and Peace Has Left Tamils with No Choice but Political Independence', Annual Heroes' Day Statement, Kilinochche, Sri Lanka, 27 November 2006.

Pontecorvo, G. (dir. and writer) (1966). *The Battle For Algeria*.

Posner, R. (1998). 'Social norms, social meaning, and economic analysis of law: A comment'. *Journal of Legal Studies* 27: 553–65.
Posner, R. (2000). *Law and Social Norms,* Cambridge, MA: Harvard University Press.
Posner, R. (2001). *Frontiers of Legal Theory,* Cambridge, MA: Harvard University Press.
Posner, R. and Rasmusen, E. (1999). 'Creating and enforcing norms, with special reference to sanctions', *International Review of Law and Economics* 19: 369–82.
Pratap, A. (2009). 'Lessons from the Tiger defeat', *The Week*, 31 May 2009.
Przeworski, A. (1995). *Sustainable Democracy*, Cambridge: Cambridge University Press.
Przeworski, A., Alvarez, M., Cheibub, J. and Limongi, F. (2000). *Democracy and Development*, Cambridge: Cambridge University Press.
Putney, A. (1908). *International Law, Conflict of Laws, Spanish–American Laws, Legal Ethics*, Minneapolis, MN: Cree Publishing Company.
Quinn, W. (1989). 'Actions, intentions and consequences: the doctrine of double effect'. *Philosophy and Public Affairs* 18(4): 334–51.
Rajasingham, K. (2001). 'Sri Lanka: The untold story. Chapter 10, Lord Soulbury and his soulless report', Asia Times Online, 19 October 2001. Available at http://www.atimes.com/ind-pak/CJ13Df01.html (accessed 11 September 2011).
Rasaratnam, M. (2009). 'Ideology of Tamil nationalism', in A. Pararajasigham (ed.) *Sri Lanka: 60 Years of 'Independence' and Beyond*, Emmenbrucke, Switzerland: Centre for Just Peace and Democracy.
Rawls, J. (1971). *A Theory of Justice*, Cambridge, MA: Harvard University Press.
RC (1994). 'World Disaster Report 1994', Geneva: International Federation of Red Cross and Red Crescent Societies.
Reddy, M. (2010). 'Ban goes ahead with Sri Lanka panel', *The Hindu*, 17 March 2010.
Renteln, A. (1985). 'The unanswered challenge of relativism and the consequences for human rights', *Human Rights Quarterly* 7(4): 514–40.
Reuters (2009). 'UN rights body backs Sri Lankan resolution on war', 27 May 2009. Available at http://www.alertnet.org/thenews/newsdesk/LR170562.htm (accessed 21 August 2010).
Reuters (2010). 'Sri Lanka rejects UN's war crime advisory panel', 23 June 2010. Available at http://www.alertnet.org/thenews/newsdesk/N23216259 (accessed 24 November 2010).
Rice, S. and Loomis, A. (2007). 'The evolution of humanitarian intervention and the Responsibility to Protect', in I. Daalder (ed.) *Beyond Preemption: Force and Legitimacy in a Changing World*, Washington DC: Brookings Institution Press.
Rousseau, J.-J. (1973) *The Social Contract and Discourses*, London: J. M. Dent.
Sandvik, K. (2010). 'Security and international law', in P. Burgess (ed.) *The Routledge Handbook of New Security Studies*, London: Routledge.
Sapir, E. (1955). *An Introduction to the Study of Speech*, Orlando, FL: Harcourt Brace.
Scott, C. and Yap, J. (2010). 'Sri Lanka: Collapse of Rule of Law', Sri Lanka Campaign for Peace and Justice, London, 8 October 2010.
Sen, A. (1999a). *Development as Freedom*, Oxford: Oxford University Press.
Sen, A. (1999b). 'Democracy as a universal value', *Journal of Democracy* 10(3): 3–17.
Senaratna, K. (2009) 'Not signing the Rome statute is not enough!', *Sri Lanka Guardian*, 10 October 2009. See also http://www.news.lk/index.php?option=com_content&task=view&id=11869&Itemid=52 (accessed 19 October 2010).
Sengupta, S. (2008). 'Take aid from China and take a pass on human rights', *New York Times*, 8 March 2008.

Shashikumar, V. (2009). 'Lessons from the war in Sri Lanka', *Indian Defence Review* 24(3): July–September.

Shaw, M. (2009). 'Camps, media . . . genocide?', openDemocracy, 30 June 2009. Available at http://www.opendemocracy.net/article/sri-lanka-camps-media-genocide (accessed 11 September 2011).

Shellens, M. (1959). 'Aristotle on natural law', *Natural Law Journal* 4(1): 7–100.

Singer, P. (1979). *Practical Ethics*, Cambridge: Cambridge University Press.

Sinn Fein (1916). 'Proclamation of the Irish Republic', Dublin.

Siriweera, W. (1980). 'Recent developments in Sinhala–Tamil relations', *Asian Survey* 20(9): 903–13.

Sitrampalam, S. (n.d.). 'Nationalism, Historiography and Archeology in Sri Lanka – A Perspective', unpublished paper, University of Jaffna, Thirunelvely.

SLG (2007). 'Iran to fund Sri Lankan arms', *Sri Lanka Guardian*, 12 November 2007.

SLMM (2007). 'CFA 5 Years', statement by the Sri Lanka Monitoring Mission, 22 February 2007.

Smith, A. (1986a). 'State-making and nation-building', in J. Hall. (ed.) *States in History*, Oxford: Basil Blackwell.

Smith, A. (1986b). *The Ethnic Origins of Nations*, Oxford: Blackwell.

Smith, A. (2003). *Chosen Peoples: Sacred Sources of National Identity*, Oxford: Oxford University Press.

Smith, C. (2009). 'The LTTE: A national liberation and oppression movement', in L. Gayer and C. Jaffrelot (eds) *Armed Militias of South Asia: Fundamentalists, Maoists and Separatists*, New York: Columbia University Press.

Smith, N. (2010). 'Understanding Sri Lanka's defeat of the Tamil Tigers', *Joint Force Quarterly* 59: 40–4.

D'Souza, F. (ed.) (1990). *Starving in Silence: A Report on Famine and Censorship*, London: Article 19, International Centre on Censorship.

Sorel, G. (1970). *Reflections on Violence*, New York: Collier Books.

Stein, G. (2009). 'Death toll at the end of the Sri Lankan conflict was 30,000 to 40,000 – Gordon Weiss', Dateline, SBS Television, Australia, ABC News.

Stokke, C. (2005). 'Tamil Eelam – a De Facto State: Building the Tamil Eelam State: Emerging State Institutions and Forms of Governance in LTTE-controlled Areas in Sri Lanka', Oslo: Department of Sociology and Human Geography, University of Oslo.

Sunstein, C. (1997). *Free Markets and Social Justice*, Oxford: Oxford University Press.

Sunstein, C. and Thaler, R. (2003). 'Libertarian paternalism is not an oxymoron', *University of Chicago Law Review* 70(4): 1159–202.

Surendiram, S. (2009). 'Humanity failed in Sri Lanka', *The Guardian*, 12 June 2009.

Swamy, M. (2006). *Tigers of Lanka*, 6th edn, Colombo: Vijitha Yapa Publications.

TamilNet (2005). 'Rules guide on use of Tamileelam National flag published', 26 November. Available at http://www.tamilnet.com/art.html?catid=13&artid=16423 (accessed 20 April 2010).

Tamil United Liberation Front (1976). 'Vaddukoddai Resolution', Vaddukoddai: Tamil United Liberation Front.

Teson, F. (2003). 'The liberal case for humanitarian intervention', in J. Holzgrefe and R. Keohane (eds) *Humanitarian Intervention: Ethical, Legal and Political Dilemmas*, Cambridge: Cambridge University Press.

The Australian (2010). 'Sri Lanka chief Mahinda Rajapakse gets total power', 9 September 2010.

The National Times (2010). 'Comments'. Available at http://www.nationaltimes.com.au/opinion/politics/policy-on-sri-lankans-ignores-the-dangers-people-face-20100412-s40o.html#comments (accessed 13 April 2010).

The Sunday Times (2010). 'ICRC chief weeps', 24 October 2010.

Thomas, R. (1986). *Indian Security Policy*, Princeton, NJ: Princeton University Press.

Thoreau, D. (1993 [1849]). *Civil Disobedience*, Mineola, NY: Dover Thrift Editions.

Tilley, J. (2000). 'Cultural relativism', *Human Rights Quarterly* 22(2): 501–47.

Todorov, T. (1986). ' "Race", writing and culture', trans. L. Mack, in Gates, H. (ed.) *'Race', Writing and Difference*, London: University of Chicago Press.

Toft, M. (2003). *The Geography of Ethnic Violence*, Princeton, NJ: Princeton University Press.

Traub, J. (2001). 'The Bush years: W's world', *New York Times Magazine*, 14 January 2001.

Traub, J. (2009). 'At risk in Sri Lanka's war, *Washington Post*, 22 April 2009.

UN (1945) 'Charter of the United Nations and Statute of the International Court of Justice', New York: United Nations.

UN (1948a). 'Universal Declaration of Human Rights', Geneva: United Nations.

UN (1948b). 'Convention on the Prevention and Punishment of the Crime of Genocide', Resolution 260 (III), 9 December 1948.

UN (1986). 'Declaration on the Right to Development', New York: United Nations.

UN (1999). 'Report of the Independent Inquiry into the Actions of the United Nations during the 1994 Genocide in Rwanda', UN Document S/1999/1257, 15 December 1999.

UN (2002). 'Explanatory Memorandum', Rome Statute of the International Criminal Court, New York, 11 April 2002.

UN (2010). 'Expert Panel for Sri Lanka Will Not Infringe on Sovereignty – Ban', UN News Center, New York, 16 March 2010.

UNDPI (2008). 'Secretary-General Urges Human Rights Activists to Fill Leadership Vacuum, Hold World Leaders to Account, in Address to International Day Event', United Nations Department of Public Information, 8 December 2008.

UNGA (1965). 'Declaration on the Inadmissibility of Intervention in the Domestic Affairs of States and the Protection of their Independence and Sovereignty', 2131 (XX), 21 December 1965.

UNGA (1981). 'Declaration on the Inadmissibility of Intervention and Interference in the Internal Affairs of States', 36/103, 9 December 1981.

UNGA (1993). 'Review of the Implementation of the Declaration on the Strengthening of International Security', A/48/49, 16 December 1993.

UNGA (2005). 'World Summit Outcome Document', United Nations General Assembly, New York, 15 September 2005.

UNGA (2006). 'International Convention for the Protection of all Persons from Enforced Disappearances', United Nations General Assembly, Resolution A/RES/61/177, New York, 20 December 2006.

UNGA (2008). Fifth Committee, 28th meeting, GA/AB/3837, United Nations, New York, 4 March 2008.

UNHCR (2004). 'Sri Lanka makes citizens out of stateless tea pickers', United Nations High Commission for Refugees, 7 October 2004. Available at http://www.unhcr.org/cgi-bin/texis/vtx/news/opendoc.htm?tbl=NEWS&id=416564cd4 (accessed 13 April 2010).

UN News Centre (2009). 'Security Council Voices "Grave" Concern over Sri Lankan Humanitarian Crisis', 13 May 2009.
UNOCHA (2009). 'Situation Report No. 18', New York: United Nations Office for Coordinating Humanitarian Affairs, 30 May 2009.
UNSC (2006a). 'The Protection of Civilians in Armed Conflict', Resolution 1674, United Nations Security Council, New York, 28 April 2006.
UNSC (2006b). 'Resolution 1706, Invites Consent of Sudanese Government; Authorizes Use of "All Necessary Means" To Protect United Nations Personnel, Civilians under Threat of Physical Violence', United Nations Security Council, New York, 31 August 2006.
UNSG (2010). 'Secretary-General to Recall Resident Coordinator in Sri Lanka, Close UNDP Regional Centre Following "Unacceptable" Colombo Disruption', SG/SM/13005, 8 July 2010.
USAID (2006). 'Mission in Sri Lanka, Democracy and Governance Program', Democracy and Governance Program Initiative.
Vssubramaniam (2010). 'Delhi more alarmed than Colombo over the Mullivaykkal massacres and Sri Lanka (SL) war crimes', *Ground Report*, 5 December 2010. Available at http://www.groundreport.com/Business/DELHI-MORE-ALARMED-THAN-COLOMBO-OVER-THE-MULLIVAYK_1/2931768 (accessed 25 January 2011).
Wade, M. (2010). 'Policy on Sri Lankans ignores the dangers people face', The Age/The National Times.com.au, 13 April 2010. Available at http://www.theage.com.au/opinion/politics/policy-on-sri-lankans-ignores-the-dangers-people-face-20100412-s40o.html (accessed 11 September 2011).
Waltz, K. (1979). *Theory of International Politics*, New York: McGraw-Hill.
Walzer, M. (1980). 'The moral standing of states: A response to four critics', *Philosophy and Public Affairs* 9(3): 209–29.
Walzer, M. (2000). *Just and Unjust Wars: A Moral Argument With Historical Illustrations*, 3rd edn, New York: Basic Books.
Weber, M. (1946). *Social and Economic Organization*, ed. T. Parsons, New York: Oxford University Press.
Weber, M. (1948). 'Politics as a vocation', trans. and ed. Hans H. Gerth and C. Wright Mills, *From Max Weber: Essays in Sociology*, London: Routledge & Kegan Paul.
Weinstock, D. and Nadeau, C. (2004). *Republicanism: History, Theory and Practice*, London: Frank Cass.
Weiss, G. (2011). *The Cage: The Fight for Sri Lanka and the Last Days of the Tamil Tigers*, London: Bodley Head.
Weiss, T. (2004). 'The sunset of humanitarian intervention: The Responsibility to Protect in a unipolar era', *Security Dialogue* 34: 135–53.
Weiss, T. (2006). 'R2P after 9/11 and the World Summit', *Wisconsin International Law Journal* 24(3): 741–60.
Wen, L. (2009). 'China crosses the rubicon', *Australian Financial Review*, 23 June 2009.
Whorf, B. (1956). *Language, Thought and Reality: Selected Writings of Benjamin Lee Whorf*, ed. J. Carrol, Cambridge, MA: MIT Press.
Wickramasinghe, N. (1995). *Ethic Politics in Colonial Sri Lanka 1927–47*, New Delhi: Vikas Publishing House P.L.
Wije, C. (2009). 'Professional conduct of a professor of politics', LankaWeb News. Available at http://www.lankaweb.com/news/items09/160209–1.html (accessed 17 November 2010).

Wijesinha, R. (2008a). 'Letter to Brad Adams, Human Rights Watch', Sri Lanka High Commission, Canberra, 14 August 2008.

Wijesinha, R. (2008b). 'The White Man's Burden: Anglo-Saxon Attitudes towards Abuses and Impunity', Geneva: Sri Lanka Mission to UN, 7 April 2008.

Wijeyawickrema, C. (2007). 'Professor Rajan Hoole's human rights award', Lankaweb, 17 October 2007. Available at http://www.lankaweb.com/news/items09/170209–12.html (accessed 7 March 2010).

Williams, M. (2010). 'Rajapaksa tightens grip on power as party wins Sri Lanka vote', *Bloomberg Businessweek*, 9 April 2010.

Wilson, A. (1989). *The Breakup of Sri Lanka: The Sinhalese Tamil Conflict*, Hyderabad: Orient Longman.

World Conference on Human Rights (1993). 'Bangkok Declaration (or Report of the World Conference on Human Rights, Bangkok)', Bangkok: World Conference on Human Rights.

Xinhua (2010). 'UN chief appoints panel of experts on Sri Lanka war crime probe', *People's Daily*, 23 June 2010.

Yogasundram, N. (2006). *History of Sri Lanka: From Pre-History to Tsunami*, Colombo: Vijitha Yapa Publications.

Index